THE NATURE OF RELIGION

THE MACMILLAN COMPANY
NEW YORK · BOSTON · CHICAGO · DALLAS
ATLANTA · SAN FRANCISCO

MACMILLAN & CO., LIMITED
LONDON · BOMBAY · CALCUTTA
MELBOURNE

THE MACMILLAN COMPANY
OF CANADA, LIMITED
TORONTO

THE NATURE OF RELIGION

By

EDWARD CALDWELL MOORE
*Plummer Professor of Christian Morals,
Emeritus, in Harvard University*

NEW YORK
THE MACMILLAN COMPANY
1936

Set up and printed. Published May, 1936

PRINTED IN THE UNITED STATES OF AMERICA
NORWOOD PRESS LINOTYPE, INC.
NORWOOD, MASS., U.S.A.

To the memory of a life-long friendship with

JAMES SETH

Professor of Ethics in Brown University
1892–1896
and
Professor of Moral Philosophy in Edinburgh University
1898–1924

and of many helpful contacts with

ANDREW SETH PRINGLE PATTISON

Professor of Logic and Metaphysics in Edinburgh University
1891–1919

PREFACE

This book has grown out of later reflection upon some parts of the topic of a course of lectures concerning the philosophy of religion. This course I had given through a series of years, mainly to graduate students and undergraduates. My earlier profession had been that of an historian. In the last few, freer, years, I have sought, at least, to orient myself afresh as to the progress of the sciences of nature in our generation.

The book takes its departure from the question which students instinctively raise: What knowledge of religion can we have? Others also raise the same question.

The second chapter deals with the question, What is religion? Here I have assumed that it is fair to take illustrations, mainly, from the one religion with which most of us are likely to be more familiar, namely, Judaism-Christianity. That these are one religion will be suggested to anyone who will so much as open a Bible. Their antitheses and antagonisms are mainly due to the fact that, like parents and children, they have so much in common.

The third chapter deals with questions which are fundamental to all higher religions, namely, that of the intuition of God, the intuition of immortality, and intuitions concerning God himself.

The fourth chapter seeks to present parallels to realities such as may be found in the pursuit of other realities and to the effort at their realization. I take for illustration

PREFACE

THIS book has grown out of later reflection upon some parts of the topic of a course of lectures concerning the philosophy of religion. This course I had given through a series of years, mainly to graduate students and undergraduates. My earlier projection had been that of an historian. In the last few, freer, years, I have sought, at least, to orient myself afresh as to the progress of the sciences of nature in our generation.

The book takes its departure from the question which students instinctively raise: What knowledge of religion can we have? Others also raise the same question.

The second chapter deals with the question, What is religion? Here I have assumed that it is fair to take illustrations, mainly, from the one religion with which most of us are likely to be more familiar, namely, Judaism-Christianity. That these are one religion will be suggested to anyone who will so much as open a Bible. Their antitheses and antagonisms are mainly due to the fact that, like parents and children, they have so much in common.

The third chapter deals with questions which are fundamental to all higher religions, namely, that of manifestation of God, the intuition of immortality, and intuitions concerning God himself.

The fourth chapter seeks to present parallels to religion such as may be found in the pursuit of other realities and in the effort at their realization. I take for illustration the quest of truth as in the sciences, the apprehension of beauty as in the arts and the bondage and high liberty of morals. I have sought to point out affinities of the pursuit of these with the aims of religion.

If any further personal word is fitting, I might say that the pages cover some aspects of the history of my own mind in the last fifty years. They record changes of opinion. A devout home, a free and happy ministry, responsible association of all my maturer years in a great university have been my background. My colleagues in both the history and the philosophy faculties taught me much. My pupils taught me more—at least, they taught me different things. Intervals in teaching afforded me, first and last, opportunity to spend, in sum, nearly two years in India, China, Japan and the former Ottoman Empire, and about the same time in Europe, Catholic and Protestant.

CONTENTS

PART I

THE NATURE OF OUR KNOWLEDGE OF RELIGION

Part I

THE NATURE OF OUR KNOWLEDGE OF RELIGION

I. THE RATIONAL

It is proposed to offer in this first chapter some pieces of study in relation to the problem of religious knowledge. Questions concerning the nature of our knowledge of religion are raised for us, parts only of a larger whole. They are preliminary to a study of the nature of religion itself. It seems advisable, however, to indicate our mode of approach, at least, to that which is our real concern in these essays — the nature of religion. Definitions of religion are numerous. The essays of the last generation alone have brought forth more than forty. None of these [illegible] seems altogether adequate. This fact does not suggest that strictly speaking no brief definition of religion is possible. A definition from the point of view of a theory concerning religion inverts the proper order of procedure. The facts must lead to the theory. New facts are brought to our attention as the discussion of religion grows. Old facts are viewed in a new light. Descriptions of various aspects of the fact of religion may, however, be ventured. Three [illegible] can be made. Religion is something different from knowledge. Religion is [illegible] [illegible]. It is resolve and power for [illegible] [illegible]. It is [illegible] [illegible] to that which is [illegible] [illegible]

Part I

THE NATURE OF OUR KNOWLEDGE OF RELIGION

1. THE RATIONAL

It is proposed to offer in this first chapter some fruits of a study in relation to the problem of religious knowledge. Questions concerning the nature of our knowledge of religion are indeed, for us, parts only of a larger whole. They are preliminary to a study of the nature of religion itself. It seems advisable, however, to intimate our mode of approach, at least, to this which is our real concern in these essays—the nature of religion. Definitions of religion are numerous. Discussions of the last generation alone have brought forth more than forty. None of those offered seems altogether adequate. This fact alone may suggest that, strictly speaking, no brief definition of religion is possible. A definition from the point of view of a theory concerning religion inverts the proper order of procedure. The facts must lead to the theory. New facts are brought to our attention as the discussion of religions widens. Old facts are viewed in a new light. Description of certain aspects of the fact of religion may, however, be attempted. Discriminations can be made. Religion is something different from knowledge. Religion is impulse to worthier living. It is resolve and power for such life. It is manifest in a life thus empowered. It is feeling for higher things. It is belief in that which is ever beyond us. It is experience that that which is beyond us, if we give ourselves to it, gives itself, in a measure, at least, to us. It alters us in the endeavor. The endeavor enhances the conception. In this respect religion is analogous to other experiences. Inspiration for and achievement of a work of art is an experience of this sort. True wisdom, lastingly proved to have been such, put forth, it may be, not without misgiving, in momentous responsibility and verifiable only afterward, is a matter of this sort. Moral or social endeavor, even when defeated, still leaves him who made it assured both of the rightfulness of the thing attempted and of his duty to attempt it. There is implication of reality in the universe corresponding to the needs and wants of men.

Religion enables us continually in the direction of the fulfillment of our moral and spiritual selves. It lifts us out of our current selves. It lifts us thus, perhaps, when we are least conscious of ourselves, when we are absorbed in the idea and our work. Yet, because we participate in this lifting, this beyond of ourselves becomes the true self of ourselves. There may thus be an inner victory even when corresponding outward achievement fails. Religion identifies us with others. It commits us to high aims on their behalf, although, or even because, this involves abnegation of ourselves. What is even more to the point, it makes us forget ourselves. It sustains us in the sense that we are not alone and do not live to ourselves. Such belief, maintained, at times, notwithstanding reasonings to the contrary, is an intuition of a sort manifest in many others of the deeper relations of our lives. Sometimes our reasonings make us uncertain of our intuitions. At times they should. This may be one of the great uses of reason —to criticize our intuitions. If, however, we let this attitude transform our characters, this may have long consequences for our friendships, for trust and love and, indeed, for a large part of all the sane ventures proper to man's life. Religion itself is only one more of those ventures. Nevertheless, in everyday affairs the intuitive is a common form of reasoning. Many people trust to it who do not reason much in any other way. They sometimes reason very soundly. Those who habitually live the grand life of rationality do well to remember that there are some things which are, initially at all events, mediated to us in the intuitive manner and in no other. We have the power, as also the responsibility, for making ventures. There are best things in life which never come to him who makes no venture. We cannot even retain what we inherit without venture.

Even these first brief paragraphs concerning the nature of religion suggest already some first things which we should here say concerning the nature of our knowledge of religion. Not all of the knowledge necessary to wise living can be described as strictly rational. Nor do we need to resort forthwith to belief in supernatural communication. The history of thought is at this point full of instruction for us. Primitive man must have been quickly made aware of the limitations of his knowledge. He was correspondingly credulous as to the world about him. It was a world in which unknown forces made themselves felt for either the weal or woe of men. As the life of man enlarged, the area of what was familiar enlarged with it. But it was long before this enlargement was referred, as we should say, to natural causes. Explanations by reference to the supernatural lay more near. There came a time when some of the Greeks in Asia Minor and in southern Italy made notable approaches to reasoned understanding of the world in which we live. Their gains may seem to us small, but they were epoch-making—for their method. In the end, especially for higher spirits, and in the Hellenic world itself, explanations were sought and in amazing measure found. Also, with an assurance not always justified, on the part of some, reference to the supernatural was viewed with scorn. The Hebrews had no training in the intellectual life such as philosophers, notably Socrates and Plato, gave to the Greeks. The supernatural had large place in the teaching of the prophets. There was also splendid moralism among the later seers. The supernatural had again large place in the Gospels. Jesus shared these views. Yet also, palpably, deep things in him were intuitions. Miracles had large place among Christians as the ancient world declined. The philosophical culture of the scholastics did little to enlighten the world in this particular. Even of the time of the Renaissance one may still make much the same remark. Yet now, men who found themselves disputing the Church in this regard abjured, privately at least, religion. The reformers seemed to themselves to have nothing to pit against the supernatural authority of the Church except the supernatural origin of the Scriptures, with also the miracle of grace in the hearts of believers. It is hardly too much to say that the long struggle against the Roman Church, with also many secular powers who made the cause of the Church their own, caused the miracle to seem only the more necessary to the life of the believer. It was against this resurgence of the supernatural in all its intensity that Deists and Rationalists and Positivists struggled. The sciences of nature in their beginnings felt the same antagonism.

Meantime, in all ages men and women have held to an enduring substance of their faith. At the same time, they have advanced to ever fresh interpretations of it with the march of knowledge from generation to generation. This is more marked, of course, within the last three-quarters of a century. Men of faith have not been carried away by what seemed the clamant logic of the moment, nor have they, most of them, taken refuge in the notion of a changelessness which divine influences entering upon human life have never shown. Mystics have been brave forerunners of modern men in this regard. They have not yielded to fanaticism, to which an easy view of the supernatural has sometimes led. By no means all, nor the best, were carried away by the craze concerning witchcraft in our own country hardly two centuries ago. The second Isaiah was the great voice for men of this kind before the time of Christ. Socrates had trusted, before all else in the inner voice of his daimon. Plato was often of divided mind. Humble people in Jesus' entourage showed the same calmness in possession of beliefs of which they could not, indeed, give logical account, but which scribes and Pharisees were unable to shake. Jesus shared this trait in a manner which sometimes makes us wonder whether the picture of him in the Gospels is not, in a measure at least, colored by apprehensions natural to the evangelists. Mystics of all ages have been dominated by this inner sense. At bottom, it is the intuitive reason which has been allowed its own place and granted its own power as over against too confident rationalization. And again, the very wonders of its insight and sound guidance have been described in enthusiastic terms, as if it had been all due to supernatural intervention. These two major paragraphs, the one upon but a few world-recognized aspects of religion, and the other upon well known varying phases of interpretation of those same aspects of religion, may together serve as introduction to our topic. The rest of Part I will deal with phenomena of religion in general and with their explanations. This has been the main direction which the discussion of religions has taken since the comparison of religions has assumed in general more scientific shape. With these facts as to the nature of our knowledge of religion, we may resume our consideration of major facts concerning religion itself. For the present, we are concerned with such facts in their universal aspects and their relation to the progress of mankind.

At the level at which we are speaking we understand ourselves as persons. We have no symbol for that which is beyond ourselves as persons save one which implies quality of person. This may seem to beg a most important question. The religious, and these of almost all the religions, have called this beyond of ourselves as persons, God. "Thou thoughtest that I was altogether such an one as thyself," a psalm makes Jahve say. The emphasis must have been upon the word "altogether." The verse covers a long chapter in the history of religions. There seems indeed to have been a period in the history of religions when this beyond was not yet thought of as person. It was a mysterious impersonal power of which, by magic, men thought they could possess themselves. For this at present a Melanesian word "mana" is used. Australian tribes have other words. Those who thus thought paid the price. They thought only of goods, not of the good. When men had arrived at the notion of personal gods, they paid another price. In polytheism there were as many gods as goods. Some of these were gods of evils which men counted to be good. Even on the attainment of monotheism, the worship of one god of all goods, this had for long ages its parallel in the fear of one spirit of all evil—with angels and devils in their respective trains. No maturer religion, save perhaps early Buddhism, has ever succeeded in ridding itself of the personal in the idea of God. And in proportion as Buddhism in India, and for a period achieved this, it tended to become a philosophy of life for cultivated men and, on the whole, a pessimistic philosophy. Even Buddhism, however, never achieved this for interests larger than the intellectual or for its own wider propaganda. The age-long Mahayana Buddhism of Burma, China and Japan is a religion of personality. The reality, God, may be more than person, but, being ourselves persons, and religion at its higher levels being so intensely personal a matter, we do not know how to think that. The reality, however, can hardly be less than person. "Our wills are ours to make them Thine." We shall take occasion later to recur to this question. Religion thus in its simplicity takes hold ofttimes of simplest natures, humble lives, true hearts, faithful doers. This form of it in its pure religiousness comes nearest to an ideal present in almost all the more mature religions. The maturest religions are in this sense the simplest. They also deteriorate when they try to include as integral to themselves either dogma, which is merely expression in thought, or ceremonial, which is only expression in feeling, or current morality, which is expression in action, and which changes. Religion itself is the abiding impulse to the realization of the good, which good also changes in apprehension and embodiment with the growth of men and the progress of mankind.

We are just now in this study proposing to speak of religion in its essence, in its universal aspects, and by no means necessarily in the one exemplification of it with which we may chance to be most familiar. Nevertheless, it may be of advantage to take our illustrations mainly from the one religion, Judaism-Christianity, with which those who are likely to read this book are more familiar,

Jesus' teaching is full of appreciation of this simplicity of religion. Parts of the Old Testament are hardly less so. Jesus loved the plain man. In a sense which we must never forget he was himself a plain man. He took a little child and set him in the midst of a company of his hearers, saying, "Of such is the Kingdom of Heaven." Yet no one was ever less a child in these matters than was Jesus. Recall his trenchant criticism of men of the intellectual sort in their approach to religion, of men of the ceremonial approach, of men of the institutional approach, of men of merely worldly and selfish approach. It is difficult to think of this as coming from one who had not thought long and deeply over these various ways of misunderstanding religion, and rejected them all as inadequate, misleading, subversive. Evidence that Jesus was not altogether of a simple mind is given also in the fact that he so well understood people who were not at all of a simple mind. It was not because, in a kind of innocence, he did not know them. It was because, as the issue of observation and reflection, of reasoning about others and himself, because indeed of experience of his own, pictured for us in the tale of the three typical human temptations—it was because he did know. If he exhorted men and women to be in their religion like little children, if he said to one of the rulers of his nation, "Ye must be born again," it was not because he was a child or wished them to be children and nothing more. He may not have sat so long as did Gautama under the bo-tree meditating. His whole working life was not long enough for that. Yet he also meditated. He was thirty years old —old for an Oriental—when he came to his ministry. He had times of meditating in the midst of his ministry. It was in intercourse, not wholly with men who came to him, but with men of all sorts to whom he went—it was in observation and reflection that he gathered his wisdom. He had not yet rejected life. He never did reject life in Gautama's sense. He had not yet come to the point where life rejected him. The joys and sufferings of men, as well as his own, led him to conclusions different from those of the Buddha as to the existence of God and the significance of life. Nevertheless, his mind was working upon the same problem. What is the evil to be avoided? Is it pain, or is it sin? What is the good to be attained? How to attain it? How to help others to attain it? Is it deliverance from illusion and suffering, or is it deliverance from sin, a deliverance of which suffering may be the price? Is it deliverance for one's own self, or is it also deliverance of others, the effort toward which is in itself deliverance for one's self? Jesus also traversed in anguish of soul the road of man's life. He returned rich in knowledge as to the simplicity and unity, the power and light in life which religion is. There is wide difference between one who faces sorrow and is glad and one who sought escape from sorrow and was sad. He brought the wisdom of a world of contemplation of men and of himself and of intimacy with God to very simple terms. Yet it could be said of him that "He needed not that any should testify of man; he knew what was in man."

Perhaps from no other point of view is the shortness of Jesus' life so nearly incredible as from this. We usually expect such wisdom of men who lived long and often sadly, some of them even badly. Some wander so long that they never get back to simplicity. He knew indeed, as we were saying, people who had found the secret of religion by journeys perhaps even shorter than his own. In those journeys it might be that they had not troubled themselves so much about the great world. He knew also people who carried the problem of the great world upon their hearts. He was one of them. But, again, he knew people who by their addiction to modes of thought scholastic, professional, and this only the more, if class influence or personal ambition entered into their thoughts, had missed the secret of religion, and with it some part of the understanding of and the power for life. They had lost the simplicity of life. He knew that secret. He knew himself. One must indeed say of him, not so much that he knew about God—he knew about God mainly in terms of the law-givers and prophets of his own faith—what one must say of him, however, is that he knew God. Much that he says of God is in imagery. And, again, it is mainly the imagery of his own Scriptures. Parts of it are also imagery drawn from an acute and poetic observation of nature. There are flashes also of reaction to men's conduct which are devastating. He knew very little about God in the sense in which philosophers, Greeks and others, had even then, for a long time, been inquiring. He knew still less about God in the sense in which theologians have, by now and for ages, been asserting things which men of science in our time, some of them, deny, and about which probably we all find ourselves puzzling. He knew about God in the terms of law-givers, prophets, psalmists of his own race and faith, and in relation to questions natural to his own time. He knew God, however, in a sense far profounder than that. It was this fact, that he knew God, which enabled him now and then to dissent so radically from that which had been said about God even by authorities of his own faith. And, just as there are these two knowledges concerning God, there is such a thing as knowing about religion, and there is also such a thing as knowing religion. Knowing about God and also knowing about religion, no matter how we may struggle against change, is always changing. Knowledge of God remains. One condition of its remaining is that it permits the other knowledge to change. The reason is in the unchanging need on the part of man of something which religion—but by no means only a given statement or practice of religion—necessarily supplies.

Nevertheless, we all company with men whose approach to religion is instinctively from the intellectual side. They approach their own questions from this side. They tend to approach every question from this side. Students, by the mere fact of being students, even if they are not yet very great students, are likely to think that this is the way to approach any great subject. Most of all must it be the way to approach a subject so difficult as religion—to approach it, namely, as an intellectual magnitude. Their constant debates of religion show this. Religion-baiting is popular. This is, however, only another way of saying that for the sake of these, at least—and, having made the above discriminations, for ourselves as well—we also should approach the subject of religion from this side. How do you know? What knowledge can we have? What knowledge can anyone have? These are the questions. Furthermore, neither teachers nor students, nor indeed the world at large, is altogether to be blamed for this state of things. Advocates of religion in the pulpit, in books, in the current press, in exhortation, even in conversation, so often do and so long have done just this thing. They have set forth dogmas, doctrines, teachings, views of religion, as if these were religion. They do not make it clear, they may not be clear within themselves, that that which they thus present is a traditional view, an authoritative view, their own personal view of religion—but a view, not religion itself. Others can hardly be blamed for falling in with this assumption. These then proceed to attack these teachings about religion. They imagine that they are attacking religion. One might almost say that they have been taught so to imagine. Still further rejoinder is natural, and this from either side. How do you present any subject except by presenting ideas about it, your own ideas, or those of someone else or of supposed authorities? You cannot present anything except through the medium of thoughts about it addressed to the thoughts of others.

I may hope presently to make more clear that one can indeed permit the matter to present itself, in its own ultimate verity, through the medium of lives which this verity guides and governs. Even this implies, however, openness to this particular kind of conviction. This particular openness to conviction, moreover, argumentation is apt to close. Men see great institutions which set forth doctrines or practices of religion, which demand submission to discipline in the name of religion, which urge corporate association with the religious. It is rather natural that men assume that these things are regarded as religion. They see also those who profess and adhere to all this and yet show but meager, and sometimes no effect in their lives, no hindrance to their doing what everybody else does, their being what people generally seem to be. At this men cavil. They are often right. But on these terms they are more clear as to what religion is not than able to form an opinion as to what religion is. This is one of the reasons why religion so often presents the spectacle of being always on the defensive. For this reason one has at times a sober feeling that the defense of religion will have to be much altered before attack upon it can really be met. The self-evidence of religion will have to be more relied on than all the evidences of religion of which we ever heard, if the misunderstanding about the nature of religion is really to be done away.

It is not that Jesus was out of sympathy with the intellectual life in its relation to religion. It is, however, against all the evidence that he lived exactly what we should call the intellectual life. The outward semblance of his life was not at all that of a life of contemplation. No more was it that of a life of mystic rapture. He was not like the Buddha. He was not like Plotinus. He established relation between thought and duty. He balanced reason and deep feeling. He found expression for this in action. He combined enthusiasm with control. But it is true that he was no theorist. It seems as if it were more often the sense of a duty to be done which led him to reflect upon it. Reflection then showed itself in a characteristic way of doing that duty and of laying it upon others to be done. His immediate followers were sometimes content with finding in him fulfillment of prophecy. Less consciously, they found in him fulfillment and enhancement of moral ideals. It was Paul, a follower who never saw Jesus, who began the process of elaborating Jesus' teaching into doctrine. He combined it with much else, for example, with reminiscences of his rabbinic Judaism, which indeed he had abandoned, but which had by no means wholly abandoned him. There are, rather rarely, echoes of Hellenic speculation, for he had been born in a Greek town famed for a school. He hardly achieved a system, or, at the most, one of which Paulsen has said that it never existed in its entirety in any mind except his own. Paul was not brought up at the feet of Jesus. He mentions the feet of Gamaliel, the greatest rabbi of his time.

Material which is assembled in the first two synoptic

Gospels puts together, sometimes in forms coinciding and sometimes in divergent forms, traditions gathered, part of them at least, from eye witnesses. The ultimate authors, however, do not seem to have been the eye witnesses. The very preposition used in the title, "The Gospel according to Mark," shows that the apostle was not necessarily the author of the whole tradition which he embodied. The third Gospel speaks explicitly of written sources, and apparently of several of them. Luke describes himself as a redactor. The Fourth Gospel is obviously the latest of them all, perhaps by a considerable interval. It is the only one which contains, and this in its preface, a more elaborate allusion to a philosophical idea, that of the *logos,* rather widely spread in contemporary non-Jewish speculation. The parallel of the *dabar Jahve,* the Word of the Lord which came to the prophets, may have made this speculation seem more familiar than it really was. The Book of the Acts plainly seeks peace after a protracted struggle in the rising Christian community. Its theme is the progress of the gospel from the home of the old faith to the center of the world. The Gospels in their measure, and certainly Paul's letters, bear witness to contemporary Jewish opinions about an impending catastrophe which should end the world. The last of the New Testament writings appears to be, except for the seven little letters to churches in the first three chapters, an actual Jewish apocalyptic writing, only slightly touched over by a Christian hand. There is every evidence that Jesus shared apocalyptic expectations which have never been fulfilled. There could be no more perfect illustration how truly Jesus was at home in the truths of religion and, on the other hand, in respect of views of world history and of many similar matters, a man of his own time. Gospels, later called apocryphal, which seem to have circulated for a time in some communities, were ultimately excluded from the canon. Apologists, often wandering teachers of rhetoric or philosophy, explain, some of them, how they came to be converted to Christianity, at a time when conversions of men of their sort were not yet common. They turn the material of discussion of Christian truth this way and that, without anything resembling unanimity as to the results arrived at. Theologians of the third and later centuries were often administrators as well. They were responsible both for interpreting Christianity to the outside world and for repressing schism within the Christian body. It was these men and their successors who gave to Christian doctrine, still later formalized and perpetuated as dogma, the forms with which we are familiar. These forms are all shot through with the inheritance of the Greek philosophers and with reflection upon metaphysical problems of which Jesus and the apostles, so far as we know, never heard.

It is not that Jesus was not a thinker, although, as we have said, his familiarity with that which we are likely to describe as thought was limited. It is that he was so much more than a thinker that we do not esteem him as quite rightly so described. It is that he gave thought of transcendent significance to concrete problems of living his own life and to helping his followers to live their lives in the spirit which religion is. He leaves us to infer that we are quite free to live that life in company with the noblest thoughts of our own age. He lived his life in association with thoughts natural to his own time, and in reaction to the one literature which he seems to have known, exclusively the literature of a devout Jew. He warns against being led off into realms of speculation such as absorbed some magnates of his own race and time and made of them what he called "blind guides." It is quite certain that he was not a man of many books in the sense in which some of his contemporaries were undoubtedly that. It is quite possible that he was a man of no book but one, substantially our Old Testament. His followers were very simple people. He was himself a very simple person. His followers are indeed called disciples. We do not think of them, however, as resembling the disciples of the great philosophers of antiquity, leisurely frequenters of the Academy or of the Stoa. One might indeed by a poor play upon words say that they were peripatetic. They do seem to have wandered over a small area, but that was partly because their Master had not where to lay his head. Followers they are commonly called. It is noteworthy how often he said, "Follow me." Not many of the world's greatest teachers have said so simply "Follow me." If others said it, they might be understood to be referring to the following of their particular philosophy. Jesus palpably meant something far profounder than that. His disciples and their disciples came later to be known as people of the "Way," that is, of a mode of life. Jesus' men like their Master seem to have worked at thought mainly by thinking of something else than thought. They thought, namely, about life which, if one is to live it supremely well, requires much thought.

The Book of the Acts asserts that it was at Antioch that Jesus' followers were first called Christians. By the end of the second century, they were widely spread in the Empire. Yet even then so great a man as the Stoic Emperor Marcus Aurelius knew little of them, and that little not good. Epictetus never alludes to them. Plotinus deprecates what he had heard of them. By the middle of the third century the Empire aimed at their destruction. Early in the fourth century the Empire came to terms with them. It will need no saying, however, that not all of the Christianity of the time of Constantine can be carried back to Christ. Also, not all that Jesus was or taught had been carried forward to the time of Constantine. It will make vivid the thing for which we are contending if one will read the Gospels, or even only one Gospel, at a sitting, and then immediately read the Nicene Creed, or better still, the so-called Athanasian Creed, which were both of them put forth as authoritative interpretations. If what we have said above is true, the Gospels are themselves, in their measure, interpretations. But they are nearest to the testimony of men who had seen the man Jesus and felt the spirit of his life. The creeds are interpretations into the mode of thought of another age and of a different world, a world which had gathered into itself all the great races of antiquity. With these the dominating culture was that of the Greeks, which was also on the verge of a swift decline.

Perhaps I should take a moment here to say, in passing, that Jesus held only less sacred than the development of the individual, of which we have been speaking, the development, which was also natural and necessary, of a fellowship in religion which was to become the Church. This emphasis also had with him its roots in life. It hardly needs saying, however, that Jesus can never have used in his discourse the word church, for an association of believers, an institution which did not yet exist. This will be discussed later. Perhaps the point now to be made is merely this. Jesus gave no warrant in religion for a solitary life. He was himself no solitary. Certainly he gave no warrant for that which would suppress the life of the individual. And beside this, there is another matter, treatment of which is also deferred, the matter of worship, both public and private. The point now to be made is that this, like that other, is manifestation, expression of religion, aid to the spirit which religion is. I do not find that Jesus was hostile in principle to noble forms of worship. He thought them ignoble if they took the place of the life of the spirit. He saw that some, concerned preponderantly with them, came to be interested chiefly in their outwardness. These probably chose them for their favorite manifestation of religion because they were themselves men of the outwardnesses of life. He sought indeed his hours alone with God. Also he spent days in company with the group of men whom he was forming. At the height of his popularity he drew about him multitudes whom he could stir and yearned to form. He frequented the synagogue. The temple, so far as we know, he visited but rarely. There, it is rather evident that he was of somewhat divided mind. The people about the temple seem to have been of divided mind concerning him. If scribes and Pharisees in the synagogue demurred at his interpretations, it was primarily priests who sought his life. One may gather that it was not the grand opportunity for worship which occasioned this division of his mind. It was, rather, that in this manifestation of religion it seemed to him that there was much manifest that was something else than religion. Certainly his last visit to Jerusalem proved that. At best worship, public or private, in its grandest expression, or, again, in its most rudimentary manifestation, is but expression. It is stimulus to the spirit of life. It is guidance for that life. It is sympathy in that life. But it is not in itself religion. To this also we shall return later.

To recur to the immediate purpose which we have before us. Jesus was not opposed to the intellectual life in its relation to religion. He lived that life, as we have seen, in some matters of grave concern and with startling penetration. There is, however, no evidence that he was greatly learned even in the lore of his own faith, in the sense in which scribes and Pharisees whom he met were learned men. Palestine in his time had many such men. He can hardly have failed to know the teachings of some of these synagogue magnates only less well than he knew the teachings of the Scriptures themselves. Some of these men drew from him stinging rebuke. It was often their vanity, now and then even their hypocrisy, which called forth his rebuke. And, besides his indignation at the kind of men some of them were, he rebuked the casuistry and misleading character of some of their methods and teachings. He did not stop even at that. More striking evidence still of his sovereign attitude toward interpretations is given in his dissent from some things authoritatively stated even in the sacred documents of the faith which was his own and which he deeply loved, devout Jew that he was. He made drastic re-interpretations of interpretations long current and associated with highest names. He did this not once, but on many occasions. "Ye have heard that it hath been said by them of old time . . . but I say unto you." No small part of the so-called Sermon on the Mount is made up of paragraphs which begin in this amazing fashion. Or, to recall another of his noblest phrases, "The letter killeth; but the spirit giveth life." Even of his own teaching he said "The words that I speak unto you, they are spirit and they are life." It is as if he would provide against inflexible interpretations of even his own words. He leaves us no doubt that the very task of the living spirit is to confirm that in men's statements, including even his own, which is true to the life for him who seeks the confirmation. The task of the living spirit is to confirm that in accredited statements, even those buttressed by long experience and great authority, which is true for a new age, even for every new man, and consonant with the sum of valid knowledges which may be newly current.

In the large, doctrinal interpretations made by the Christian generations in their long sequence have been conditioned in the contrarieties which they were made to meet. They have been consonant with, or perhaps we should say necessitated by, the mode of thought of the times which produced them. Those familiar with the history of thought see these great deliverances in their setting. They do not seem so strange as they may do to those to whose minds they are the only representation of modes of thought of a given era widely separated from their own. It may also be true that, even for the unlearned, if such statements were isolated, they might not sound very convincing. But they are not isolated. What convincing character they may have is for simple-minded people due often to associations, say of youth, or again, in the depth of personal experience, before critical estimate set in. One might even think of such statements as carrying us all the way back to the apostles or even to Jesus. This is, of course, true only in a very small degree. But thus it may come about that the believer, whether he is conscious of it or not, thinks about the religious life in a manner different from that in which he thinks concerning anything else. This is perhaps the first step toward not thinking naturally or sufficiently about religion at all. Almost uniformly the greater statements have been brought forth in controversy, sometimes controversy for the very life of the faith. Now it has been forgotten what the controversy was all about, indeed the persons of whom we now speak possibly never knew. To put it more justly, the man of whom we are speaking probably lives the life which is the life of his own time with all his energy. He lives the religion which is life—the life which is religion. This is something which he understands. Of this religion he thinks in terms natural to himself. Even if they are limited terms, they are consonant with his own time. He is in fellowship with others who work at the problem of the religious life in the same way. He probably thinks, it may be that he even knows, extremely little about the creeds. At all events, he leaves this subject to those whose business it is, as he supposes, to know about them. Meantime, others over whom living religion has no such hold as it has over the man of whom we speak, may take these classic statements of religion for religion. They have heard it said that these statements were made in crises of Christian history by the most illustrious teachers of their day. Furthermore, eminent teachers of religion in our own day insist that these are permanent statements of what one may or must believe. They may feel that they must reject the religion along with the statements, if they arrive at too sweeping criticism of these. Or, contrariwise, they may esteem that they need have no thought about religion at all except to assent to statements which they admit that they do not understand. This is not from either side a very satisfactory state of things.

We have been taking our illustrations from the history of Christianity as that religion which is most likely to be well known among us. Impressive parallels may, however, be found on the very face of the history of other religions. Judaism rejected Christianity, or rather, rejected Jesus before there was anything which bore the name of Christianity. Jews rejected Jesus because he did not fulfill the ideal of the hope of Israel as the vast majority then cherished that hope. They came to cherish only a more and more lurid hope as the ruin of their state and the dispersion of their people came upon them in the time, first, of Titus, and finally, of Hadrian. But Christianity also rejected Judaism. Paul led the way. He rejected more of it than did his Master and retained more of it than he himself knew. Certainly Jews have had many centuries in which bitterly to complain of hostility, even of cruel persecution and of aversion of many Christians to this day. The rift is still wide. This is perhaps less excusable for Christians, or at least for normal Christians, because in our Bibles we have the Jewish sacred literature always before our eyes. Our sacred literature is not in their Bibles. It is hardly open to a Gentile to say how much sounds strange to him in a synagogue. It is certainly open to him to say how much is familiar and dear, for example, the Psalms with much of the literature of the prophets. Our own Puritan ancestors would certainly have said even the Mosaic law. Quite apart, however, from our common inheritance, common ground is created and perpetuated by the life, which is the real religion, that devout Jews lead, and which is not widely different from the life that devout Christians lead. We know also that many of them feel in this same manner towards us. At their best the two lives are very much alike. Persecution and prejudice have done much to drive devout Jews in upon themselves. They have made permanent things which would otherwise naturally have changed. But it is not to the undevout Jew that we go for understanding of his religion. It is not of an undevout Christian that a Jew would seek to understand Christianity. There is not a world of understanding of any religion to be had from those who have none.

The Buddhism which conquered China and Japan was not the Buddhism of Gautama. The rejection of the idea of God and the refusal to accept life had at one time in

India many followers. It has now but few. It never travelled far. It was a Buddhism which had place for deity and promise of something more than mere escape from life which converted other peoples. This Mahayana Buddhism had its own doctrine of salvation. It was this which was the secret of the conquests which the old Indian teaching made among the two greatest peoples of the Far East. This is the secret of the immense vitality and high service of Buddhism in Japan today. It had and still has a power of adaptation to changes which we do not always think of in Oriental faiths. It is this which has in a measure transformed Buddhism in Japan, even since the Meiji era. It was the idea of the Boddhisattva, one who renounced the immediate enjoyment of Nirvana in order to preach the good news to miserable men, which went before the historic propaganda of the old faith. There might be many Boddhisattvas. The Japanese Kwannon, the woman who could not herself enter Nirvana because she was a woman, but who could by a good life be reborn a man, she also gave herself to an endless pilgrimage through recurring births to bless humanity. Besides these saints, imitators of the Buddha, was the still more wonderful figure of Amida. In another universe and in an inconceivably remote age, a monk, by many lifetimes of sacrifice, earned merit to admit him to Nirvana. He held it worthier, however, to refuse and to continue earning merit which should redound to the salvation of those who put their trust in him.

Or take the example of Islam in Turkey at the present moment. Until recently there were the usual evidences that the faith of the prophet had place in public life. It held sway also, perhaps it holds sway now, in the old way over devout hearts. Those who lived long in Constantinople knew that there were Moslem saints. There have always been such. They lived before all things the inner life which is religion in a manner parallel and not altogether dissimilar to the life lived by Jews and Christians. What they did with certain pages of the Koran must have been much the same that Christians do, and long have done, with fierce nationalist pages in the prophets, or again, with much of the apocalyptic of the New Testament, particularly of the Book of the Revelation. Just now, in the awakening of intense national and modern feeling and in hostility to Europe, secularism is not tolerant of the deeper things even of Islam—hardly more tolerant than it is of Jews or of the Greek Church or of Western Christian missions. Something similar may be said of Russia at the present moment. Ecclesiastical institutions, on the whole, had lamentably lagged behind. Long ago Peter the Great had made the Procurator of the Holy Synod a layman. Peter, not himself devout, may have thought of this as a measure for modernizing the Church. The last Procurator does not seem greatly to have concerned himself with that work. The spirit of the modern world in its acutest form has in both these nations, for the moment, thrust religion from its place. What they, either of them, may think of bloody pages in their own earlier history, in which fanatical religion had a large place, must be somewhat similar to that which we think of bloody pages in the history of our faith in various parts of the world, not too remote from our own time. In either case, there seems to be, for the time, but small appreciation of the religion which is life, which certainly lives and will live again in the minds and hearts of many men of all these faiths. In a measure it must have been the holding fast to the forms, whether of belief or of practice, or of both, the identification of religion with those forms—this was conspicuously true of Russia—which leads men of the new mind to esteem that religion itself must be done away.

We ourselves shall perhaps fare better than we deserve if our secularism with its alienation from religion, or, at all events, its profound misapprehension concerning religion, is not to have parallel effect upon the life which religion is, and so, in the end, upon the religion which is life. Adversity may be good for us in this regard. It has often been so in world history. One can but recall the gibe of Gibbon, that if anything could prove the divine origin of Christianity it would be that it has been able to survive the errors of its followers. It is at times the externalization of religion which is the contribution of some of those most conspicuously identified with the cause of religion to its general peril. Long continued repression or, as at the present moment with us, a mere alienation and suppression in a secularist movement which has come with the marvelous advance in the external aspects of civilization, does depress the life which religion is. This is, however, not so harmful as that which sometimes seems the very betrayal of the nature of religion, the externalization of religion itself, the identifying of religion with its forms, whether doctrinal or ceremonial, and perhaps most of all, the grasping of religious organizations at social or secular power. Misfortunes, short of being too cataclysmic, are likely to bring about again the recognition of what the spirit of religion means, as also the need of it in which men and nations stand. The need of it is only the greater for men of varied and rich life who feel no need of it, and for nations completely absorbed in furtherance of outward aspects of civilization. It is often perversions of religion that turn men against it in secular movements which undermine, and in revolutions which would destroy religion. For the moment there may be something like common ground between enemies and friends of the cause, in attacking that which the former propose to destroy while the latter aim, by elimination of evils, to restore religion to its purity. Neither of these aims is in the light of world history easy of accomplishment. There may be —there has at times been—a great idealism, something in itself resembling religion, in the effort to destroy religion. One reads Voltaire and not a few of his contemporaries, with the feeling that they understood religion in no sense except as formalized in an institution which they distrusted and sometimes feared and hated. If the matter had been presented in just this way, Voltaire might possibly have demurred. He himself had, or thought he had, at least at moments, a perception of religion. His effective attitude was, however, always the same, "Crush the accursed thing." It was the end of an age in which representatives of religion had flouted reason in the interests of authority. This was almost as true of some Protestants as of any in the Roman Church. It was no great wonder if representatives of the rights of reason flouted religion. Both parties to the long dispute failed to make distinctions which have grown quite clear to us. Rousseau's sentimentalizing of religion borders often on the ludicrous. But at least it was in the direction of recovery of the place of feeling in religion. Schleiermacher also sought to recover the place of feeling in religion and for a century has been praised among Protestants for so doing. Opponents were, however, not wholly to blame. They were confronted with representatives of an institution which often claimed, officially at least, that the institution was the religion. There was pith in the saying of Madame Roland—incidentally, later beheaded by other revolutionaries—that her religion was the Republic of France. The ultimate tragedy was that in the resurgence of religion after all these tribulations, and again especially in France, the old forms came back, and this in the political and social as well as in the ecclesiastical world. Even Napoleon had to come to the Concordat. The Pope also came to the Concordat. Further wrestling with the problem devolved upon coming generations. Probably it will always be so. The significant thing is that despite these concurrent and opposing mistakes, the spirit survives.

Underlying more modern movements at which we have hinted which are also secularist in tendency, is a vastly enhanced knowledge of nature and an incredible augmenting of man's power through application of this knowledge. For the moment, there is something like an infatuation with the use of this power. This knowledge has altered the whole picture of the life of man. Perhaps we merely use the language of tradition when we describe it as secularist in its tendency. Why should it be secularist? If religion could show a like vitality, this obvious increase of power would entail merely a like measure of idealism and consecration. This obvious increase of power demands, however, nothing less than that we shall make place for the new learning in the organized whole of knowledge. Or rather, perhaps we should say, since the new knowledge has taken its place, we have to see to it that it does not altogether discredit the old knowledge, with its aims and ends in life. The new learning must find place in our thought. But there is no reason why it should take a place which it cannot ultimately keep. It must be reckoned with in the ideals which we hold before ourselves, and so, in the end, in our view and practice of religion as well. The new knowledge has put us in possession of powers which even our own fathers never imagined. It is, however, the use which we make of this power which changes the outlook and even the inner consciousness of men. It is the absorption of some men in the pursuit of this new knowledge only, and mainly in the outward use of it, which is the perilous thing. It is true also that some who are thus themselves absorbed have enthusiasm in aiding their fellows to avail themselves of these new powers. Quite naturally, however, if left to itself, this enthusiasm also works obliviousness of other interests. It works to the extrusion not alone of religious interests. It works to the disadvantage of higher aesthetic concerns. It compromises even the intellectual life in all save a limited area. It relegates ethical concerns. It may not touch even the sense of social responsibility, save again in the rather superficial way in which one may desire to see others started on the race for liberties, comforts and pleasures which the possessor himself so much enjoys. Philanthropic sentiment at this level easily mistakes itself for religion. It needs something more to make it such. This is the fundamental criticism of what just now calls itself the new Humanism. This is in somber contrast with the great outburst of Humanism four centuries ago, as also with the humanitarian enthusiasm of the end of the eighteenth century.

And, finally, it is true that some, and, on the whole, a growing number, of those who have made greatest achievement in the new learning have a place also for religion and lead in the effort to point the way to a reconciliation of the two. For it hardly needs saying that the remedy is not in crying for the rejection in principle of any of this new knowledge or of the powers which it confers. The remedy is not in an austerity of life which would separate religion only the more completely from the life of the world by arbitrary and artificial denials. The mediaeval world, without knowing any science or sharing, in the least, the power which it confers, tried that. The monastic movement brought forth indeed individual characters of great loveliness at a time when the temptations of the world were less manifold and alluring than now—at least they seem so to us. It utterly failed, however, to transform society save upon its own terms. In its denial of reason, in its reaction against progress, in the segregation—not to say the childlessness of the best—it retarded the world. In its attitude toward new knowledge, and this particularly in the period of the dawn of the sciences, it had its own share in alienating the Renaissance from the Church, and again, in the convulsive movements of rationalism in the eighteenth century. In its rigorism and exclusiveness, it is one of the things which has given us much to struggle with even in the twentieth century. The attitude of austerity toward life has had its share in driving some men of the rising sciences into atheism or, at least, into a contented agnosticism. The ascetic mind which is, to be sure, not much in evidence just now, but which might become so by reaction, failed to realize the significance of the vast expansion of the world. The remedy is nothing short of the inclusion of all this new knowledge, and of the powers which go with it, in the moral and religious purposes of men. One of the signs of our times is the disappearance of the word *agnosticism,* and this even in face of the fact that some of the contention for religion itself has been, to say the least, obscurantist. The remedy is nothing short of the dominion of spiritual aims and moral ends over the new elements in life, which, it is already manifest, can neither be abandoned nor ever be made satisfactory ends in themselves. They are merely means of a fuller life of the individual and of society. They are such means to those only who desire a fuller life. Such dominance of moral and spiritual ends over the manifold, changing and enlarging means of life, has, in the past, many times been imperilled. Sometimes it has seemed to be lost. It has generally been recovered. It will naturally never be regained in the old forms. When, however, it is not regained incalculable changes in the life of humanity must take place.

What is more significant even than this vast increase in the quantity of our knowledge, if we can use such a phrase, is what we may call the newness of the area of large parts of it, and, as well, the contrast presented in the method of arriving at it. Nevertheless, it is a fundamental conviction that, whatever be the boundaries of our knowledge, or the enhancement of it through new inquiries, along with the inevitable rejection of much that has been taken for knowledge, knowledge, if it is really such, must be a whole. The unity of knowledge is axiomatic, however far this man or that man may be from having unified the various phases of knowledge within himself. Most of us are far enough from such unification. There is, however, only one cosmos to know and ourselves, the microcosm, to know it. The old adage *homo sum* might stand us again in good stead. Physics and metaphysics were not long ago thought of by many as opposing modes of approaching the problem of the universe of things. To describe the matter graphically, although also with a simplicity that is almost humorous, men thought of metaphysics, philosophy, somehow as a manner of reasoning from the top downward, from general conceptions to their various applications. And men had long ages in which to discover how mistaken that view was, if it were isolated, and how injurious its consequences might become. Think of the stagnation of medicine from the time, roughly speaking, of Galen to the time of Harvey. Read only Burton's "Anatomy of Melancholy" to be convinced of this, or again, Sir Thomas Browne's

"Religio Medici." Then men came to think of the sciences, notably physics or chemistry or biology, even astronomy, as reasoning from the bottom up, that is, from detailed observations to an hypothesis, which presently took the form of a doctrine, and then became a dogma—until it was disproved. Comte thought but poorly of philosophy—so poorly that he must have taken pleasure in calling his resumé of the sciences "A Positive Philosophy." In somewhat similar fashion he entered also the precincts of religion—"invaded the borderland of religion," was the phrase used of his effort in his own time. That was interesting in its time. For a brief period and a limited circle, it was influential. Under the impact which Comte's effort represented, philosophy, which was really such, wavered. Philosophizing took different directions. Differences of direction have been maintained almost down to our own time. Schelling's effort had been in contravention of Fichte's idealism. This was before the time of Comte but in the same general direction. Hegel had sought to unify the two tendencies and, for that matter, to include religion as well. But one needs only to recall the dates to realize the futility, then, of such an attempt. Since then, and perhaps because of Hegel's premature endeavor, there has been, one might say, no unity of movement in philosophy. Systematizing theology literally stood still for a long time. Then in some efforts, to be sure, it sought to recover its old place, and in some to make place for the new. Here, also, one may say, and with even greater emphasis than in the case of philosophy, that there is no unity in the endeavor as yet.

With all of our contention for the unity of knowledge there is, nevertheless, a knowledge which is central to religion. There must be. Theology was only too often and too long an attempted metaphysical formulation. Its logic was, like that of philosophy, deductive. It has found it growingly difficult to maintain connection with the newer aspects of philosophy. And in general we may say that its connection with the advance of the sciences leaves much—some would say, almost everything—to be desired. Through ages, one might say always, the reasoning has been from God to man, from the top down, from the far side to the near, from assumptions as to God to facts as to man. One has only to open one of the manuals of theology current in many of our schools in my own youth. The chapter on God stood first in all the older systems of theology. And certainly no man to whom morals and the life of the spirit are the ultimate magnitudes will dispute that, in the sense of logic, the sublime words with which the book of Genesis begins, "In the beginning God," have their own supreme right. But it is a right in logic which is a very different thing from being a right in history. The past of the universe, and with it the history of man, is to us only a little less mysterious than is their future. But if we are trying to say more definite things about God, things in which all that we are now continually learning about a perpetually evolving universe, with also all that a tragic and glorious and unfinished history of man has to say to us, we cannot be content to begin with a dogmatic or even with a poetical beginning. No more can we say that we will begin at the end. For, exactly because there is God and because we believe that the best of man is before him and not behind, we can only dream what the end will be. And in the light of the sciences, we repudiate many of the dreams of our forefathers as to what the end is going to be.

We have to begin where we are, in the middle, and work both backward and forward from that. But in fact that is just what we do with everything else. We do not for a moment think that "In the beginning" all the animals just as we know them were there assembled to receive their names or that the trees were just the same that we ourselves could familiarly name. History is longer than that, and the history which went before history is longer still. Poetry, the language of emotion, is old, and the emotion which made language is older still. But if we are asking for noble insight and forecast with the still nobler intuition and hope about God, we have to draw these from the noblest we have seen and the nobler still that we imagine. Upon such thoughts, mainly poetical—whether man knew it or not—men have fed their souls since man began to be man. One might add that it was by the aid of art, since there began to be any art, and then we should have to add and multiply beyond that. In this sense a chapter on God in our theologies should come last and not first and *finis* should not be written at the end of it. We should be with the lapse of time prepared to add appendices, or even to re-write the whole chapter. Most of all, the chapter on God should come after the chapter on Christ in whom we think we find what religion now most needs to know about God. We should be content to hold that even Jesus taught only that which mankind needs to know or can apprehend about God, and perhaps we might add, only that which Jesus himself apprehended about God. For the rest we wait. We assume that Jesus waited. It is over against the background of science—and fully admitting how much science has yet to learn—it is against the background of what science, as yet, teaches, and not, as did the Hebrews, against the background of a garden in Eden, that we have to think of the beginnings and progress of man. No more can we think of the end of the world and the consummation for man in terms of the apocalyptic views which Jesus also seems to have shared with the men of his time. When he escaped those apprehensions of his time, it was into the world of intuition and emotion whither we also can follow him. Certainly it is more than evident that the fate of humanity, not to say also of the individual, will depend upon man's moral and spiritual qualities far more than upon any elements in his environment. It will depend far more upon his soul than upon his body. Or, to put it differently, it will depend upon his having made his body the instrument of his soul, and an expanding universe the environment of enlarging purposes of his spirit. It will depend far more upon that for which God stands as symbol than upon anything which a man or the race can otherwise attain or achieve, although the symbol also will be constantly changing with our achievement. It will depend upon our inner and higher life for which all achievements in man's outer life and world are only means, but never ends. It will depend upon the life of the spirit in respect of which, of all created things, so far as we know, man stands alone, and each man alone, before the face of God, who is spirit.

Most of us accordingly think that the paragraph upon God should come last. But indeed in some systematic statements the paragraph concerning man is not easily recognizable, even by some of the really religiously minded, as containing quite an adequate description of man. Surely a part of the knowledge of religion must be approached from the side of facts concerning the nature of man. For three generations one of the greatest achievements of science has been in the establishment of the relation of man to nature, in the revealing of the emergence of man out of the context of nature. It is only upon the basis of the inclusion of such material that we can rise to a philosophy of religion at all. There is indeed no good reason for confusing theology with philosophy of religion. But the two sciences can hardly be built upon precisely contradictory principles. In our generation, some men who had prepared themselves to teach theology availed themselves, if opportunity offered, of the chance to teach instead philosophy of religion. This was, possibly, because of the greater liberty accorded them. But the impression as to the lack of liberty in teaching theology, as some theological schools are organized, is unfortunate. No one asks that theology shall regain its old ascendancy, achieve again the solitary majesty which it held in the Middle Ages as the queen of the sciences. But it needs to take its own high place in the world of the sciences. A philosophy of religion must reckon, and theology, no less, must reckon, with the advance of real knowledge with every generation. Such a theology will certainly wear a different aspect from the dogmatic theology upon which some of us were bred. Religion is natural to man. It is necessary to the fulfillment of the nature of man. It is one of the forces working for that fulfillment. So old is this view that the religious themselves, those of them who welcome the aid of the new sciences, and especially the gains due to the study of the history of religions, have indeed received manifold correction of their views from these sources. But by no means have they waited for results of these investigations to be convinced that there is such a thing as religion, nor indeed to learn the best of what they know concerning its high qualities. Experience of their own, the touch of other men's experience, the experience of the world with religion and of the world without religion, has taught them something of that. A profounder knowledge of man's self and a truer knowledge of religion only illuminates a man's own valid religious experience. But the having of some religion of one's own illuminates the religion of others. All life illuminates religion as, indeed, religion illuminates life.

2. THE INTUITIVE

There is, furthermore, a knowledge of religion which is immediate, intuitive. It is not discursive. It is as of something self-evident—to him to whom it is evident. It is reached by processes of thought not formal, perhaps not always conscious. This also must claim mention in this prefatory chapter. It is perhaps the witness to religion upon which the deeply religious most rely. Origins of it may be in inheritance, or again, in association. It is not by this fact discredited. The man who is accustomed to reasoning processes, anxious on behalf of reason exactly in relation to religion, may question the validity of his intuition. He may esteem it a survival of earlier prepossessions. With some it is that. He may regard it as a substitute, thus far with him unconscious, for rational processes. He may wonder at the commanding power of intuition in himself. He may note the absence of it in others of equal cultivation with himself. He will note that the intuitions of other men may relate to other matters as, for example, of artists to art, of musicians to music, of poets to poetry. He is aware that his own intuition in the matter of religion has diminished as his rational interest has matured, or again, in proportion to the decline in himself of any interest in the matter. Nevertheless, in moments of dismay his intuition may resist his perplexity as if there were about it something irrefragable. Through its outward results in conduct it is at times the evidence which may carry most conviction to the least religious. This is partly because it brings no opposing theory into action. It is not itself a theory. It may cause the listener some amazement. It does not, however, initiate argument. There is no rejoinder to make to it save indeed the one which the man who is thus convinced may himself be actually making. He may be looked at askance who thus trusts an intuition which many of his fellows of like cultivation do not share. His compeers may not know the divided mind within himself. Perhaps that is just what intuition is—an intimation of other or, at all events, of further possibilities. Most men look askance at intuitions which they do not share. Some men, at times, look askance at their own. We should go still further, and say that all intuitions ought to be brought to the scrutiny of man's other powers. And yet high achievements in art, new developments in music, great tentatives in science have often begun in this dim sense that all was not well with our reasonings. What has been thought or said thus far had not reached the limits of the possibilities. Discoveries are rather apt to give intimation of themselves beforehand in this way. They most safely give this intimation, however, to the man who is conversant with the reasoning thus far. The man not conversant with the reasoning may be receptive. He is not likely to be creative at this juncture. He is more likely to be misled.

We touched upon this matter when we spoke of the life which is consonant with religion, of conduct which follows upon conviction, of the influence which men of this sort exert even upon some who are not aware of being thus influenced. It is, after all, no wonder that the good life based on deep feeling makes impression. Similarly, it is the life guided by the intuitions of religion which may trust that these will somehow either be confirmed or, conversely, be refuted. Experience may support an intuition. It may confute it. It may greatly alter it. It is this which happens in practical affairs of life, in the initiation of new ventures, in one's friendships with men, in the life of love, in association with those whom we trust. Experience will refute it in the case of those whom we become convinced we should distrust. The refutation will be rational, but it may expand into an intuition the reverse of the first. The living of a life based upon this sort of practical conviction may, in the end, undermine what has been to us a happy confidence. By contrast, it is the living of a life based upon this sort of practical conviction which may confirm him who lives the life. It confirms him in such manner that, even in face of argument which he cannot always answer and of contrarieties which he does not overcome, he remains assured. He would say perhaps with emphasis, that he knows. He means not merely that he took one of several possible ventures and that experience has justified the venture which he took. He would probably say that he was inwardly sure when he took it. It would be easy to reply that he could not possibly have been thus sure. That would prove merely that we all use the word know in two senses. We do this in many relations.

Religion has this kind of self-evidence—for those for whom it has this kind of self-evidence. Even those who have not, or not entirely, committed themselves to a life which comports with such conviction may have moments of a sense of its validity. They may have this sense even though arguments for another course in living may have preponderated and, in the end, prevailed. Our intuitions sometimes haunt us after decisions have been made. It must have been the sense of the rewards, and likewise of the perils, of this kind of knowledge which made the Master say, "Blessed are the pure in heart, for they shall see God." Religion may have this kind of self-evidence to many a pure soul, no matter how widely cultivated. It certainly has this kind of self-evidence for many persons of meager cultivation. With these it takes the place of a kind of knowledge of religion which they may perhaps never acquire. On the other hand, it is quite true that the claim of self-evidence may be, and often has been, the occasion, rather, of delusion, an excuse for pretense, a justification for fanaticism, whereat reasoning men are gravely offended. We may recognize, however, that with many men, and more particularly with youth, this, of intuition, is the initial religious experience. Such is often the beginning of the religious life. Perhaps we should say, rather, that it is the beginning of the awareness of the religious life. How much this may have had to do with the atmosphere of devout homes, with startling experiences, with the contagion of other people's experience, is commonplace. Commonplace is also similar experience of mature men, either in disillusionment with the life lived upon opposing principles, or, again, through contact with potent religious personalities. Parallel are other awakenings as of genius in art, of a mastering proclivity in life or discovery of a unifying principle in work. Parallels are not lacking in other relations in life.

Men sought a generation ago, especially in this country, to capture the evidence of this religious awakening. They thought to subject it to rational inquiry and to tabulate results. The effort was an interesting one and has proved instructive. It had its origin perhaps in the feeling that the new science of psychology might help us here. The endeavor was to get away from formulations of doctrine of established religious communities. These the novice might be merely repeating as best he could. It was recognized that doctrines are but formulations. No less, however, the vocabulary of revivalists contains formulations. The language of religious instruction now widely current in our churches also has formulations, only sometimes less, rather than more, circumspect. Of course, the Wesleys and Whitefield, Finney and Moody, had also sought by inquiry to assure themselves of the reality of the experience of the masses of their converts. It remains that some of those named were themselves men of something like religious genius. They had a kind of divination, some of them, at least, of the thing which they were seeking. And perhaps the most drastic thing to say would be that they had a kind of divination for religion, but not for psychology. It was thought by psychologists of religion that they also might make direct appeal to experience, and this from the new point of view. Questionnaires were widely circulated. As one reads these, one is profoundly impressed how difficult it would be—or at least should have been—to make such a questionnaire. Naturally, the unsophisticated promised least prejudiced results in statements of their experience. Incidentally, more reflective persons did not answer. Perhaps they shrank from revelation of such intimate matters. Possibly they felt that the language of the questionnaire did not exactly fit their case.

In the end, and after volumes of tabulation, it was found that the answerers were rarely able to describe their experience except in terms of some description already known to them—often rather naive, sometimes distorted—but formulation after all. Often one could tell in a general way from what religious background the answerer came, what hearsay it was that he had in mind. It was discovered, what students of mysticism already long since knew, that the power to describe an inner experience is rare—perhaps the greater the experience, the rarer. How many people can tell anything, that is, to third parties, about being in love? They show it, that is all. And they are generally shy about showing it. And if they are not shy about showing it, one might almost wish they had been. Sometimes the answers to the questionnaire were less intelligible than those which it had been intended to avoid. It was not experience which was described. It might be rather pathetic imaginings concerning that experience, conventional language about it, even when the fact of the experience might be quite genuine. The mass-aspect of revivals also certainly tended to produce this result. The disappearance of the questionnaire may be connected with the disappearance, at present, at least, of the revival. The mechanization achieved by the method of the questionnaire was, however, formidable. It brought into clear relief only the same thing which had often baffled inquirers in the atmosphere of sympathetic personal concern. But the paper questionnaire was not exactly sympathetic. There is in fact no mirror, except a sympathetic personality, upon which one can get the reflection of pure experience. Instead, what you get, especially from immature and unreflective persons, and in a mass endeavor, is just what you are seeking to avoid. It is not undistorted reflecting of experience. It is almost certainly reflections about experience, sometimes naive, often repetitious, conventional, something quite other than the experience itself. The unanimity, which was sometimes praised, is the very thing which was misleading. People are not exact copies of one another. Especially is this true in the deepest things in life.

There is indeed considerable difficulty in discussing that of which no entirely satisfactory statement can be made. The great mystics have been quite right in feeling that. Experience and the statement of it are two different things. They take place, if one may so say, at different levels. Mystics have grown eloquent in the effort to express the inexpressibleness of their experience. But even that is no exercise for a novice. Ineffable is one of the commonest words in the mystical vocabulary. Upon the precise point which we are now making those who are not mystics will readily agree with them. And how could people little trained in expressing anything express the ineffable? Of course, it remains that some men, and perhaps more often women, in the ranks of the great mystics, have achieved grand and original description of the religious experience. More often still they have achieved the witness to its consequences in their lives. Those whose descriptions are thus immortal belong, however, to the class of those who brought to the discussion of their religious experience, sometimes an intellectual quality or, again, an emotional quality, and, most rarely of all, both qualities together, which, it needs no saying, the wholesale questionnaire was not exactly seeking and practically never found. No person of the quality of which we are now speaking would ever have answered a questionnaire. He would have written his own poem—whether in verse or prose would have made no difference. He would have painted a picture or, best of all, he would just have lived a life which was his poem. The point is that the ineffable expresses itself mainly in life and conduct, in character. It shows itself in the exalted spirit of those who often feel nothing so much as an indescribable quality of the impulse which has taken possession of them. If they add to this intellectual and emotional power in greater measure, if they feel driven to express their experience, the result has been given to the world in forms which are sometimes immortal. In the highest sense the expression is to the experience what the statue is to the sculptor's sense of beauty, the specific beauty or greatness the idea of which he is trying to convey. It is what the poem is to the thing which the poet felt driven to try to say.

The distinction which we make may be compared to the score, or even to some surprising rendering, of great music, like Toscanini's rendering of Beethoven's "Missa Solennis," and this, as related to the still greater majesty of that which was in the composer's mind. We have to remember the sense of despair which sometimes overtook Beethoven at his failure to express that which his whole nature felt. It is the supreme witness to his nature that he did thus feel. What he did was the best he could do. It is the best that the orchestra and singers can do, to try to help to convey that which so moved the composer. But with it neither the composer nor the musicians are ever quite satisfied. The rendering moves also the souls of listeners, but each in his own way. It moves the same soul differently in different moods. Perhaps what the musician in listening most deeply feels is how much could not be said. That is also the listener's most touching tribute to the greatness of what has been said. The music says different things to different people. It says more and less to the same man in different moods. It says nothing to some men in any mood. From the appeal to the Muse in the first line of the Odyssey to Milton's prayer in the opening words of "Paradise Lost"—

And chiefly Thou, O Spirit, that dost prefer
Before all things the upright heart and pure,
Instruct me, for Thou knowest . . .
. . . What in me is dark illumine,
What is low raise and support,

one hears the same note of disparity between the aim and that which the poets find, or even hope for, in the performance. Their appeal is to that which is beyond themselves. It is that their utterance may be, if only in some measure, comparable to the high thing which has possessed their hearts. It is not like a mathematical demonstration or a lawyer's argument. It is like the coal on Isaiah's lips which, through burning his lips, might enable him to speak. Even that phrase has a dash of imagination about it—the speaking best through burnt lips. Paul, who was only at times a mystic, says of himself that he heard words which no man could utter. Pascal returns to that again and again. Perhaps it is exactly for that quality in what Pascal wrote that men recur in the crises of their spiritual lives to Pascal. It is for that quality that men turn again and again to Augustine's Confessions. They hear him say of certain experiences of his inmost soul what no man who ever lived has said so well. It is for that quality that Luther turned to the "Theologia Deutsch," whose author we do not even know. There is all the difference in the world between Michael Angelo's "Last Judgment," at the altar-end of the Sistine Chapel, nothing less than titanic in its symbolism, and what Michael Angelo, through his symbolism, was trying to make men feel. There is the same difference between Dante's boiling and freezing hells and the immortal, inviolate moral distinction which he means to make men feel. We are not compelled to think that Dante looked upon these symbols as quite so purely symbolic as we do. I doubt if we ought to think just that even about Milton's hell. Both may have had a sense of something which might be quite literal about it—a sense which most of us lack. Both had, however, something so awful to say, for the moral and spiritual meaning of man's life, that they make the reader feel the inadequacy of the symbol just because he feels the truth which is so much greater than any symbol can ever be.

We ought to make clear to ourselves that all of this of which we are now speaking takes possession of us in the manner of intuition. It may be quite impossible to express it in the manner of rationalization. It takes hold of us in poetry which we perfectly well know is poetry. It takes hold of us in painting, in music, and above all, in idealistic action. The religious man, at his best, often turns to ventures in life which have no final satisfaction in this life. That is the enigma which he presents to the non-religious. He turns aside not because he is thinking of other compensations, streets of gold, gates all of one pearl, trees bearing their fruits every month—in another life. He recognizes that that also is just picture, poetry. He is just as uncertain as any other normal man as to what is beyond death. He may even be uncertain as to whether there is anything beyond death. But whatever is beyond death must be congruous with the sense which he has of living the highest life. That satisfaction in a measure he gets now. That satisfaction, now, is enough for him, or perhaps I should say, it is enough now. He does not know the end. He is sure that he does know the way. The real witness to religious experience is not so much words about it as character attained through it, life proceeding from it, soul to whose experience that life contributes, and also testifies. In that case, there is something here which is not at all difficult to take hold of, but which is probably not taken hold of by definition or by argument. It takes hold of us in poetry, painting, music, in every effort after the ideal in life. If we have this kind of sensitiveness, it takes hold of us as probably no argument ever does. Appeal of this sort takes possession, moreover, of men of little cultivation and perhaps of no other power of expression of their deeper selves. Things of this sort have taken possession of men in all ages and at all levels of experience. Compared with this witness words are unnecessary and may be quite futile. Their very futility may have effect exactly opposite to that which is proposed. The Master's teaching is replete with admonition on this point. "By their fruits ye shall know them." "He that doeth my will shall know of the doctrine, whether it be of God or whether I speak of myself."

After all, there is nothing surprising here. Intuitive judgment often lies at the basis of the commonest ventures in life. The commonest people often make those ventures. Initiative, courage, resourcefulness in difficulty, tenacity of purpose, are qualities necessary for success in any worthy thing we try to do. It is amazing how often a venture which, at the outset, had none too much of rationalization to go upon, is justified. This is true in the most ordinary affairs of life. Why should it not lie at the basis of the religious life? After all, religion, at its best, is the greatest of our mortal ventures. Some men are always trying to make it cease to be a venture. They would make it a bargain between ourselves and heaven. But that is not the highest view to take of the promises of God. The surprise which sound natures feel at the success of a risk which they took is paralleled only by the surprise at their failure often felt by those who merely take no risk. The most distressing failures among men are often of just this sort. They beset those who could never bring themselves to trust the unknown, some part of which will probably always remain unknown. Some of it may remain ill understood even after the goal has been reached. To trust one's intuition, and, incidentally, thereby to develop one's intuitional faculty, to balance this with one's rationality, so far as this is in any way possible, and yet to persevere in face of that which is not yet rationalized—this is what is necessary. But this is necessary to success even upon commonplace levels of life. In the commonest language of the world we call that trust in men and things. It is the venture which gives our rationality something actual to work upon.

Faith in religious matters has been described as knowing things which are not so. There is a great deal more truth in that description than we might at first admit. Faith is, at all events, the being sure of things which are not yet so, or again, the being sure of things which cannot now be proved to be so, or still again, of things which will never be proved to be so—or, else, proved not to be so—save by the man who takes the risk. Yet such faith—call it courage, what you will—is the only entrance upon the course by which these things can be proved—or, alternatively, disproved. He who will not trust himself to ventures has no right to expect a clear issue either pro or con. As the Epistle to the Hebrews says, Faith is the being substantial to us of things which are only yet hoped for. Their substantiation comes later. It is the being evident of things not seen. To those to whom that phrase is a flat contradiction, it is just that —a flat contradiction. But they illumine only themselves who say so. Those who are not willing to make a venture never find out what is at the end of it. How should they? Even supposing these things do exist, they become evident only to one who sees them in this manner and decides to try them out. And if they do not exist, this is the only way to find that out. The commonest matters in life, and to the commonest man among us, are thus constantly proved, and many of them are disproved, and all in this one way, and in no other. He who does not take the main ventures in life upon this basis does not take them upon any basis. He himself makes them false for him, all the while that they are being proved true for others. Those who are disappointed in life are, before all others, those who disappoint life.

Therewith is not said that those who do not themselves thus render their living futile do always, or perhaps ever, get just what they thought they were going to get, the object of their endeavor precisely as they envisaged it. Probably in the vast majority of cases they do not. They get something—it may be different, it may be better, it may be worse. But they have made themselves in the process, and that is probably something better than any thing we ever get. The other man in his refusal of effort, or in his setting lower objects before his effort, has, at all events, failed through lack of effort to make himself, or has even made himself worse by unworthy effort. This may be one of the reasons—and there are other reasons —why the venture of religion is easier for the common man than for men of far greater intellectual training. The venture of religion is to him more like all the other ventures which he has to make if he is going to live at all. To think that we never know anything except through intellectual formulation might be called the deliberate provincialism of the intellect. It is a provincialism rather widely spread among the learned. We are often entirely convinced of things for which we spend the rest of our lives in seeking the evidence. We do well if we find evidence enough to keep us going. If not, we should, as we say, lose faith. That is correct. That is exactly what we do lose—faith. But we lose also that to which faith alone could ever have led us. To the end, we may never have entirely cleared away the mystery. Of the greater issues of religion, this is, of course, still more true. To the end of life we shall certainly not have cleared away all, or perhaps even much, of the mystery about those issues. But what is the use of religion? Clement of Alexandria declared that faith is the assent of the soul. Henry Jones interpreted that: Faith is propulsion. It is more than insight. It is the beginning of action. If such is the common experience of ordinary men in mundane affairs, why should we expect it to be any different in religion?

Furthermore, it is in this manner primarily that we know persons. Persons best worth knowing are never profoundly known in any other way. To have formed in advance a theory of a character, to be unwilling to modify the theory we have formed, is perhaps the surest of all ways of never coming to know the particular man. Perhaps, in the last analysis, this is the surest of all ways of never coming to that most important of all knowledges which we describe as the knowledge of men. Our initial impression of qualities of character is almost always of the intuitive sort, before we begin to give ourselves rational account of it. To allow the prejudices of another—or, for that matter, our own—to weigh against our initial impulse to keep an open mind is certainly surrender of our own judgment. The play of reason, the instruction which experience brings us, may confirm, as also it may fail to confirm, our earlier impression. We have various names for this sort of judgment in advance. We call it suspicion when it turns out badly. We call it divination when it turns out well. We use the word know in either case. The truth is we do not know. We could not know. Reasoning in such a matter is, however, mainly confined to the confirmation of our intuition, or else to the refutation of it.

Finally, God, the Supreme Object of our concern—unless we decide not to be concerned about God—the

Infinite Object of our search—must be in some sense counterpart of the personal in ourselves and must, therefore, be approached in somewhat the same way—by intuition. If there is no counterpart for the highest in ourselves, then why should we count just this, our personality, the highest in ourselves? The idea of God as having relation to our personal qualities is, by some, easily disposed of. It is said that children and primitive men naturally project this quality of themselves, as persons, into their surroundings. Children talk to chairs and find fault with that over which they stumble. Their immaturity and our present inability to think the matter through projects them, and, quite as truly, us, into difficulties of thought which as yet defy us. Nevertheless, at the highest stage of civilization men and not things, persons, precisely in their quality as persons—in their intelligence, their initiative, their responsiveness, in their responsibility and trustworthiness, in their sympathy, their companionship, in all the qualities which call out our trust, in their freedom in it all, and our freedom as toward them—men and not things are the most significant element in our surroundings. It is from this angle, again let us say, that the emptying of the universe of that for which the idea of the personal is, at all events, the only symbol that we have, is such an impoverishment of life. It may well be that the words which we fling out toward this mystery are only symbols. It is certainly true that we know persons mainly through their limitations. We might even say that we distinguish persons largely by their limitations. And then, to speak of unlimited personality, draws near to being a contradiction in terms. Yet, if there is nothing in the universe which is the congener of this highest in ourselves, then why is this quality of person in ourselves, with the same quality in others, the thing most necessary in our little personal universe, and the most indispensable to the fullness of certain aspects of our life at all?

It is indeed difficult to think of the universe with a personal God. It is more difficult to think of the universe without a personal God. To put it differently, if it is difficult to think of God as personality—which is certainly true—it is still more difficult to think of the impersonal as God. On these latter terms, why is it not rather, as some indeed think it to be, this very personal quality of ourselves which is the most vain and illusory thing about ourselves? At intuition it stands—and let me say again at the risk of constant repetition—for those for whom it stands. It is vain to say that we shall never get the last verification until we pass into that other mystery about ourselves, namely, whether there is any life and consciousness for ourselves beyond the present life. But normal people do not sit still contemplating that mystery. We acknowledge it as mystery, and then we proceed to fulfill our present life as best we can, and esteem this the best preparation for another life, if there is any other life. I might add that this is also, obviously, the best thing to do if there is not another life. The evidence of so much as that is in this life. It is not the worst disposition to make of this life even if this life is all. What we think has large share in making us the men we are. But what we are determines also in good measure what we think. We cannot too often repeat to ourselves that in regard to these greatest things—and many smaller ones—we never get wholly beyond intuition. "From that bourne no traveller returns"—or even ever communicates, as most men soberly think. It may be that some who hold to this intuition about further life—that is a better phrase than future life—Wordsworth called it "intimation"—do so because so many intuitions in our life have proved true.

Others may claim that this tenacity of faith has its source in the fact that so many other intimations have proved not true. Either way, at intuition it stands. But of many other things besides God and immortality that remark is true. One of the best evidences of profounder rationality is that we do not come altogether to distrust the great intuitions of life. Why should we stake all upon the love of any human being? For, it is quite true, that the quality of love must some day be shown in relations which are still unknown to us. Certainly one of the great duties of rationality is to guard, to clarify and, upon occasion, to refute what we may have thought to be an intuition. Intuition often goes before, it sometimes follows after, and, most often, it is acknowledgedly contemporaneous, with the premises and processes of pure rationality. We have moments—and some matters—in which intuition begins to appear to us like the only possible rationality. The contrary seems irrational.

It seems not to admit of question that all of our profounder relations are to persons. Even the most self-centered lives, those ruthlessly set upon exploiting the possibilities of power or gain, have usually had a few persons, some one person, on whose behalf, for moments at least, they imagine themselves to be making their endeavor. With these they share, even if it be grudgingly, their success. Without them, they would be more lonely in their failure. To these they are forced to expect, since all men are mortal, to transmit their power when they themselves shall be obliged to yield it. Such meager reservation from an all-devouring selfishness may indeed make the prospective legatee, also, something of an abnormality. Just so, however, a richer nature may assume responsibility on behalf of others, for men whom in their multitude he cannot know, for the sake of a cause, for country or faith, for future generations. It is for men, mankind, that one abjures advantage for himself, even in moments when he may doubt his own wisdom, or is not assured of success. He may be confident that, at least, the spirit he is of will raise up others to serve enlarging purposes. It cannot be illusion that we think this the good life. We know that it is such a life that creates great personalities. It is personality which creates such a life. The very ideal of personality thus points beyond itself. It is open on the further side.

It was surely natural that, once men had passed beyond the stage of mere conjuring—the stage of magic, in other words—then, they began to imagine personal beings more like themselves as ruling the phenomena of nature and determining issues in the lives of men. They peopled the world unknown to them with beings more or less like themselves. These were objects of worship, recipients of sacrifice. They were thought of in very human fashion, pictured even in terms of objectionable human personalities. It was true that for the religious in Israel there was that which Jahve could not do—or would not do. But there was little that was obvious to the ancient world to make masses of men think of God as bound, in his own way, by his own world. There was little to lead them to think of the Maker and Ruler of the universe as then most exalted when he showed inviolable allegiance to moral and spiritual law. Yet this was something which he, less than any other, exactly because he was God, might ever go against. One has only to know something of mediaeval literature and, for that matter, of Reformation theology, to realize that the conviction was still far down the horizon that there is thus at the heart of the universe that which the Omnipotent can never do. This is the thought which makes so many of the arguments about the sovereignty of God, of which Calvinists, for example, made so much, not only bewildering but actually misleading. We all know men and women for whom there is much that we are perfectly sure that they will never do, nor think of doing. Their freedom is not to do it. There is much also which they can be relied upon to do, even at all costs of suffering and heartbreak to themselves. Yet not merely mythologies but whole theologies have proceeded upon what we must now think a gravely unwarranted assumption, namely, that God can do anything. There is a phrase of transcendent insight which occurs in the second Epistle to Timothy, long attributed, even in its present form, to Paul: "He abideth faithful. He cannot deny himself." The phrase is used concerning Jesus, the incarnation in a supreme sense, as Paul thought it, of God. Yet even with the picture of Jesus before us in the Gospels, one cannot view the history of theology without seeing that things have been long and widely attributed to God which do not comport with that which we should infer as to the character of Jesus, nor, indeed, with quite all that we think we must hold as to the best of men. Taken seriously the character of Jesus rules out certain ancient and widespread conceptions concerning God.

For various reasons relating, in a general way, to current theories of the universe, the picture of God which philosophers and theologians have made appears, now and then, to have lagged behind the insight into character, with also the feeling of the nature and influence of character, which was granted us in Jesus two thousand years ago. Much of the rest savors of speculation, of abstraction, of that which men assumed to be postulates of reason, about God. Some of these assumptions are still with us. In some theologies abstractions still figure which withstand all that we have come to know of the nature of the physical universe and of the history of mankind. They withstand what we know of the evolution of morals and government, of the application of science to life, of the history of faiths and of our own faith, of the criticism of our sacred literature, of the knowledge of similar literatures, of enlargements of conception which have come to us as to the mind and life of humanity. It needed no saying "that God is not the author of confusion, but of peace"—to quote Paul again. But, to avoid confusion, our ideas of God must ever anew be brought into harmony with the body of ideas and principles of which an ever-advancing knowledge puts us in possession. We cannot bring our advancing knowledge into harmony with the pre-judgment which belongs to a stage of knowledge which has long since passed away. We may speak of an unchanging God, but we change. As a result of these changes in ourselves, we should not like to admit that we are the less competent to understand God. If our knowledge of nature and of man advances, we have difficulty in believing in a God who does not fit into the nature in which we now believe. Perhaps it is the very imagery drawn from ourselves, imagery which describes God as Maker of laws, establisher of moral distinctions, executant of the Supreme Order, which creates difficulty for our thought at this point. But is not this just imagery? It is very ancient. It was at one time very natural—but natural to what? To a view of the complete divine transcendence. It is a remnant of the thought of God as anterior to, and in some senses at least, exterior to his universe. Again let me say, how natural! But let me also say how, occasionally with older thinkers, and more frequently in modern times, both philosophers and religious men have made earnest with the thought of immanence. Perhaps mystics have always leaned to the thought of immanence. Spinoza's teaching had no room for anything but immanence. Pathetic personal consequence for him was that he was almost as vigorously repudiated by Jews as by Christians.

The universe must be one. That unity was intended to be emphasized under the title of the sovereignty of God. But at least it must be the universe itself which reveals to us how that sovereignty is exerted, and still more, wherein it consists. Men have been misled by analogies of autocratic government—governmental notions which, also, by the way, have since the middle of the eighteenth century largely passed away. Abstractions concerning God may serve their own purpose in philosophy, although here also they are often misleading. Philosophies, like science, may be trusted to change, both of them, and in their mutual relation, with the lapse of time. It is true that the tempo of change in philosophy has been for a hundred and fifty years much less rapid than the corresponding evolution in science. Also the changes have been less coherent. Fewer still of the best minds have been devoted to the evolution of theology. In a measure perhaps this has been because of the assumption that theology does not evolve. But does it stand still while the world goes on? In the large, however, the progress of thought has always been like that. There are secular alterations in emphasis. The identical area of religion is the conduct of life, the development of character, contribution to the character of others. It is quite clear that religion, even our own religion, has been lived under ideas concerning man and the universe quite different from our present ideas. If I may say it in all reverence, it was so lived by Jesus Christ himself. But it cannot, or at all events it cannot so well, be lived by one of us if we think it necessary to live it according to ideas regnant in the time of Christ or, again, of any of his great servants, reformers and theologians of intervening ages. The body of a living man is said to renew itself entirely once in seven years. The embodiment of our religion, whether in thought or in activity, ought to renew itself, perhaps not in quite so short an interval as that, but at least the principle is clear. It is the religion and not the theology which is the thing which is alive. It is this which made certain formulations alive at one time, and causes religion to need other formulations at another time. This is the thing which may be said to make Jesus alive to us, while many successive interpretations of Jesus and reasonings about God no longer live for us. The point is that it is the intuition concerning God and the good life which lives and perpetuates itself from age to age. But it is not any formulation which the intuition has ever received or ever will receive.

God is in the very highest sense and by his very nature less free than the most problematical of men. In a sense God is not free at all, if you prefer to say it so. He is bound by the highest, the highest being the only perfect expression of himself. In this sense God is changeless. Yet what God can give to the world of men changes ever because the world of men changes, and, perhaps we might say, because no two men are alike. It changes in a sense which is most significant for us by very reason of that which God has already given to us and done for us. Even the good man is far from being so free as is the man who is forever wavering between good and bad, and is more than likely to come, in the end, to be bound by the bad. In that same sense, the good man is also, and more and more, bound by the good, only he feels this being bound by the good to be what Paul calls "the glorious liberty of the sons of God." We have to think of God in terms of Jesus, and not as men have prevailingly done for almost two thousand years, to try to think of Jesus in terms of God—or rather, what actually happened—to think of Jesus in terms of what men then thought about God. Jesus accepted defeat and went down to death because he could not win some men at all, nor any men to complete allegiance to his thought as to his own and their own relation to God. Somehow thus, assuredly, we have to think of the relation of God, the Supreme Goodness, Wisdom and Grace, to us. We have to think of God's powerlessness to make any man good who does not wish to be good, who does not strive to be good, who does not grow in goodness and God-likeness, by his own resolve, even though it may also be by God's aid. From this point of view, election, predestination, have, to say the least, a very different meaning from that which we used to assign to them. At-one-ment has for us a different sense from the one so long and so insistently urged as atonement. We have to think of the Infinite Goodness as far more universally intended, and also as far less externally efficacious, than some traditional theologies would have us suppose.

The particular point here at issue concerns the freedom of God, as apprehended by us as that of a personal God to whom our personality is analogous. We come upon the conviction, perhaps startling in the light of our previous notions, not indeed that God is less free than we, if you choose to put it in that way. But he is, at all events, more supremely bound in the response of his whole free nature to the good and true than the wisest and best of men can possibly become. Yet, in their own small way, good men approach that. They are free but they are also bound, bound iron-fast in their own free will, their own allegiance to the good. The better they are, the more they are thus bound. Paul loved to describe himself as the "bond slave of Jesus Christ." It is not however but that he was very proud of not being of the slavish mind. It was his free mind that made him the bond slave of Jesus Christ. He was that by his own sovereign will. He gave himself freely to Christ, as Christ had given himself freely to Paul. He gloried in that attitude of mind, in that disposition and effort of life. Certainly that type of mind was characteristic par excellence of Jesus. We should miss the deepest sense of the sinlessness of Christ if we for a moment believed that he could not have sinned. On that basis his sinlessness would make him no model for us. In the experience of goodness there is a point where freedom and obligation are fused into one. The man is the more free because he is under one supreme obligation. And the converse is as strictly true. The man is under one supreme obligation exactly because he is free. He is free to the highest and free from all else. If you like the phrase one might say that the better men are, the more they bind or have bound themselves. But that phrase is not quite so true as the other. The better they are, the less they have need of separate decisions. Their fidelity we might perhaps liken to that of the needle to the pole. But, in truth, it is exactly not like the needle to the pole. The needle is not free. It only appears to be so. The man is free, and he is free exactly because he has bound himself. The fidelity to God and to the good is the infallible expression of his own free nature, of his own unvarying volition. That is an ideal which we none of us attain, but it would seem as if it must be the ideal of God.

We do not know quite how to think of the Supreme, the Almighty, as being the most bound of all natures in the universe, under the most perfect, if also the most glad, subjection to demands which his own nature and, quite as much, the needs of man and the whole nature of the universe, impose upon him. Yet also the ideal parent is just that, most bound and yet most free, binding himself or better still, bound by an obligation he assumed in becoming a parent. The true parent views this as the most precious aspect of his relation to his child. The best parent is completely absorbed in doing the best possible for his child. But that best possible for the child is certainly teaching the child to do the best for himself. Therefore, also, the best possible may become the actual for the child only by suffering him to take the consequences of not having done it. And the best possible for the parent may be suffering with the child. Perhaps the oldest language of the world for the relation of God and man is to this day the most illuminating language that we have. "Father of gods and men," Homer said. "The God and Father of all men," Paul said. "Our Father, your Father, my Father," said Jesus. Of course, there is such a pitiful thing as a father's weakness through what he mistakes for affection. We cannot attribute that to God. The more clear is his insight, the more certain is his aim. The more true is it that there are things which he will never permit an indulgent love—an all too human love—to lead him to do. Popular revivalistic conceptions have sinned against this austere view in one way, and the old formal theories of atonement sinned against it in another. It may be objected that so strict a rendering of salvation in terms of moral achievement, of transformation of character, postulates that which some men—and among them some who most need it—do not bring in any greater measure to the moment of their awakening. Indeed not all such famous cases, if we may allow ourselves that phrase, have had much time after their awakening. Sometimes in undue measure the triumphs of grace have been celebrated in the lives of just such men. It might also be responded that in just this disproportionate emphasis may lie one of the secrets of the alienation of some right-minded men from such a theory of grace. A man may have none too much of goodness himself, but he thinks that somehow goodness, before or after, is fundamental to the matter. It is very necessary to respect God. To be sure, Jesus on the cross said to one of the thieves, "Today shalt thou be with me in Paradise." Obviously in such a case Paradise should not then be thought of as only a prolonged rest in pleasant surroundings, with no problems, although it must be owned it is sometimes so depicted. Certainly what comes after life can be worthily depicted only as more life and worthier. And this is true not least but most for those who start upon that life somewhat at disadvantage.

May I seek in the remainder of this chapter to give an illustration of the way in which intuition supplements, and in the end may abolish rationalizations which have done duty for centuries in the interpretation of a cardinal doctrine of Christianity, the doctrine, namely, of the atonement. It would not be possible for us to find a more central example. And it is one which has parallels in other religions. I have given the impression thus far that intuition is likely to precede the rationalization of great truths in our lives and, more particularly, in our religious lives. The example which I now give may illustrate how our intuitions may follow and modify our rationalizations. The great historic theories of the atonement illustrate this. I think also that they illustrate several things besides. It is this general view which I wish in the remaining paragraphs to apply to what is ordinarily assumed to be perhaps the most fundamental doctrine in theological thought. If any example is central to Christian theology, it should be this one.

The Anselmic doctrine of the atonement assumed that in the sin of man the honor of God had been impugned. Offense was infinite because of the infinite nature of the offended God. No satisfaction rendered by man could suffice. Satisfaction could be rendered only by one who shared the nature of God. Thus Christ's sacrifice was accepted as vicarious for men, who then, in gratitude, bound themselves in allegiance to Christ. But surely this is, with absolute frankness, the framework of feudal society. The theory of Arminius, shared by Grotius, substituted for the thought of an offended sovereign that of violence done to an eternal foundation of human society, namely, inviolable justice. Without God's unvarying justice, human society could not exist. Jesus assumed the guilt of man in order that, at once, both the justice and the love of God might be made plain. Surely here is the emergence of the idea of the sacredness of human society, one might say, of the obligation of both God and man to that sacredness. Of this idea Grotius, perhaps the first great international lawyer, was the protagonist. And yet, in this case as, in the other, we cannot rid ourselves of a sense of arbitrariness, indeed of injustice, on the part of God toward Jesus. The advance is great indeed from the idea of a personally affronted God. Here what is manifest is the solicitude of God, as well as of men, for the supreme interest of humanity. The real objection is that, in the isolation of Christ's vicarious sacrifice on our behalf, it puts this, which must always happen in the conferring of all highest benefits, as if it happened but to one man and for all time. It is not as if God could accept one sacrifice in place of all. It is rather that the spirit and example of one is intended to inspire all. It is indeed that the spirit of all good must be held to have supported Jesus in his insight into a law and life of sacrifice whereof his death was but the seal. But it is the same God who waits to inspire and uphold other men, all men if they will, to see life and themselves and God's grace in the same way. It is "at-one-ment" with God—and this with "a right God," to quote Bushnell's anguished phrase, as he struggled over the doctrine of the atonement. It is at-one-ment, heart and soul, with Christ and God, and this is open to all men who will have it so. It is not a sacrifice to an offended God which is sought. God is both too great and also too good to be pictured as merely offended. His grief must be for us and not for himself. And the overcoming of that must be through something which the sense of his changeless love moves us to do and be, and, doing and being that, to find ourselves at one with God and God at one with us. It is not even, as with Grotius, a sacrifice to the ideal of human society. It is a sacrifice of what is selfish in every man to that which is selfless in every man who would follow Christ and be at one with God.

But now what do these examples show? Is it not that all interpretations given in the past of this aspect of our truth bear—and how could they fail to bear?—the marks of the prevailing modes of thought of the ages which produced them? The difference is between the Anselmic view of God as an offended feudal monarch whose honor must be sustained, his offended majesty appeased, on the one hand, and, on the other hand, the Arminian view of God as indeed too great ever to have felt the sin of man as an offense against himself, but as an offense against a fundamental truth, a priceless verity, which men must see. This indeed marks a great advance. It represents God as having felt the issue of man's sin not as affecting himself but as cutting man off from the fulfillment of himself. Society cannot exist without the ideal of justice which all men must serve. And yet the Arminian view is also still entangled in the sense that somehow the sacrifice of Christ availed with God for all men. The truth is rather that it avails in each man by each man's own obedience to an eternal principle. It is a principle which indeed his sin has enabled him to discover. But once the principle is discovered, he has made himself by God's aid a free man, of his own will to pursue it. Even MacLeod Campbell, an epoch-maker in this discussion, only a century ago, could never rid himself of the word satisfaction; satisfaction to God, satisfaction for sin, although, frankly, the word bore no meaning whatever which had real relation to Campbell's own theory. Bushnell's discovery, nearly contemporaneous with MacLeod Campbell's, in its grand insistence upon a "right God," seems to have been his feeling that somehow satisfaction in any of the various meanings which had been attached to it was not congruous with the notion of a "right God." "A right God" would not demand satisfaction for himself. He would ask of men only that which would restore them to their right relation to himself and themselves. He would help them to regain that relation.

But why do we no longer hear of a still more ancient view of this same transaction, the atonement? Some theologians all the way from Irenaeus almost to the time of Anselm, and some greater names among them, interpreted the sacrifice of Christ as a ransom paid to the devil. It is simply that for us this whole framework of thought has long since passed away. Many of us no longer believe in the devil. But in some sense almost the whole human race did thus—and long—believe. We do not believe that a man is in bondage to the evil except through his own acts. And correspondingly, we do not believe that a man can be rescued from that bondage except, again, through his own free acts or, better, through a state of mind and heart which those acts signify, through the power of the example of better men, through the inspiration of Christ, and by the aid of God in his own endeavor. We fully believe that God, the Spirit of all good, helps a man. We do not see how even God can help a man to a moral victory, to an inward personal life for the good, except as the man wills it and will help himself. Certainly it is clear that the apostles personalized the power of evil. On the face of the New Testament, it is quite clear that Jesus himself thus believed. He frequently talked of the devil. But is it disbelief in Christ to decline to believe in the devil? He shared with the men of his day many other postulates of thought which we no longer share. We ourselves still say that the sun rises, although we know very well that it does not. But when Jesus spoke of the sun's rising, there is no reason whatever to suppose that he thought of it in any other way. How can we think of him as truly a man of his own time unless we think of him in some such way? It is equally true that in some other ways he was incredibly far in advance of his own time. But it is for his amazing insight into things which have no time, which are true for all time, it is for this that we think of him as unique in his nearness to God, and find in him, now, just as then, the power and grace to bring us close to God, if only we will freely follow him. It is somehow here that the greatness of Jesus lies, the greatness of the spirit of God in a man, "very man," as the old creeds rightly say.

The progress of philosophy with the knowledge of history have contributed much to the resolution of the kind of difficulty to which we have just alluded. The old humanist and rationalist movements had their share. Literary and historical criticism of our own sacred books, comparison of these with the sacred books of other faiths, these, too, have had their part. The progress of the sciences of nature in the nineteenth century, the vast expansion of such knowledge within our twentieth century, has done its part. Together they have contributed to set in a new light the ancient question of the natural and the supernatural. They have changed the boundary between the two, which used to seem so clear, or rather, in the light of advancing knowledge, we wonder whether there is any boundary such as we used to conceive. They have put a new construction, as we have intimated, upon our thought of the relation of God and man in the nature and life of Jesus. We are able to think of an incarnation of the God, who is spirit, in a man who is true man of the spirit, without lifting him out of participation, full and entire, in the life of man. On the other hand, we are able to think of him as bringing purity and power and peace, the very spirit which is God—which God is—into the life of man, and thus setting an example, conveying power to the whole world of men who freely and with a whole heart follow him. Other ages found possible, indeed natural—why should we not say intellectually necessary?—interpretations of that great aspect of the work of Christ of which we have just spoken which are no longer necessary for us, and for some of us no longer possible. The fact itself, asking ever for new interpretation, abides the same. What is it which makes theories of the sacrifice of Christ which dominated minds of the greatest men of the faith for centuries seem so remote to us in the present day, so artificial, and no longer viable? It is intuition. It is unformulated feeling, keeping pace with the vast advance of knowledge, that this truth also must find relation to other truths within our world of thought. It is undeniable that they do thus seem—these older interpretations—no longer viable. They do this indeed to men who have not made the long journey through the history of thought which we have above described. On the whole, it may be that some of those who have not made this long journey of thought are rather likely, when impressed by this sequence of different embodiments, to surrender the living kernel of the truth itself. But it is the living seed within which accounts for the succession of the forms. They were always only reasoned shells, which indeed, with the lapse of generations, some of them, have become but husks. But it is the man whose religion is a living thing who is most likely to feel that there is in this strange series of forms something which still lives. Else how could it have lived so long and made for itself so many different shells? He feels that it does live exactly because it has outlived its forms. He has intuition of a truth which lives ever and needs only to find new formulations in a new world of thought.

Now it is, of course, of purpose that I have called up the memory of these four great historic views which have been held, each in turn, to be the true view of a central truth of the Christian religion, namely, the atonement. It has been by way of validation of the claim that doctrine and dogma are in their nature interpretations. But there must be some truth to interpret. Doctrine and dogma are not in themselves the thing which is interpreted. They are intellectual formulations of a vital truth. Because they are intellectual formulations they partake of the character of the intellectual life of the age which produced them. They are congruous with that character, marked by its traits. Because they are so marked, we recognize them as part of the warp and woof of the life of their time. And it is exactly for that reason that they did exert so great an influence upon the thought and life of their time. And then, for precisely the same reason, they exerted a diminishing influence upon the life of subsequent times. Changes in modes of thought are ordinarily slow. Conservatism is great. Nowhere is it greater than in the area of thought concerning religion. Moreover, great institutions have lent all their weight on the side of this conservatism in respect of forms of thought. Even intuitions rest—or rather, they seem even to some intuitive people to rest—upon the preservation of formulae. Exactly the contrary is true. It is intuitive people who in the area of a new life of learning find their way out. The formulae in their succession rested upon living intuitions. But what is it that "grows old like a garment?" It is the formula which was, after all, just that—a garment for a thought. What is it which is living and casts the garment? It is intuition, constantly renewed with the generations of devoted men. What is it that may grow bewildered, dissatisfied with a half-accepted, or even once enthusiastically accepted interpretation? What is it which may turn rebellious and die to the interest of the truth itself, because it does not know that it is dying only to the form in which that truth has once been held? It is a faith which has identified itself with forms and now must set itself free to find an expression which is congruous with a new life and time. It is the living religious intuition which, if we may so say, does no more than breathe the atmosphere of a changed intellectual world. But it does breathe that atmosphere. It is the living intuition which comes to feel that old theoretical solutions, which were once reigning doctrines, or even official dogmas, no longer satisfy. Humble people may still live on in the just conviction that, after all, feeling and conduct are religion. They are right. But people who are not quite so humble, taught an insistent dogmatic solution from which, nevertheless, they vaguely differ, grow indifferent. People still less humble may discard in militant fashion the religion along with the dogma, with all the untoward circumstances which that may entail. Is not that one secret of some of the opposition to religion, and still more of the indifference to religion, which we observe in our time? In the end those arise who—because of their competence can, and because of their sense of responsibility will, contribute their share toward a new statement which in such circumstances must be found. Statements change. Religion abides. And surely this is the final index of the fact that religion is for man and that man is made for religion. How far have we passed beyond many of the theoretical positions of St. Augustine? It was Augustine, however, who said, "Thou, O God, hast made us for Thyself, and our hearts are restless till they find their rest in Thee." And Pascal said, "I had never found Thee, O God, hadst Thou not first found me."

3. THE SUPERNATURAL

May I be permitted here a bare word as to my sub-title —the supernatural. It is clear that the idea of the supernatural is correlative with the idea of the natural. The progress of the knowledge of the natural alters the area, and perhaps even the idea, of the supernatural. I have not myself been able to find that the word which gives us our word supernatural occurs in classical Latinity. Nor have I been able to ascertain with certainty when the word first emerges in Christian discussion. This is not at all because the distinction which the word describes was not present to the mind of the ancient world. And perhaps it was even more clear to the early Christians and to the mediaeval mind. That distinction was fundamental to both. It has remained fundamental for many minds almost down to our own time. The contention for "natural religion" which characterized a good part of the eighteenth century was in the end defeated by the fact that it overshot its own mark. It treated this antithesis as if it were absolute and not merely relative. It drove religious men to say, not that the vaunted "natural religion" was not in its own sense natural, but that it was not in any sense religion. The parallel of what has happened in the world of the phenomena of nature is at this point instructive for us. Many events out of the ordinary in the course of nature—perhaps one might say some events within the ordinary course of nature—were by many, and this almost down to our own time, attributed to direct supernatural agency. The development of the sciences of nature has enabled us, and practically all men, to esteem processes and events which had been immemorially ascribed to divine intervention as part of the marvelous order of nature itself. They reveal a power and purpose in nature which our own ancestors never imagined. The case is surely similar in the life of the minds and souls of men. The mind is quickened. The soul gains in insight and vitality. The impossible becomes possible. It becomes actual. The impulse spreads. Others share the inspiration. Life rises to a higher level. It gains new scope and energy. Higher aims are possible, loftier achievements actual. What seemed beyond nature becomes natural, definitively so, for the life of humanity henceforth. God gives himself to souls who give themselves to God. Men give themselves to one another in this same way. But it is not as if he to whom impulses thus given were himself suppressed or superseded. Quite the contrary. He is enlarged, empowered, enabled. It is not a word or an act, not an outward fact, which is bestowed upon him. It is a touch of the spirit which is God, to man who is spirit, too. The deed comes from God, but it is the man's own deed. From him it becomes the spirit of other men and deeds, of a new world. In that sense we can hold that such issues are supernatural. But this is exactly because they are natural, fulfillment of the nature of man in God, expression of God in and through men.

The writer of the Epistle of James once used of God, whom he calls the "Father of lights," the noble phrase, "with whom is no variableness, neither shadow which is cast by turning." James was not an author of the intellectual quality of Paul or, again, of the author of the Fourth Gospel. It suited the turn of his simple argument, however, to throw out a noteworthy phrase. It is that, even in the limited application which he probably intended his reader to make of it. It is from the side of the thought of the unchangeableness of God that we, at all events, propose to approach the problem of the supernatural in general and of the miracle in particular. The miracle has often been thought of as the cardinal evidence for the supernatural. On the face of the Gospels there is no doubt that Jesus believed in miracles. He believed that he himself performed them. It was by the power of God that he performed them. The Gospels, as we have them, are probably Greek translations of Aramaic originals. The third and fourth Gospels, bear each of them, evidence of unity of authorship. In the one case the author was a cultivated man who explicitly says that he used many sources of the tradition. The fourth Gospel shows throughout a definite principle of selection and interpretation. The first and second Gospels may be compilations from earlier sources, or at least traditions. They also have characteristic modes of approach. The second leans to the recording of mighty works. The first deals rather with moving discourses of Jesus. It often alludes to prophecies which in the narrative are fulfilled. Both make the impression of a certain primitiveness which we may ascribe to their sources, and which we gladly hail. The first Gospel takes its departure from a genealogy of Jesus which begins with Abraham. The list divides schematically, fourteen generations from Abraham to David, fourteen from David to the carrying away to Babylon and fourteen from the carrying away to Babylon, through Joseph, to Jesus. It speaks of the perplexity of Joseph, of the animosity of Herod, of the flight into Egypt, and, after the death of Herod, of the return to Nazareth. It is in the third chapter that the narrative of the ministry really begins. This tells of the preaching of John the Baptist and, after the baptism of Jesus, of the inauguration of his ministry. The third Gospel also has a genealogy of Jesus which is, like the other, a genealogy of Joseph. It pursues the inverse order, beginning with Joseph and reaching back to Adam. Even in the part of it in which generations are parallel, the names are in many cases different. The genealogy is, moreover, at the end of the third chapter. It follows a longer narrative in which occur three poems of immortal beauty. These have become treasures of the services of worship in the Church, the Magnificat, the Benedictus and the Nunc dimittis. There is also at the beginning of the third chapter a passage of priceless historical worth in which events are set in connection with personages in world history, the Emperor Tiberius, the Procurator Pontius Pilate, the Tetrarchs in the subdivisions of the province, and the notable fact that there were two high priests. Allusion is made to the ministry of John the Baptist. The baptism of Jesus at the hands of John is described. There is an artistry about the Gospel which makes it a part of the great literature of the world. There is that also about the Fourth Gospel, with its selection and interpretation of teachings of Jesus, with the play, in its introduction, upon one of the most pregnant forms of philosophical thought then current in the ancient world, with also a mystical rendering of the last facts recorded concerning Jesus. These give to this Gospel also a place among the greatest treasures of thought of the world.

Belief in wonderful works as attestation of the personality and witness to the authority of Jesus' teaching was natural in his time, more especially in view of the Messianic expectation. Belief in such attestation would have found relatively few to question it among those who believed in the Gospels at all, almost down to our own time. In Jesus' time and world few would have been found to question the significance of such mighty works. His enemies attributed them to the devil. How much the weight of this form of attestation of Jesus' person and teaching had to do with the early spread of Christianity, it might be hard to say. The work and teaching of Mohammed had also for his believers the same form of attestation. Islam may have been moved in a measure by the example of Judaism and Christianity. It is due to the present ascendancy, in part, of literary and historical criticism, in part also of questions arising from the side of the modern sciences, that we look upon the interpretation of these events as questionable. The feeling of the antithesis of traditional views of the origins of Christianity, with views both of history and of scientific thought widespread in our time, have caused the question of the miracle to assume an importance, and this exactly for believers, which it may be said that the question has never before had. Once a support of faith, miracles have now become for some a problem of faith. The Hebrew words which in most of the Old Testament, particularly in Deuteronomy and the Psalms, set forth in this manner God's power and praise are rendered into English as signs and wonders. There are also two Greek words which are constant in the New Testament. These stand in our English translations in general with the same English equivalents. The Vulgate used almost uniformly *miraculum*. English translations as far back as Wycklif generally render the two Greek words by the words miracle and sign. Emphasis is clearly either upon the emotion with which the event is viewed, or else upon the interpretation of it as evidence of God's presence and power. That Jesus himself, in high consciousness, ascribed the power to do his mighty works to God working in and through him there can be no doubt. His disciples viewed it in the same manner. Later they are credited with having themselves wrought such works. There is allusion to a certain place in which Jesus could do no mighty works because of the unbelief of its inhabitants. One may conjecture that the chroniclers of his activity might have been disposed to set wider boundaries to the use of his power than he himself observed. The fact seems to be that even in the exigencies of his life this power was never exerted on his own behalf. His works are mainly typical of his compassion for others. They seem also to have been wrought mainly upon those who manifested a receptive attitude toward himself. These were convinced, however they interpreted it, of his wisdom and power and, again, of his truth and goodness. There are works like the raising of Lazarus, or, again, the supreme fact of his own rising from the dead, as to which it is open to us to doubt exactly what happened. It is open to us to wonder whether the former account may not be an actual misapprehension. The latter might be due to a great prepossession as to a Messiah and his work, an expectation which took him, with some of his deeds, outside the usual in the course of human life and work. Even so, there is an array of things related which have for us no explanation save in the extraordinary power of his personality, to which surely corresponded a receptiveness on the part of many of his following. Despite the amazement occasioned by such acts as are recorded of him, no one ever attributed to him traits of character which the exercise of such vast and strange powers seem to have brought to some men. He himself believed, "I could pray to my Father and he would presently give me more than twelve legions of angels,"—"But," he adds, "How then should the Scriptures be fulfilled?" He was only thirty-three years old, perhaps only thirty-one. Release was not the way to the fulfillment of his purpose. No word recorded of him is more typical.

If we look at the background of Judaism in the Palestine of Jesus' day, if we realize the intensity of the Messianic expectation, we shall not be surprised at the acceptance of signs and wonders, interventions of God on behalf of his oppressed and suffering people. Apocalyptic literature, especially in the later days of Israel's subjection, fostered such hopes. An apocalypse stands at the end of the New Testament. It has even been thought by some to be a Jewish writing, only slightly touched over by a Christian hand. It was a book loved by some Christians when the persecutions came on. So, perhaps, it found its place in the New Testament canon. Yet its place in the canon was long and sharply disputed. Again, while there are in the Gospels also whole passages in this apocalyptic vein, what is related of Jesus' own utterance is rather differently oriented. In his great vision of the Last Judgment, he speaks the language of his time. Yet what he says is levelled against evil men as such, and not against the enemies of his nation or against enemies of his own or of his little group of followers. With all his high consciousness of being the Messiah, he never claims outward advantages or rescue for himself. It is the moral and the universal which everywhere preponderates. It is the compassion of Jesus, the thought of the love and mercy of God, which everywhere in his mighty works has the first place. He has a long view of the moral judgment of individuals and of the world. Yet he never loses his sense of his own place in the life and faith of his time. It was exactly in these respects, in which he transcended—and disappointed—the expectation of many of the zealous in his time, that he has been a guide and refuge to men of all time. One might say that if ever a man had a right to expect intervention of God on his behalf, it would have been Jesus in the Garden and in the crisis on the Cross. He claimed Messiahship. But he was far from expecting privileges, immunities, divine aid, deliverance, such as the popular imaginings pictured in connection with the work of the Messiah, when he should come. This is one of the things which makes the teachings of the Second Isaiah about the suffering servant so wonderful, by contrast with much of the rest of the prophetic literature. Also this is one of the things which makes what is related of Jesus so wonderful by contrast with that which we might almost expect his humble and dismayed followers to allege.

The expectation of great deeds, great privileges and

immunities, an accompaniment of the marvelous for great men and epochs, was far from being prevalent among the Jews only. One may indeed point to majestic figures among the Greek philosophers whose investigations of nature, primitive as they now seem to us, with also their grand reflections upon the life of man, assumed an attitude quite different from that to which we have referred as frequent among Jews. Jews thought of themselves as the nation of God's choice and of the destiny of the world as involved with their destiny. But witness, for example, what Plato writes in the "Apology" concerning the last hours of Socrates. Few modern men can read the "Apology," follow the reasonings, feel the spirit of Socrates while he waited to drink the hemlock, without wondering at the parallel that those majestic moments offer to that which is related of Jesus' own approach to death. Later again, the two great religious figures among the Stoics, the slave Epictetus and the Emperor Marcus Aurelius, say something of the same sort to us. Stoics, however, arrived at their convictions by quite a different process of reasoning. There were, of course, and had long been Romans who scoffed at miracles and regarded them as mere subterfuge of priests. It would be too much to say that the populace, whether in Greece or Rome, shared either those lofty or these sinister views. This would be no more true of them than among the masses of Jews. With the decline of the Empire and the decay of learning, superstition resumed its wide and unreasoning sway. Miracles are frequent and paltry in the history of early monasticism. Legends of saints and martyrs are full of such evidences of God's recognition of their characters and work. Certainly the great reformers, and again, the popular teachings of Protestantism were not far behind in this regard. Presently prevailing views of Scripture, along with that of the nature of inspiration, sustained the opinion that, however we might expect no miracles in our time or in other relations, we must acknowledge those recorded in the Bible, and, most of all, those which had to do with the life and work of Christ. It is only fair to say that such views, at least in their perpetuation, had to do with a theory of inspiration which earlier reformers did not all share, but which became characteristic and appeared to be necessary almost down to our time. This is the position in which many Christians even in these later years find themselves. Meantime, knowledge of the laws of nature, of which one might say that the ancient world had little and the mediaeval none at all, has grown in the modern world. It establishes presumptions concerning events, whether contemporary or historical, and not merely in the world of matter but in the world of men as well. These presumptions neither the learned nor the unlearned oppose. These would hold even in relation to the most amazing event, and even if it were sustained by what is represented as irrefragable testimony. It is not good that, while all events outside the Scripture should be viewed as belonging to the wonderful context of nature, even if the laws of such events are yet to seek, those which are in the Scriptures should be viewed in a different manner. This cannot be good for the influence of Scripture or of the truth which Scripture contains. It does not enforce respect for the attitude of faith. It sets Jesus apart from the context of life in a way which is disastrous, and which may be said, so far as it goes, to contravene the purpose of the incarnation. It makes the incarnation seem to have been incomplete. It makes faith to rest in too large measure upon things which are sometimes of small consequence and the testimony concerning which may be differently understood.

The argument for the miraculous rests upon the belief in the power of God and in the love of God for the children of men. The argument against the miracle rests by no means wholly upon the modern view of the order of nature, with the conviction of the inclusion of man in the context of nature. It is true that these views do create a presumption. But weightier, by far, is the conviction as to the character of God, along with the belief that the highest concern of God is for the characters of men. Only too plainly we see that the conduct of men one toward another is often at cross purposes at this point. Solicitude may inspire a course which leads directly away from the emphasis upon the inviolable nature of the right, and, with that, of the necessity of a man's recovering his own inward relation to the right. Nobler natures among men may vacillate at this point. Men may in their affection "undo with their hands" that which it is their heart's desire to do. We cannot soberly think that of God. Forgiveness and pardon are not to be confused. Forgiveness may be in its proper moment a helpful, a healing, a creative frame of mind. No attitude is more constantly enjoined by Jesus. But certainly it is a mistake to suppose that pardon always leads to the recovery of character. It may quite as easily contribute to the defeat of its own hopes. Perhaps the reason why the two ideas, that of forgiveness and that of pardon, are so often confused is an entail of the long dominance of inherited notions of legal, and one might say, external relations between man and God. Such might be the relations of a sovereign to us, but not the inward and vital relations which the word father, so much preferred by Jesus, would imply. The parable of the prodigal son is surely often misread at this point. The picture of the unprodigal son is not exactly prepossessing. But neither is the portrait of the prodigal son altogether prepossessing. We learn that the yearning of the father, wounded in his spirit, pictures something about God. It is something which small and rigid men may not always appreciate. One might add that it is something which prodigal sons, when they are not in distress or again, when they are out of distress, do not always fully appreciate. The more prodigal they have been, the more possible it is that they may be willing to play upon this forgiving disposition of the father. What is certain is that free forgiveness by no means pictures all there is of God. Austere and faithful recognition of the condition of recovery of character pictures the rest. If even men feel that, God must feel it all the more. And in respect of the recovery of character, God is as helpless toward mankind as was this father, or as is any father, toward his son.

Forgiveness may draw a prodigal toward the recovery of himself. It may also lead a prodigal to think that nothing more is necessary. If we do not permit ourselves to talk merely about getting to heaven—whatever that may mean—if we think more about fitness to be there, and perhaps even about possibility of staying there, or even probability of wishing to stay there, that would be more obvious to us. And after all, we do not know what became of either of the sons. The picture stops at the frame. Jesus said many things which enforce a single lesson, or even only, as here, a part of a lesson. Aristotle is reputed to have said that no simile goes on all fours. But life goes on. Forgiveness may be a gentle beginning of what is in the end an austere matter. The austerity must be met by ourselves. Paradise can hardly be an enclosure, although Milton, certainly an austere man, spoke as if it had high walls about it. Did even Milton lapse for the moment into thinking of the walls as serving merely to keep the unfit out, and forget that they should not also keep the unfit in? If Paradise is a moral world, if the very conception of it is moral and spiritual growth, it must be quite as free for men to go from it as it is to come—unless indeed we assume that they will decide never to come, which, I might add, seems to be a thing which happens. This more or less questionable playing with images may point, nevertheless, in the direction of what I have most seriously to say. Whatever may be the case as to the miracle in the physical world—we may leave that to the scientific people—it is clear that confusion arises from imagining that any miracle can take place in the moral and spiritual world. The beginning of the physical life we might, if we choose, describe as a miracle—although it is clearly an event in the plainest order of nature. But as to the beginning and the continuance of the spiritual life, if we are free agents, this must be still more clear.

But belief in the physical miracle would seem to have had upon some minds the effect of making belief in what men have called the moral miracle easier still. As a matter of fact, this last is vastly more difficult to conceive, not to say that it is vastly more important that it should not happen. A view of the world of nature which makes it possible for men to think that God would, or could, suspend the orderly working of nature, in the interest of purposes of grace, has had deplorable consequences for men's view of the inexorable working of facts in the area of their moral lives. It has been only too easily assumed that if intervention with benign intent could happen in the world of outward fact, then similar events could all the more easily take place in the realm of men's characters and purposes. But is that true? Is not the fact just the contrary? In the phenomena of nature, as we assume, at least, we have merely forces to deal with. In the phenomena of grace, which we must remind ourselves are the phenomena of our spiritual nature, we have to deal with man's free will. Many of us are prepared to say in all gentleness, that the physical miracle seems to our view improbable. But we feel bound to say that the moral miracle is impossible. We may please ourselves by calling the amazing results which sometimes take place in the whole attitude of a given man toward life, his ceasing to do evil, his learning to do well, his being transformed by the renewing of his mind—we may please ourselves, I say, by calling that a moral miracle. Yet certainly nothing of that kind takes place without the co-operation of a man's own moral nature. Paul himself went through just such an experience of radical change of mind. "Transformed by the renewing of your mind," is the most perfect phrase which he has given us. Converted is the usual word, far older than the use which Jesus or the apostles made of it. It is an event more significant by far than any physical miracle could ever be. Yet in truth it is not a miracle at all. It could by no possibility be a miracle. It requires the concurrence of man's own free spirit. It is impossible if he does not concur. It is reversed if he ceases to concur. No doubt we do well at times to cherish the impression that something re-creative has happened. Slow or swift, transformations of character are the secret of the progress of the world. In all such things the individual is before the mass. But whatever be the emotional language which we use, we are well aware that such transformations do not take place without the free concurrence of everything in the make-up of the man himself. Nor are they continued without his continuing of that altered mind and will which they imply. Nor are they consummated without the absorption of his very being, the consumption of his years, in the endeavor which they entail.

It is a saddening observation to which one is sometimes forced exactly as he reflects upon the literature which has made much of phrases like "the miracle of grace." Whatever may be the figurative language in which we may indulge about the beginnings of this life in the spirit, the living of it is no figurative matter. The living it is in taking the responsibility, in doing the work of a man in the world in the spirit which came to him in that experience of renewal. We were all too young to know it when we were born—physically. But some of us would certainly feel that we had missed something if we had been too young to know it when, in the great old phrase, we were born again. Then we came alive to certain distinctions and resolutions which have shaped our living ever since. We should miss something if we were unable to remember when we passed from the drudgery of being kept in after school to the enthusiasm of the life of the mind. "The achievement of immortality" was, a few years ago, a phrase at which some took umbrage. It was easy to quote the phrase "The gift of God is eternal life." But it would seem as if there must be some qualification. There must be some achievement of immortality or else it could not worthily be called life. We cannot be so completely mistaken as to what constitutes a life worth living. Even Paul who, if anyone, might be described as a miracle of grace, said, "Work out your own salvation with fear and trembling, for it is God that worketh in you both to will and do of his good pleasure."

It is well known, although not always recalled, that Protestants in the period immediately following the Reformation, having repudiated the authority of the Church, took, and in increasing measure emphasized, a practically identical view of the origin and authority of Scripture. Luther in the earlier years of his reforming work had held an opinion on this question natural to a really learned man. He was influenced in no inconsiderable measure by opinions current through the revival of learning. The first editions of his translation, issued in 1521 and following, show this beyond question. The stress of the conflict with the Church, however, and no less, the necessity of repudiation of views and conduct of the more violent among his own followers, as at Münster, led him, after 1529, to adopt a view in marked contrast with his earlier opinion. He dropped a critical preface in which he had recognized differences among the Scriptural writings. He had roundly condemned, for example, the Epistle of James as an "epistle of straw." Melancthon seems never fully to have agreed with Luther's change of view. Erasmus, for this reason,—and several others—withdrew the measure of sympathy which he had once had with the reforming movement. When fifty years had passed, the Protestant bodies were almost everywhere committed to a view of inspiration which made of both the Old Testament and the New a divine oracle. Yet upon the basis of this view of the inspiration of Scripture, the Formula of Concord, arrived at with much labor in 1577, to allay strife among Lutheran adherents, betrays so plainly the differences of interpretation of an inerrant Scripture that it has sometimes been described as the "Formula of Discord." The claim concerning the inspiration of Scripture, as it stood in the popular mind and ruled for more than two hundred years, even in learned discussion, might almost be compared with that which had been said almost eighteen hundred years earlier on behalf of the famous translation of the Old Testament known as the Septuagint. The legend ran that the seventy translators had worked, each in a separate cell, upon the grand task of rendering the Old Testament into Greek. When the seventy copies were compared, they were found to differ from one another by not so much as an accent. Students of the history of the Commonwealth, and more particularly that of the sectaries and the Rump Parliament who were the despair of Cromwell and, as well, those who are familiar with the early history of Puritanism in this country, know how the prevailing view of Scripture was that of a miraculous determination even, one might say, of vowel-points in the originals. The Scriptures were authoritative as nothing else in the world was authoritative. The influence of time and circumstance, of human individualities, might be found in anything else, but not in the sacred documents, nor even, some thought, in the translations. The care of God vouched for that. These phrases have been repeated in my lifetime. It is small wonder that the apostle Eliot, for example, writing from Roxbury to an acquaintance in the Long Parliament, said that the troubles of the Parliament would never be solved until the Commonwealth, which was then the government of England, should be remodelled after the pattern for all states and for all times, given of God in the legislation from Mt. Sinai. The extraordinary group of scholars who, in the years before 1611, had produced the translation popularly known as the Authorized or King James Version, would certainly never have taken so extreme a view. But, at all events, the popular mind in that turbulent period took more and more the form we have described, until the bigotry and nonsense of the Rump Parliament brought about the return of the monarchy, in the person of even so deplorable a figure as was Charles II.

There were great critics of the Scripture in the age of

the Reformation and afterward. Particularly in the seventeenth century there were such in the Roman Church as well. The criticism of that age was, however, almost exclusively grammatical and lexical, hardly at all historical. The historical and literary criticism, as such, which occupied the minds of scholars everywhere in the nineteenth century, came somehow to be called the "higher criticism." It is not evident in what sense it was higher. It was certainly different and had its own place. But the great Biblical critics of the seventeenth century put the world under quite as great obligation. They made possible other phases of the work in later times. It was, however, the age of Reimarus and Lessing, say the last three decades of the eighteenth century, before literary and historical criticism, as such, was taken up. This criticism prevailed still later in England and latest of all in America. When this historical criticism was entered upon, it was at first the occasion of strifes bitter and sometimes destructive, for example, in the later works of Strauss and in those of Renan. Time has worked wonders. In large and increasing measure opinion of Scripture reckons with this historical and literary criticism. Many who could never follow the processes are familiar with the results. So much is this the case that, on the one hand, some feel that the Scripture has no particular authority at all. And, on the other hand, an episode like a famous trial in Tennessee, only a few years ago, seems already almost incredible. An historical view of Scripture feels its inspiration and authority for no external reason which would set it apart from other literature. It feels that authority in its truth and beauty, in its power for the recreation and guidance of men's lives, in the spirit which it reveals and conveys—to those who will receive it. It notes the changing manifestations of that spirit and its progress within the Scripture itself. It marks the incomparable influence of the Scripture in the life of humanity as well as in the souls of individuals. It does not believe in their miraculous origin save in the sense in which the movement of the spirit of God upon the souls of men is a part, and the greatest part, of the mystery of life. Still less, of course, can we believe in the miraculous preservation of Scriptures or in their inerrant transmission or translation. We find the sign which they are and the wonder which they work in the spirit they are of, and in the effect of that spirit upon the minds and lives of men.

In impressive way this same one hundred and fifty years has wrought a great change in our view of the universe, through the light of the advancing sciences—by the light, we might add, of new sciences which have been developed within the period which we name. Problems of which mature men less than half a century ago never dreamed now beset us in the universe with which astronomy deals. They meet us in the areas of which physics and chemistry treat, as also in biology. Just now a new science like psychology, on the margin between the physical and emotional world, presses them upon us. Settlements once deemed irrefragable are now esteemed untenable. The province of the natural sciences once seemed possible of limitation. Questions now emerging seem illimitable. Old solutions are abandoned. New hypotheses affect almost everything. New methods are adopted. Newer ones are sought. One looks back, say only fifty years, and recalls radical antagonisms. These were indeed in part due to prepossessions of the religious. Perhaps in equal measure they were due also to assumptions —sometimes one might fairly say presumptions—of scientific men as well. One realizes with some difficulty that even the greatest of scientific teachers then at Harvard, Louis Agassiz, who died only in 1873, never accepted the hypothesis of evolution. I write indeed from the point of view of controlling interest in religion, but the sources of misunderstanding are not all on the side of the religious. It is small wonder if, by the number and magnitude of the achievements of science, in the sweep of new and newer interpretations, some men were carried away. One's preoccupations become the source of one's limitations. The great encomium upon men of the scientific side might be bestowed for the readiness with which they have changed and continue to change their hypotheses. It is rather obvious that religious men also should change their hypotheses. It is of still greater moment that both should recognize that statements which have been held as doctrines, and even made fundamental as dogmas, are often of the nature of hypotheses. After all, what men call the truth is often only a statement of truth for which one's earlier training, his later preoccupations, or for that matter, the present knowledge of the world, may not yet have given us material for re-statement. What is of first importance is to know that both the hypotheses of science and the statements of faith are statements. They all have been made in the light of the times which made them. Much of what was instinctive antagonism between defenders of faith and seekers after fact has passed away. Even that sentence is liable to objection, in so far as it might seem to imply that defenders of faith are not also seeking after fact. They have fact in their experience. Such facts are often unfelt by those whose preoccupations have been exclusively of another sort. One thinks of the period of a book like "Supernatural Religion," and of Mrs. Humphrey Ward's "Robert Elsmere," as also of Matthew Arnold's painful repetition of his phrase, "The trouble with miracles is that they do not happen." One feels that that period was about the nadir of mutual misunderstanding in which both parties can well afford to share the blame.

Somehow the phrase "Law, or laws, of nature," so much upon the lips of scientific people fifty years ago, has not stood up very well under the wear and tear of subsequent discussion. One almost thinks that the scientific people must in their zeal have borrowed the word from the theologians. For law would seem to imply some law-giver or law-givers—which was hardly what the scientific people were just then trying to prove. "Order of nature" would do better. It does not commit us to so much. Law, however, does not answer so much better in the discussion of religion, as we now clearly see. The atmosphere of maturer religion, at all events, is freedom and not law. The conception of God for maturer men and races is not so much that of a law-giver. It is that of an inspirer, guide, fulfiller of something in the nature of man in respect of which man shares the life of God. The idea is not that of an injunction whose purpose it is to control men. It is impulse which quickens, inspires, guides, helps men. Obedience to it re-creates, fulfills men. The conception of God is thus of one who, in the last analysis, guards, guides and confirms the liberty of men. God would seem to care most for things which cannot be achieved except through liberty. God is all that, while, at the same time, he is under the last sad necessity of letting men destroy themselves if they will so to do. One might, therefore, seek a substitute for the phrase about the law of God. One might speak of the order of nature, the nature of man, with also the nature of God. One might reflect upon that phrase of Browning's, "All's law and all's love." That is surely the level at which we most nobly think of the relation of God and man. At this level what has been called the miracle of grace becomes the re-creative influence of a personal God upon persons. It is an influence liberating, enlarging, fulfilling. It has no need to be a sign or wonder in the sense of contravening the nature either of God or man. By the same token, it is something much more wonderful than is the common apprehension of a miracle.

It is not surprising that what we called intuition should have been described from the subjective side as divination, and from the objective side as supernatural communication. The origins of it are subtle. Limitations are uncertain. Insight is so different from what may seem the pedestrian processes of rationalization. Moreover, men of insight are, sometimes at least, men not trained in reasoning processes. And conversely, men long habituated to rationalization may have lost, or at least impaired, their faculty of insight. We ourselves use the word divination in a manner quite colloquial, but which conveys our sense of being taken by surprise at this way of being sure of things. We use picturesque language. We say it is borne in upon us. But it is the sober sense of the sound play of reason over our intuitions, and equally, it is the just sense that our intuitions may help, or else give pause, to our reasonings—it is this which maintains, for a well-balanced mind and an experienced character, a just relation between the two. It is this which makes us feel that the ascription of an intuition, without further ado, to a source beyond ourselves, the apprehension of it as preternatural or supernatural, is a mistake. It is this which makes us feel that intuition is the normal response of one side of our nature, primarily perhaps the affective and emotional side, an impulse, say of caution, or again, of enthusiasm, deterrent or stimulating to us, in that which we may—or may not—have arrived at by conscious reasoning. Modern psychology has made much of the subconscious and, up to a certain point, with good reason. Rational processes are typically conscious and methodical. In matters, however, in which memory and hope, regret and anticipation, contrition and enthusiasm, have large part, there is "below the threshold" in our minds that which desire or aversion contributes, which memory stimulates, which passion molds, something in which we surprise others and, indeed, quite as often, surprise ourselves. It comes up from below the threshold, as it has been called, of our present reasonings, perhaps even from the world of long buried hopes. It is moved by the history of our emotions, a history perhaps forgotten by ourselves. It reveals something in which past hopes or old convictions are newly formulated. It may well be that this is to be our guiding light henceforth. No wonder that men call it inspiration. It stirs the depths within us. It lifts us to heights which have not been our own. It is no wonder that men thought of it as coming immediately from without and above. Socrates had his daimon. One reads Plato's "Apology" to this day, in vain, to make out whether Socrates thought of the monitions of his daimon as wholly from within, his better self, or from without, from beyond, from above himself —or both. He constantly uses phrases about being true to himself and also about being true to God. So do we.

The history of the idea of divine afflatus is full of instruction for us. The naive view of external communication was natural to earlier races. It survives to our day in highly sensitive natures. It is constant in books of the religions, by no means those only of Jews and Christians. Mystics have often been confident of it. The sibyl, oracles, are kindred conceptions. The period of the decline of classic culture saw both the complete loss of the hold of these ideas upon some and, conversely, the reassertion of them in full power for others. After the fall of the Empire, the ages which we call "dark" saw their resumption in formidable force and often in crassest form. The Renaissance, for some, broke with them again, poured contempt on them, on necromancers and even on priesthoods which, in their claim for supernal knowledge, suffered like reproach. But perhaps the greatest force for the resuscitation of related ideas came, now and then, among the really cultivated of the reformers. This was in the interest of the sustaining of the authority of Scripture on the part of those who had broken with the authority of the Church. The right of private judgment, emphasized among Protestants, gained thus a supernatural support. George Fox drew his amazing insight from an inner source the connection of which with the deity he never doubted. Saintly John Woolman never doubted it. Rise of the sciences of nature, truer apprehension of history, criticism of Scripture, have done their part for most Protestants to alter this situation. But to the devoutest Protestants surely this is by now quite clear. Divine inspiration can never have been found in books except as it has found its way into the books from a devout heart. The guidance of men's hearts is not miraculous in the sense of an external miracle. It is not supernatural at all in the sense in which that word has commonly been used. It is the very highest reach of the best of men in contact with the things of the spirit and with God. It is natural in the noblest—the only really noble—sense of that word.

"There is a natural and there is a spiritual," as Paul said. God, who is spirit, moves men in the depths of their spirits toward himself. Men rise toward the "life which is hid with Christ in God." This is not for a moment to say that Paul did not believe in the supernatural. I assume that Jesus believed in the supernatural. His belief takes its form from the belief of his time. Difference in form, for the same belief, is for us imposed by a knowledge of the world of nature and of some aspects of the life of man, which Jesus did not have. Knowledge of the world changes. Things of the spirit remain. The manner of presentation of them, however, does not—or not wisely—remain the same, to men to whom the whole apprehension of the world has changed. The word supernatural has a long history. In that history it has connoted something given to us, superimposed upon all our knowledge, as from a part of the universe to which our knowledge could not attain. But natural and supernatural are for us relative, not absolute terms. The spirit of man lays hold upon God. God takes possession of the spirit of man. The divine manifests itself in and through the human. There are qualities of God which cannot be manifested except through the human, the life of man in the spirit. Nothing else in our world is kin to those qualities. But was that true once and for all—once only—in Jesus? Was Jesus as personality an unresolved, an irresolvable miracle, "two natures in one person forever," as the Nicene Creed says—and the Athanasian Creed is even more insistent? Was Jesus less, or was he more, himself when he communed with God and fortified his soul to drink the cup which might not pass—and drank it? Or was he then most like to God and showed to us most perfectly what God is like? It is the advance of the sciences which has most vividly taught us how all our knowledge shades off by imperceptible degrees and in all directions into mystery. That sense of mystery on the margins of all in our human nature grows for us from day to day. It is the sense of mystery on his margins which sometimes seems to us to mark the difference between man and beast. There is, on the contrary, the sense of a definite boundary between the natural and the supernatural which our traditional usage of this latter word conveys, the sense of "two worlds," as Keble called it in his hymn. We mean that the supernatural penetrates the natural. What we have is the sense of a zone, forever changing with the advances of our knowledge, different for the knowledge and experiences of different men. This is only another way of saying that the natural rises into the supernatural in all the higher realms of the natural. Most of all in the realm of man's life and spirit, mystery penetrates the natural. It is clearly so in our relation to personalities. No one who has ever thought about his greater friends would deny that. We do not know all there is to know of them. That is the very ideal of friendship and love. How is it between ourselves and Christ? How must it have been between Jesus and God? "It is by this," by the notion, that is, of a radical difference between the natural and the supernatural, writes Professor Henry Jones "that the demand for the intervention of the divine in special circumstances implies his non-intervention in ordinary circumstances. That is a demand which cannot be made by one who believes either in the permanence of relation of antecedent and consequent in the natural and moral world, or in the divine omnipotence, finding the evidence of this on all hands in the world's ordinary course." And again, "Providential interference implies a separation which is intolerable to the spirit which knows the longing of devoted love and feels the constant need of God. Deism, with all its errors, taught one permanent truth. That truth is that the moral life must be entrusted to the moral agent. If a man is to learn goodness, then he must be left to carry out the ethical experiment in his own way. This is the sense in which morality is a most solitary enterprise."[1]

What is borne in upon us is that we are right as to the principle of the fulfillment of the life which we live here and now. It is the principle of our own free devotion to ever purer ideals, ever loftier purposes. It is the attainment of increasing powers and, above all, the necessity that such a life shall be free and responsible, our own chosen life. We are convinced that it cannot be fundamentally different with the life beyond this life. In a sense of principles of life, we do not think of the transcendent world as different from the world in which we now live. Or rather, these principles thus witness to a transcendent element in the life which we now live. By the experience and qualities of which we speak, we live now in the transcendent world—or may so live. In this high sense also, we have no need of a moral miracle at death. Indeed, in respect of principles of character, we can understand no such miracle. There can be no such immediate and complete reversal of the principles of moral and spiritual life. It is only a man himself who can reverse himself. There is enough to wonder at. There is enough that intimates God to us. It has been the achievement of science for two generations to increase our wonder beyond any imagination which our fathers had, concerning the marvel which we perceive that the world is and, most of all, the wonder that we realize that we ourselves are. It is this attitude which counts, with also the opportunity which such a life affords. The same must be said of the privilege and responsibility of moral life when this life is over. We assume that these wonders,

[1] "A Faith that Enquires," pp. 170 and 171: Macmillan. Reprinted by permission.

even if we can never here find out about them to perfection, all belong to the order of the universe to which we belong. That order of the universe is the sublime revelation to us of certain qualities of God, to which his world in general, and men in particular, are witnesses. It is the very order of nature which proves God to some. To these, suspensions or reversals seem quite unnecessary. Most of all, complete reversals in the moral order and in the fundamental characters of men are things which we are unable to believe. I confess to a sense of surprise, which does me no credit, in having found, after writing this chapter, in Campbell Fraser's "Philosophy of Theism," a passage which says practically all that for which I have contended. It is the more noteworthy because the book was published in 1896, the volume of Gifford Lectures delivered before the University of Edinburgh, 1894–1896. The author was already emeritus, the Nestor of philosophical instruction in Edinburgh. "If they"—[miracles]—"are neither outward events that are naturally bound up with the divine cosmical system, nor divine inspirations latent in the spirit of man, they seem to be incapable of connection, unfit to harmonize with the moral and filial path which I have put before you as the eternally reasonable attitude." Moreover . . . "As events that are only occasional and that are supposed to be absolutely isolated, so far as natural causation is concerned, our information about them as past miracles can be only external and empirical, dependent on human testimony, that is, gradually becoming inaudible, if indeed, it is not now unheard after the lapse of ages."[1] Compare also Edward Caird, "Evolution of Religion," Vol. I., p. 310, published in 1893.

These writers—and there are many more, all deeply

[1] Published by Blackwoods, Edinburgh. Reprinted by permission.

religious men—are in substantial agreement for reasons which are partly philosophical, and partly, as we should now say, psychological. To me the psychological reasoning seems, on the whole, the more conclusive. This is, no doubt, in part because in these later years psychology has received the larger measure of independent development. It has emphasized more and more its relation to the sciences. It has itself become a science. It would seem that even divine communication to the minds of men would be along the lines of the nature of the life of the minds of men. It would not present an abrupt contrast to the normality of the life of the mind. The externality which the age-long theory assumed would have been as natural in former ages, as is, for us, the seeking to ally even divine communication and uplift with the normal processes of the spiritual life of men. For, more and more we are convinced that God is spirit, even as man is spirit, too. Even in the relations of men to one another, we do currently—and correctly—use the same word, inspiration. Men inspire us, illuminate our minds, quicken to new life our whole nature, re-create our spirits. And we may well speak of men as the instruments of God in doing this. We speak of the Scriptures as instrument of God in doing this. But it is not as if in so doing, we reverted to the old view of the miraculous character of Scripture. It is not at all a denial of God, or of the re-creating, enlightening, stimulating, upholding of the God who is spirit, which is involved. It is only the emphasis upon God as spirit which is urged. And it is the recognition of ourselves as spirit also which is claimed.

PART II

NATURE AND MANIFESTATIONS OF RELIGION

Part II

NATURE AND MANIFESTATIONS OF RELIGION

NATURE OF RELIGION

In the previous chapter we spoke of the approach which to one of us seems natural to the problem which religion presents. We sought to begin where our generation stands. How do we know? In this chapter we are to speak of the nature of religion itself. And when we speak of the nature of religion we must, so far as we are able, begin with the beginnings of religion. This may seem a far cry. The beginnings of religion are indefinitely far removed, not merely from the modern mind, but in some respects from modern manifestations of religion as well. Current theories of the history of religions are indeed in some part made up from observations and reflections relating to our own religion. They are derived also from observation and reflection upon the facts relating to other religions, theoretically, at least, to all religions. Many of these facts were quite unknown to the generation of our fathers. Those known were not always considered in the light in which we consider them. One religion to some minds excluded all others. One was true, the others false. The modern discipline of comparison of religions brings within the range of our reflection a great body of facts concerning other religions which are manifestly cognate with facts observable in our own. This alters our mode of reflection upon aspects of our own religion as well. We gain a new interpretation of familiar facts. But it is an interpretation. In still greater degree is this the case with a vast body of facts newly brought to our attention concerning other religions and, especially concerning primitive religions. New interpretations of old facts concerning our own religion may be hindered by prepossessions. Interpretation of what we take to be facts as to other, and especially as to primitive religions, is different. It is not easy for us to put ourselves in the place of primitive men. Moreover, we are constantly gaining new information. It is quite clear that we must take cognizance of all known facts. It is clear also that we must seek to begin at the beginning. It is perhaps these facts which give to this new chapter the semblance of sharp contrast with the previous one.

From all that we know of history, religion appears to have been an immemorial feature of the life of man. It has been one of the constant forces in the development of civilization. Equally, civilization has been a constant force in the evolution of religions. In its earliest manifestation religion emerges as an element in community life. In its higher apprehensions it is a secret of the individual soul. Feeling of wonder and awe, turning easily to fear or, conversely, to reverence and trust, appears to have been the rudiment of religion. It is the sense of the mystery and power of that which confronts the ignorance and weakness of man. It is the sense of something beyond and above his world and himself. Furthermore, this feeling, whether of fear or of awe, manifests itself first of all in action. It is in doing something that the feeling finds its outlet. That which a man does will be as crude as himself. It may seem strange as a sign of religion to men who have behind them unnumbered generations of the progress of the race. Furthermore, it is in doing something which others do that the action finds its suggestion and its corroboration. The force of the community is regulative and in a sense creative of customs and rites which are, at this stage, the expressions of religion. Thoughts about these ceremonies, with also beliefs as to their origin, come later. On these interpretations, again, the tradition of the group, the mind of the tribe, exerts determining influence. Example of the family, authority of the clan, must long have outweighed impulses of slowly forming individuality. One notes this in the few savage peoples still extant. Loyalty to the tribe, identification with the tribe, is unquestioning. The tribe is the obvious thing which is beyond and above the man. What we observe among the few rudimentary peoples which still remain, with what we learn as to the relatively short period concerning which we have any record, suggests what we have to think concerning the vastly longer period as to which we have no information. One of the most certain traits of that period, however, must have been the slowness of the development of individuality. The breaking of the power of the community must have come very gradually. Emergence was late of men who differed effectively from their fellows and began to put life, with religion, upon a better plane. Probably in no area of life would individual opinion have been more slowly formed or personal initiative less naturally resorted to than in just this of religion. Observances symbolized the relation of a man, and of all his fellows with him, to a world which he, and they, understood far less than they understood the world of the quest for shelter, for means of livelihood and defense, desirable as men found it to be to stand together even in these.

Statements have been made that we may think of man as having been upon the earth for, say, half a million years. We have evidence for anything which we could call civilization covering hardly more than perhaps twelve to twenty thousand years. There are grave uncertainties about both these figures. Can we, even with ever so many ciphers, tell where to draw the line between man and his pre-human progenitors? Was there any such line? Was it not a broad zone—and how broad? And again, how much do we mean by civilization? Writing certainly introduces a strong line of demarcation. Perhaps speech, which lies much further back, should be taken as our point of departure. But here again, how much speech and of what sort? Even as to picture-writings we have no fixed sense of their beginnings. Materials used in them have been in all save a few cases very perishable. Even allowing for these large queries, such assertions may still throw some light upon that which has been said above. Certainly civilization is the result of the reaction of individuals upon the community, as also of the community upon individuals. But how long a time was it before this creative antithesis of community and individual appeared? Or is it only evidence concerning earlier stages of this antithesis and, with it, of the emergence of rudimentary civilization, which is lacking? Such evidences as we have seem often only by some chance to have survived. At all events, apparently, we must think of mankind as having lived for unnumbered generations under conditions of group life, before the period from which we have any materials whatever for history. Conditions of group life must enter into our idea of primitive religion. Nevertheless, we have to recognize that groups of men did not remain mere hives or herds. We may make every concession to the continuity of man with the animal world. Yet mind emerges and, almost certainly, feeling before mind. The work of bees in a hive is wonderful. So far as we know, however, it is the same wonder that it was when men, who were hardly so closely knit in co-operation as the bees, and probably by no means so industrious as the bees, first observed it. The method of attack of wolves in a pack has, so far as we know, undergone no improvement. From the point of view of our progenitors it probably needed none. But men who were weaker in one way learned to protect themselves in another. Nature clothed the animals. When this covering did not suffice or climate changed, they migrated or else died. Men migrated, too, but they had learned to clothe themselves, and this largely with the skins of the animals. They built shelters. They learned the use of fire which, so far as we know, no animal has ever learned. The ancients were right about Prometheus. They made implements which, again, so far as we know, no animal has ever done save in the most rudimentary way. They improved weapons. They planted crops. They built boats. It is not easy to draw the line between instinct and reason, but reason emerges. Reason does not go far without the emergence of differences which not merely divide the group from the animals but separate the individual from the group. Leadership of the group then falls naturally to these growingly varied and potent individualities. The rudimentary family, incipient stages of government, origins of language, are inconceivable without the influence of something with which the animals have nothing, or very little, which is comparable. And again, and more than ever, under the influence of personalities, mankind developed capacity for adjustment to varied circumstances and power of control over circumstances. Men inaugurated whole new phases of life, made history in chapters more ancient than any we shall ever read, and perhaps we might say, more significant than any we shall ever write. Religion must have kept pace with these developments.

The earliest stages of the comparative study of religions in modern times, like those, say, of Max Müller, made much of the mythologies—of nature myths, to be sure, but still more of legends of the deeds of heroic personages in the past of a tribe or race. Figures which we know in legend may well have been leaders of this sort. Memory and imagination of grateful peoples conjured up the poetic forms in which we receive their histories. Projection into the unknown of figures of men who lived and wrought heroically may be one of the reasons of the anthropomorphic cast which early religions came almost uniformly to bear. Like thoughts, however, concerning the dead, even as to those who were not leaders, but dear to the circle of their intimates and to whom, in love or fear, or both, continued existence was ascribed, would tend in the same direction. This last more general doctrine of animism was thought by some earlier archaeologists, rather than legends of heroes, to be the origin of the notion of gods in human form. But after all, with primitive people what other forms should the gods have taken? It was to this relation to the dead, with the hope of their continued life, with trust in their beneficent influence, or again, in fear of their jealousy and revenge, that the very origins of religion were ascribed by Tylor. At present, however, it is a widely accepted view that, back of this stage of actual personalization, lies a period in which the object of fear or of desire was not yet thought of as person, but merely as force or power. Of this a man could possess himself by deceit or violence, as when one ate the heart of an enemy. Or again, he conjured to his own advantage through his fetish, in which there was only this awesome power without any relation to the thought of deities. Strength and skill to accomplish one's purposes, to escape ill, to bring evil upon others, was thought thus to reside, even if only temporarily, in some otherwise trifling object. If the fetish failed to perform its duty, it was thrown away. For this vague force which lay back of rudimentary magic, Codrington used the word *mana*, taken from the language of a Melanesian tribe among whom he had lived. Similar beliefs have been found in Australia and among North American Indians. Furthermore, it is now generally supposed that between this stage of fetishism and the period of animism of which we spoke, there had been a period in which animal forms were those which were present to the imaginings of men. Almost all folklore reaches back into a time when men were supposed to have held converse with animals. Special powers were ascribed to beasts or birds. Animal legends current among the blacks in our Southern states, not more than two generations ago, have rather recently been published. The singular fact to be observed is that the animals in these legends are American and not African. Particular relations were held to subsist between certain animals and a tribe. Taboo existed between the tribe and a particular animal, just as it existed also between man and man, or between man and woman. Totemism also belongs here. The animal forms with which we are familiar in the great monuments of Egypt and Assyria and, again, forms half animal and half human, may find their explanation here. Association of a certain bird or beast with this or that god, like the owl of Athené in Greek religion, points perhaps in the same direction. No notion concerning the world beyond the world of common experience could be more natural than was the attribution of powers of nature to personal deities. Rain, sun, seasons, tempests, the mystery of the fertility of animals and plants, powers decisive of battle or of the safety of navigators, were thus referred. Gods and goddesses had all the qualities, bad and good, which men met among their compeers on the earth. To Xenophanes are ascribed famous lines in which he says, "Mortals think of the gods as having voice and form. If lions had hands and could draw, they would draw the shapes of gods like themselves. Each animal would draw the bodies of gods like his own form." Voltaire once said that the Bible, having declared that God made man in his own image, man has ever since been endeavoring to return the compliment. Anthropomorphism is, however, far from being the only thing with which we have to reckon.

To other questions touching origins of religion we may return later. One thing is, however, even at this point clear. We grant that rudimentary religion is feeling. We are sure that the earliest manifestations of religion were social rather than individual. The authority for these manifestations was with the community. Ideas, or rather, imaginings, concerning that to which or those to whom such homage was due were varied, crude and in some cases revolting. Yet it is a mistake to suppose that the farther we trace religions back toward a common origin, the nearer we get to the pith and substance of the matter. Quite the contrary. Diversities and contradictions of the religions, one with another, in their later history, may lend a fictitious charm to this mode of simplification. Origins are not final in this sense. They would be no more final even were we more sure than we are concerning the facts as to the origins like those above set forth. Such theories have verisimilitude. But they are mainly inferences from a rather scanty array of facts.

Anthropologists and archaeologists will be presenting us with new facts. These will demand new interpretations. There is a more important consideration for those of us who hold without reservation the doctrine of the evolution of religions and of religion. We need to consider that to which religion has evolved quite as truly as that from which religion has been evolved. The doctrine of evolution as applied to matters much simpler than the one with which we are concerned had, at first, the effect of leading men to lay more stress than was proportionate upon the beginnings of things. The nature of anything is more fully learned from its flower and fruit than from its seed. We may concede much to the anthropoid, but we know a great deal more about man since he parted company with the anthropoid. There is also a great deal more to know. The descent of man is important, profoundly impressive. The doctrine seemed at first to many, and still seems to some, to be subversive. We know, however, a great deal more about what Drummond rather happily called "the ascent of man" than we do about the descent of man. The history of the world since man appeared—or rather, since history appeared—puts material into our hands for consideration of that question. This remark is true even of the physique of man and of his most rudimentary institutions. It is still more true of the higher aspects of his life and spirit. The history of religions is far less a matter for imagination than is the origin of religions. Its later stages, despite their complexity, are far more intelligible than are its earlier stages, despite the apparent simplicity of these. Perhaps also this impression of simplicity, alluring as it seems, is to some extent accounted for by our ignorance.

In the phrase now common in the discussion of evolution, factors which could never have been forecast have emerged. Mind and spirit of man are among these. It is the faith both of science and religion that these have emerged because of that which was about and before men, even more truly than because of that which was already behind them. For example, religion in its earliest manifestations of which we have any knowledge was without doubt a matter of the community. It showed itself mainly in ceremonies. This does not prove that the whole essence of religion was thus manifested. It is from this point of view that the theories of the Neo-Compteans, Durckheim and Levy-Bruhl, are inconclusive. We are quite prepared to claim the contrary. All that is proved is that religion thus naturally expressed itself in the environment which it then had, men being what they then were. Times changed. Conditions altered. Men advanced. Religion has shown itself in the life of morals, in the life of thought, in the life of art. It has manifested itself in organizations and in forms of worship. These were, and are, germane to the differing stages of community life, and, as well, to different dispositions and purposes of individuals. Compared with these materials for the study of the nature of religion, the origins of religion seem less important. They are less important, except for the fact that, without these studies of origins, we should perhaps not be so clearly convinced that religion had origins and evolved along with the rest of the life of mankind. What appears to be certain from this line of argument is that all manners of worship, rites, ceremonies, customs, whether rudimentary or fulfilling every condition of spiritual maturity, have something to tell us about religion. All modes of thought about God or about man and man's relation to God, all types of institution, the most primitive as well as those congruous with high civilization, and with varying civilizations, have something to say to us. We should not let familiar antagonisms blind us to comprehensive truths. All modes of life which religion implies, or rather, which imply religion, whether self-centered and ascetic, repudiating the world and seeking happiness in another, or, for that matter, seeking only Nirvana, the happiness of not being unhappy, have something to say to us. Or again, those which reveal religion in sacrifice and devotion to others, and in labors for mitigation of evils in the world, speak to us. All ecclesiastical organizations, whether aiming at solidarity and discipline, or fostering liberty and self-realization, have had relation to needs of their own times, or again, they may have failed to satisfy those needs. Not any of these, nor all of them put together, are religion. They are at most expressions, manifestations, embodiments of religion. They are conditioned in the temperament and character of those whose expressions they are. They are conditioned in the forces and needs of the age in which these men lived. They were fostered by the environment in which men worked, by the tasks to which they addressed themselves, by the aspirations which they cherished, and finally, by the reaction of all these factors upon men's other qualities.

Observations upon the nature of religion which have engaged us thus far might be tested by brief illustrations from other areas of human experience. Group forms of government, patriarchal and tribal, with usages related thereto, are the earliest which confront us when we try to trace the course of the evolution of the State. No one thinks that rudimentary forms of government, because they are the oldest that we know and because they are everywhere much alike, are the most satisfactory illustrations of the State. Permanent need is implied in the existence of government at all, and as well, in the sequence of changes in the form of government. These suggest as source of earliest tentatives, and also of subsequent modifications, reactions of individual minds upon the interests of the group, and as well, of interests of the group upon ideas and aims of the individual. The group had at times obvious interest in the suppression of differences of opinion, in the subjection of the man to the mass. It was likely at times to be blind to the opposing concern, that, namely, which forecast changes due in order to meet new contingencies or to provide for further realizations. Authorities are apt to be entrenched. Those who differ are apt at first to be isolated. It has been so also in the history of religious institutions. The price paid by men who saw further than their fellows has been much the same in either case. No one thinks of even the latest experiment in government as anything but an incorporation, imperfect at that, of the hard-earned results of experience. We think of it as the attempt to realize an idea which is itself only progressively envisaged, as to what government should be and do in the changing circumstances in which men find themselves. There is no such thing as a last term in the series. There is only a latest term in the continuous effort of mankind to combine and co-operate, to escape dangers, to achieve advantages, for the good of society as a whole and of the individual as well. On grounds of myth or tradition, or again, for reasons of selfish interest, men have thought of this or that form of government as absolute. States have alleged divine right. Churches have asserted divine competence, sometimes even obligation, to deal with secular affairs. Religious institutions have carried on the whole a more retarding burden in this regard than have their political compeers. Both have acted as if divine right could ever be an external warrant, and not rather merely an intellectual and moral competence to meet the issues involved. Religious authorities have more often declared that their revelation was something heard only by the ears of men of the past. Less often this has been conceived as something borne in upon the spirits of men struggling to meet the issues of the present and to provide for those of the future. Men of religion have been fain to declare that inspiration was a closed chapter. If not that, it was limited to a ruling class. It was behind men rather than before them, above them rather than within them. Divine right of monarchy has often enough been appealed to in the same manner. Divine right of democracy is now sometimes thus vociferously proclaimed, even on the lips of some with whom the word divine, at least, can hardly be more than a pungent comparison, or even only an ironical phrase. The permanent ideal would seem to have been, amid and by means of continuous change in measures and even in aims of government, to achieve the highest liberty of the individual consonant with the stability of society. On the long road to the fulfillment of that purpose all forms of government have been and are and will be only embodiments of a purpose to meet the unified and yet manifold, the constant and ever changing aims of mankind, as man and as mass.

Something of the same sort may be said of the evolution of morals. The assumption is common that to be true to itself religion must give evidence of itself in morality. That is certainly most true for us. But there is a good deal of history against it. On the other hand, it is often taken for granted that the sanction of morals is in religion. It would be a bad case for morals at the present moment, even in our own midst, if this were accepted as true. Not even in the case of the higher religions has that first assumption been uniformly true. The history of morals contradicts the second of these contentions. Both in rudimentary society and, again, in higher civilizations, there have been morals without much relation to current religion. Conversely, primitive religions seem to us to have been extraordinarily lacking in moral sense. Even the great religions, and even though they may have arisen in a moral awakening, have sometimes sunk far below their own level in this regard. Morals and religions have contributed to the clarification each of the other. But the history of their connection is sometimes baffling. The fact is that here, just as before, the rudimentary moral impulse seems to have been social and not religious in its nature. It was loyalty to the interest of the group long before it was expression of conviction of the individual or sense of allegiance to the gods, that guided men's conduct. Earliest gods would have been bad guides for conduct of even half-civilized men. The words morals and morality are derived from the Latin word *mores,* which primarily meant manners and customs. The Greek word *ethos* has much the same sense. The Latin word seems accurately to have connoted the consensus of opinion of the group, with also the course of conduct which followed upon it. It describes the things which were done. It warned against things which were "simply not done." No society can exist, a primitive society perhaps even less than a more highly developed one, without some kind of expectation on the part of the social body as to what men will do and, again, without at least a general compliance of men with that anticipation. Morals at this stage represented what the group found consonant with the general interest. It was this which men were punished for departing from. It was this which men wished to transmit to those who were to come after them. It was this which these in turn received with corresponding reverence. The gods on Olympus were cheerfully described as guilty of deceit, cruelty and flagrant vice, long after families on earth were doing much better. Of course, the explanation of that also is quite simple. The myths of the gods remained what they were, an inheritance—not exactly sacred, as we should think—of imaginings about nature-powers and tribal heroes. In the meantime, even rudimentary societies on earth were bravely progressing. They must rise above the example of the gods if men were going to live together in peace and quietness at all. What wonder that faith in such gods faded away. When man's ideal was strength, his gods were stronger. When his ideal was shrewdness, his gods were shrewder, even if they were distinctly less scrupulous. It was only when a man's ideal was goodness, no matter how far he and, for that matter, everyone else, might fall short of being very good, that his gods came to be thought of as good, and, indeed, far better than the best of men. The moralizing of men set the pace for the moralizing of the gods, who must accord with an ideal of their worshippers, on penalty of being no longer worshipped. Goethe said, "God is always the best that we know." Plato in his "Republic" would have nothing of the gods because they demoralized men. It was by convictions such as these that Plato came to speak of God in a fashion altogether different from that of many of his predecessors. It was thus that he became himself an authority for morals and an inspiration for a truer religion of his race.

It is not clear that at this stage we need go far in search of sanctions. Loyalty to the clan was beyond question the earliest sanction. It was rewarded by the loyalty of the clan. Infractions were punished. Life was cheap. Vengeance of the tribe was all in order, as also revenge on the side of the family. Besides this, some infractions of the current morality punished themselves. The possession of stolen goods brought bad luck which no one could escape. Any disease could be attached in superstition to any offense. Even no further back than the time of Livingstone, one hears of an African who died in a day of sheer fear, brought upon him by something which he had done, or rather, by the fact that he had been found out. Anything was permissible in war against another tribe. Common was the murder of all the men of a tribe who survived a defeat, of women also if this was thought expedient, although more often their lot was slavery. The plunder of non-combatants if there were any, the levelling of cities with the ground, the killing of babes, all these things were exalted as virtues. You may read of them in the history of Israel where they stand as ordained of Jahve himself, the God of the tribes in the conquest of Canaan. Indeed this trail goes far down into the history of the Kings. You may read of it also in the history of Egypt, in the Code of Khammurabbi, in the tradition of the Greek invasions and in the cheerful pages of Homer. This last may be in some measure because Homer is supposed to be so much older than is the majestic verse in which we read Homer. But Pindar, on his part, mourned a better past of his people. He may have been right as to some of his people. Time came when the dramatists were the real moral teachers of Greece while some priests, at least, were by some people left to their pottering. To the great tragedians the myths of the avenging gods were poetic material for a great moral idealism. Even the populace recognized them as such, and nobler spirits still more. No one would say that Socrates had no religion, but it was far from being the religion of his forbears or even of the mass of his contemporaries. Aristotle's ethics set a standard. The time came also when, under the prophets of Israel in the eighth and seventh centuries, there was an outburst of moral idealism. The literature of that era has become part of the ethical inheritance as well as of the religious impulse of the human race. It stands, this literature, for our instruction, incorporated in the Hebrew Scriptures and in the Christian Bible, side by side with the record of those injustices and atrocities of the Hebrew people when they were but a wandering tribe. The salient thing about the prophets is that with them both morals and religion became inward and spiritual. Just because they were inward and personal they assumed also a universal character. They became guiding light and spiritual power for all humanity. The thing which aroused the pure passion of these prophets was the tyranny and perfidy, the savage cruelty, which sometimes in contemporary society went along with the splendors of ceremonial worship, of unheard of wealth, and with a fatuous ambition to play a part along with the greater nations in the politics and warfare of the world. Disasters chastened some into a legalism which is, after all, not the same thing with morality. It drove others into a passionate nationalism which is not the same thing with religion. Men comforted themselves with lurid prophecies of the victory of Israel and a rule of Jahve on earth from which all but Israelites would be shut out.

Then came Jesus, last of the prophets in some sense, but different still from the best of them. He rejected much. Also he gathered into one coherent whole much of what they had taught. But his orientation was different. Offenses against the law had been so brought home to the minds of many after the captivity that they judged the national disaster to have been due to their disobedience. As a moral thesis that might well be true. But it was not altogether good for men. They grew anxious and punctilious. They substituted the petty and superficial for weightier matters of the law, exactly as Jesus said. This was Phariseeism as Jesus met it. He handled the law in its letter with a freedom which seemed to them scandalous. He himself had and desired in others a heart so full of the love of the good and of the joy in doing it that it could be expressed in no code. It was a life. To others it might be a bondage. To him it was the highest freedom. This thing and Jesus' daring interpretation of the word *kingdom* are perhaps the pivotal points of his whole gospel. To Jesus the kingdom of God was a rule of the spirit of God in the hearts and lives of individual men. It was a rule of God in society only after that. It was in vivid contrast with the revengeful apocalyptic, often as Jesus used apocalyptic pictures —perhaps in a literal sense, and perhaps not—in moments of warning to his generation. It is upon such points that the Christian ethic turns in its inwardness and in its universality. Yet it will need no saying how often and how sorely the Church itself, and with it the world, has fallen off from this high ideal of morals which drew its inspiration from one of the simplest lives the world has ever seen. Nothing could be more impressive in closing this paragraph about morals than an allusion to Roman Stoicism. Moral idealism has never reached a higher level than in the two great Stoics, Epictetus and Marcus Aurelius. The one was a crippled Greek slave, the other the master of the Roman world, at the end of the period of which Gibbon said that he doubted if the world has ever been better ruled. Neither found much help in the welter of Oriental cults and superstitions which by their day Rome had become. Is it possible that they thought of Christianity as just one more of these? Had Christianity already then begun to take the road toward other-worldliness, or else toward ecclesiasticism and dogmatism, so decisively that neither of these great men seriously considered it? Who knows? The one never mentions Christianity at all. The other speaks of it once only to reproach what he heard of the Christians' unnatural view of life and duty. Yet the purity of the ethical philosophy of the one and the supreme fidelity to a world-wide duty of the other seems for them to have taken the place of a religion. But just so, the profound and all-comprehensive religion of Jesus took for him the place of an ethical philosophy or, for that matter, of a political or social philosophy as well.

Turning again from this brief comparison of certain aspects of the evolution of government and of morals, we can but be confirmed in parallel judgments concerning the evolution of religion. Organizations, and laws to provide security, justice and opportunity for the group, or again, manners and customs touching, in the first instance, conduct of individuals, these all can be traced through long processes of modification. They deal with their respective problems on the basis of impulses and necessities of men in the mass, groups, tribes, races. Or again, they deal with necessities and opportunities of the inner life of individuals, when these are either oppressed by the mass, or, conversely, aspire to lead the mass of their fellows to better things. Conditions change. New responses take the place of old ones. It is this process in particular which brings out capacity and responsibility of individuals. Masses of men feel what is immediately necessary. Forecast of what will be necessary, of that which is, therefore, already desirable, is more likely to be accorded to individuals. Insight into the real meaning and consequence of what is happening is almost always an individual gift. Moral evolution would seem to be guided in major degree by what is about it, in less degree by what is behind it, and least obviously of all, by what is before it. The least obvious is, however, in the end the most potent. These observations apply to the history of religion as truly as to that of other phases of life. The present gives itself to the common man. The past may rest like a weight upon him. Forecast of the future seems to be reserved for the uncommon man. Our older language had a treasure in a word which we now seldom use, the word *seer*. It describes one who sees into ordinary things farther than most and foresees things which the majority are not apt to see at all. The word has been somewhat spoiled for us by the superstition that some sort of magic enables a man thus to see. When religions possessed themselves of the word, it often embodied the assumption that such knowledge came by external and supernatural conferment. Not dissimilar, however, has been the fate of the word prophet. It has wavered between meaning one who spoke for God and one who foretold what was going to happen.

The lives of the great prophets of the Old Testament impress us as lives quite natural and intelligible. They appeal to our instinctive sympathy for the heroic devotion of some of them to the cause of the true and the good in their day. We have no difficulty with the language which was natural to their day. God said this or that to the prophet. The word of God came to the prophet. What the prophet spoke was the word of God. So it was. In a profound sense we also can use that language. But when later generations ponder the pages of history, when cruder men heard prophets' words, the interpretation was different. It assumed that larger knowledge, loftier enthusiasm, deeper sense of responsibility, had come to men in the way of miraculous communication. It was perhaps natural that mankind should have viewed wonders of insight and foresight in this way. This view, however, separated the world which we know and in which we act from a world of which we need to know and with reference to which we must act, as if this difference were in kind and not merely in degree. It was as if the way of ascent of man to duty and to God were closed to him unless it were open to him from above. It is the old antithesis between nature and the supernatural of which we spoke at length in the previous chapter. Every right-minded man knows what is meant by that which is beyond the actual, beyond even the possible, at the present moment. He sees men striving in this high sense in every area of life. He knows what is meant by a flying goal. He assumes that the highest goals will always be flying goals. Therein lies the greatness of life. Man receives his noblest impulse from God when he has ardently set himself to find what the will of God is and to do that will. In doing that will, he fulfills his own nature as truly as he receives something of the nature of God.

It is exactly this, however, which a traditional view of religion and inspiration has often obscured. It has caused men to assume that God literally spoke in former times, but never speaks now. He moved men in other places, but not here. His spirit works now only through dogmas and constituted authorities of religious organizations. Or else, he works through emotional responses of individuals who do not always take account of the intellectual or even of the practical conditions of the case. It is assumed that workings which are plainly history, and which are more luminous when historically understood, are, even down to minute detail, miraculous, infallible. It is as if for such minds the monition became more impressive for not being understood. Traditions of governing bodies, forms of doctrine, manners of worship, are carried forward unchangeably by an institution. They are invariable because institutions have accepted them as such. The cause of religion carries a handicap in this regard. Most other phases of life and thought have also in their time borne this same handicap. That is something to be remembered. They have now practically all discarded it. It may be that this manner of thought harks back all the way to the period of prevalence of group forms of thought and action. But without doubt institutions have also had their part in maintaining this opinion, from the point of view of preservation of their own authority. The truth is, however, that it is exactly religion which currently needs nothing so much as inwardness, spontaneity, adaptability. When one thinks of it, it is exactly this which we should expect the religion of the spirit to furnish. Abuse of liberty in precisely this connection in our day, revolt against tradition and authority, zeal for self-expression on the part of many who have not, or not yet, much serious self to express—these things are, to say the least, widespread. The turning away from religion because it claims to be a form of allegiance—which, indeed, and in a far profounder sense, it is—these things are rather characteristic of our time. It is more than doubtful whether the recovery of needed self-control can ever again come about through mere outward discipline. And this also is ominously true for some of those who most need that recovery. It must come again through the development of self-control and normal human insight and foresight, which it may easily be that only the experience of disaster through "uncharted freedom" can teach us.

To further consideration of questions of revelation and inspiration we shall turn later. The purpose of allusion to them, even in summary manner, at this point is merely to emphasize the contention of this chapter. That contention is that historic expressions and embodiments of religion, churches and creeds, modes of life, even the Bible, are not religion itself. They are manifestations in one aspect or another of the spirit which religion is. They are aid in it, stimulus for it. The Scriptures are not themselves oracles, although Paul once called the Old Testament the "oracles of God." That did not hinder him, however, from separating himself radically from the Old Testament religion. No one knew better than he that the Scriptures of his people were not like the utterances of the sibyl. They were literature, chronicle, lawgiving, poetry, eloquence of the great men of his nation through centuries of a long and noble past. No one knew better than he what a yoke the law might become, and what a hindrance to the life of the spirit it actually had been to him. His writings are full of that contention. His very words convey at times the sense of the intensity of his revolt. As to the New Testament itself, did not Jesus say, "The words that I speak unto you, they are spirit and they are life. The letter killeth." And is not the New Testament itself obviously a literature, the literature of an epoch-making movement, biography, history, correspondence, prophecy? We cannot even turn to Jesus himself as person in the sense that we can act as he acted in the circumstances of his life. This is because both of the disparity between him and us, and also because we can never exactly reproduce his circumstances in our lives. A devout book of the past generation, "What Would Jesus Do?" is evidence enough in this regard. We can follow him only by being of his spirit and then taking our own responsibility. We may comfort ourselves with that. He, too, was a manifestation, incarnation par excellence, of the spirit of God in the life and world of a man. Even Paul, whose theory of the relation of Jesus to God few of us now share, said of him exactly that, that he was "God manifest in the flesh."

The contention that religion is spirit is not, however, equivalent to the contention that religion is spirit only. Religion is outwardly tenable, practically effective, only through its embodiments. Its embodiments are the things in which, indeed, it is affected by the world, but also by which alone it produces its effect upon the world. Indeed, it is through its embodiments that it keeps its life in the world. A disembodied religion, effective, creative, sustaining, an actual force in the world, is unthinkable. Expressions, embodiments, are a part of religion itself so long as the conditions of our life remain what they are. Total repudiation of forms of religion is an exaggeration. In it one may do lip-service to the spiritual magnitude which religion is. Yet in the end it brings atrophy to the religious life of him who holds that view. It limits him, moreover, to an influence mainly destructive upon the religion of others. This also is not unknown in our day. Such a view seems at the opposite pole from that which people are fain to describe as bigotry. In plain speech, it is itself sometimes only another form of bigotry. It is a rather current form of Phariseeism, the extreme revulsion from that which it loves to call Phariseeism in others. In its eagerness for purity and impartiality, it refuses to reckon with life as it is and to contribute to the work of the world as this gets itself done. In this conviction we may, therefore, return to certain general considerations of the forms of religion. We do so, however, from a point of view which is quite different from that which runs risk of confusing religion with its forms. Paragraphs touching the necessity of worship, the need of doctrine in the interpretation of religion, with also the historic succession of its organizations, I have put for primary consideration into this chapter on the nature of religion. They are manifestations of its very nature. Without them the history of our religion would not be what it is. One may doubt if, without them, it would have had any history. Certainly without them few or no religions have had any long and fruitful history. They are the primary means of articulation between the fundamental religion which is the inner life and the actual religion which men have to live in a world of time and change. In the remaining portions of this chapter, we shall deal with the succession of forms, both of worship and of organization, and these mainly from the point of view of their history. They have a history which is profoundly instructive. If I were to make a distinction, I should say that worship is the more vital of the two. Without worship religion apparently cannot long exist. It has existed with many and very different forms of organization. But, again, it cannot exist for long or very effectively without any forms of organization.

Private prayer is indeed a manifestation of religion at the level of an intimacy which may find no other adequate utterance. "Every heart knoweth its own bitterness, and a stranger intermeddleth not therewith." Yet few who pray are likely long to continue in such practice who do not find reinforcement through joining in the prayers of those who constitute with them a fellowship of the religious life. Conversely, it is difficult to keep public prayer above the level of mere formalism if participation in it ever comes to be a substitute for the heart's own "crying out for the living God." It is on the road to become mere ceremony. For one who becomes conscious that this is the nature of his participation, it is on the way to become a pretense. Symbols of religion, like the sacraments, are to those who participate in them, either symbols of something or else they are themselves nothing. In the first case, they are often of profounder meaning and more potent influence than a spoken word can ever be. They are plastic like a work of art, unlimited like the sublimities of nature. They suggest different things to different people. They suggest different things at different times to the same people. They are alive to those who are alive to them. We lay into them meanings which we never thought of before, but most need now. On the other hand, old aspirations, sacred associations, possibly long forgotten, rise again with them. We draw from them inspirations which are for us alone. At the opposite extreme, at the level, that is, of mere routine conformity, they are always on the point of becoming just that, conformity. It was in some part to avoid this that Protestants diminished the number of the sacraments. They reduced the frequency of those which they retained. They unfortunately stripped them of something of that which appealed to the sense of majesty and mystery. To be sure, in this they felt themselves to be combatting a magical theory about the sacraments. So they were. Nevertheless, they sometimes went far toward destroying their power, whether for the corporate or for the personal life. We are on sure ground here. There is little enough in the rest of life as it is now lived, by many at all events among us, to say *sursum corda.* Here, far more than in preaching, if the two main aspects of the usual Protestant service are to be compared, there is common ground for souls of most varied needs, passing or permanent, for lives of every phase of experience and responsibility. Indeed it is in spite of, or maybe because of, the multiplicity of our human exigencies that we find ourselves not alone in our distresses, even though there may be not one in the worshipping company whom we ever saw before or of whose particular need we have an idea. The blessing is that they have no more idea of our need. By this sense we are one with those who in like need have sought God in every generation since Christ walked the earth. We are in "the company of all believers." There are not too many sermons which, in Coleridge's phrase, "find us." There are prayers which in the profoundest sense do nothing else but that. They find us and help us to find ourselves. They are the heritage of all the ages of believing, suffering and triumphant men. Protestants retained of the seven sacraments the two for which they found warrant in the New Testament. Some went so far as to reduce the communion to a mere memorial. In the measure in which they did that, they risked the loss of a mystical element wherein resides something of its protean power over the ever changing emotions of men. Surely it must have been this which Jesus meant when, standing with the bread in his hand, he said, "This is my body." The men of the reform were moved to deny the miracle of transubstantiation. Luther parted company at Marburg in 1529 even with Zwingli, naming his own doctrine of the sacrament consubstantiation. Calvinism leaned in general toward Zwingli's view. The divergence was sharper than would now seem necessary.

The same reasoning applies to doctrine and dogma. These also are expressions of religion. They are that on the intellectual side, just as the sacraments and prayer are its expressions on the emotional side. Both are interpretations. But the sacraments are in the universal language. The creeds are too definite for that. Besides, the older ones were given in circumstances very different from our own. We all know men who go to the communion with joy but who follow the creed with remonstrance. There cannot be verbal allegiance for most of us. And perhaps we should here discriminate between the two words doctrine and dogma which are often used, especially in the redundant verbiage of denunciation, as if they meant one and the same thing. Doctrine is that which someone, presumably in his time fit to teach, has taught. Dogma is that part of doctrine which a religious community in its organized capacity has singled out as that which must be taught if men would teach under its name. Leadership is natural even among those who think. Guidance is desirable for those who do not think. Long preoccupation with the matter, on the part of one solicitous concerning it, does not go for nothing. Something like common ground of conviction is at least one of the foundations of usefulness for any teaching institution. The effort to awaken the mind and gain assent in thought of those who are under instruction, as also to keep the assent of the thoughtful, is surely one of the aims of the Church in its teaching function. Vital participation in thought about religion on the part of those who participate in the life of thought in general should be the aim of instruction in this regard. This is the more true because religion is the great interpreter of all deeper experiences of life. It is the more true also because adults remain under the instruction of the pulpit, supposing that it is instruction, as in most cases they do not in any other relation in life.

But certainly those who broke away from the authoritative tradition of the Church and then promptly substituted in its place authority of a verbally inspired Scripture, and presently added, as they supposed, authority each of its own particular sect, did not better the matter so much as it was hoped they would. The churches which are uncompromising as to their authority take cognizance of the fact that up to a certain point some men need authority. They are by now also probably aware that some men are fain to avail themselves of authority. These thus escape, or at all events divide, responsibility for themselves. Furthermore, almost all men are, and this almost unconsciously, subject to authority, even questionable authorities, in matters to which they may think that they have to take up some relation and about which they had never much concerned themselves. The matter is not so simple as it looks. But two things are clear. In so far as it is proposed to make of religion an inner guidance and not merely a leading string, it must awaken the intelligence of men for themselves. It must support them in the use of their intelligence. In the second place, if thought about religion is to serve as an interpretation of life, it cannot be content to offer in the way of doctrine the same interpretation which it offered to men four hundred years ago, or fifteen hundred years ago. Life has changed in a manner which demands of us candid recognition. In fact, it is quite futile to refuse this recognition. It is vain to offer answers to questions which men no longer ask, or if they do ask them, ask them in quite a different sense. Interpretations must change. Certain truths will remain the same, if you choose to say that, but the statement of them cannot always remain the same. The world is not the same. We ourselves are not the same with our ancestors, or even with our own fathers. We are not the same even with our own selves as we were half a lifetime ago, that is, if we have been alive to the matter under discussion in the meantime. If we have not moved in our thought in respect of religion, while we have made the march of men of our generation in other regards, we are on the road to atrophy of our religion. We are, or soon shall be, without influence upon the religion of others or, at all events, without influence for the good. Men are now saying just that about others. Some are saying it about themselves.

In Protestantism preaching was universal, obligatory. The sermon and the two sacraments became the signs-manual of Protestantism. There were times and places where not even a burial service was to be read without an address. This was part of the warfare against mere repetition and routine. It would seem to have been assumed that if a man spoke on his own initiative it must be because he had something to say. That is, however, an assumption which we have all heard disproved. Furthermore, in the struggle, generations long, against the entrenched power of the Roman Church some Protestant ministers formed the practice of exposition of a whole system of Protestant dogma covering apparently every Sunday for one or even several years. But strikingly enough, this custom flourished in places on this side of the sea where there was practically no Roman Church to combat. The reason there may have been that in some regions schools did not then exist. In more modern times, the task of preaching takes quite other proportions. One easily falls into the mood in which he is prepared to say "Who is sufficient for these things?" The placing of the whole burden of preaching upon one man and this for years or a lifetime, complicates the situation. Claims of pastoral work, co-operation with every form of charitable, philanthropic and reforming endeavor, not to say of effort for social and economic righteousness, and even political co-operation, are either thrust upon or sought by the minister. Some withstand the strain better than others, but no one can fail to see the direction in which reform must go if the best of men, rare and fit spirits, are to choose the ministry. This is the more true since there are so many other ways in which one can do his part in serving God and man. Larger churches, men of differing gifts in the ministry of one church, would seem to be the obvious solution. But Protestant tradition, and also rivalries, stand in the way. It has often been said that the way to win great men to a great task is to show how great the task is. Here it is—certainly none in our time greater—and also no greater privilege. But one must, as things are, really concede the circumstances. Of course, there was great preaching in the Middle Ages —immortal utterance, especially in mystical circles, of a grace and power which the world will never forget. Still more of it from before the time of printing may well have been lost to us. Heretical circles, when they dared, took this way of disseminating their views. Wycklif deplored the neglect of preaching to the poor and ignorant in his own land. When he was banished from his post at Canterbury College in Oxford to Lutterworth, he took this task of preaching in that little parish for his entire work. Lollardry was spread in this way. But Lollardry turned more and more to political agitation. In general, in the long and disastrous period of corruption in the Church which preceded the Reformation, it would appear that preaching reached a low ebb. The Reformation marked a revival of preaching. This left a mark upon Protestantism which to this day has not disappeared.

On the Roman Catholic side, the Society of Jesus, especially, accepted and accepts the challenge. It maintains famous preaching centers but generally on the principle of rotation of preachers.

In the last paragraphs, the religious community in its aspect as organization, institution, has come more and more into view. We shall deal with the religious organization as such in later paragraphs, as also we shall speak more in detail of the history of worship. Meantime, in concluding this portion of the chapter, relating immediately to the nature of religion, we should speak of some other things which we may still characterize as manifestations. We should speak of them here from the point of view of their propriety, even of their necessity, to the continuance and well being of religion and of the desirability of the co-operation of serious men in them. Witness to this is vividly presented in the experience, ever repeating itself, of some whose impressionable years were indeed spent in devout homes and churches. They have then, perhaps in revulsion or perhaps merely in the process of maturing and in an enlarging life which followed, through purpose, or through lack of purpose, demitted practices of religion. It is easy to minimize influences of this sort, to emphasize the inwardness of religion as against its outward forms, to assert freedom, to weary of routine, to take offense at ineptitudes, to ridicule those who observe mere formalities. It is easy, on the other hand, to exalt some who, condemning all observances, nevertheless, lead useful and unselfish lives. Still, it remains that there are few phases of life which come to their best by giving no sign of themselves. Fashions change in the expressions of religion, and not always for the worse. We are in our day rather fain to be content that, among us, manifestations of religion should be rather underdone than overdrawn. We had rather have more religion than we show than show more religion than we have. People who are not self-conscious, however, are not quite shut up to this rather bald alternative. Those who are thinking more about the work there is to do, about the duty of somebody, possibly of themselves, to do it, are more likely to find the true line between an expression of religion which may be pretentious and an expressionlessness which is impoverishing, and also perhaps pretentious. In the long run, hypocrisies are rather likely to be found on the side of that which is popular. It is not altogether to the disadvantage of the cause of religion, particularly in some of its traditional manifestations, that it is, on the whole, at present rather unpopular. That may turn out to advantage. It may lead to the rejection of manifestations which have served their day. Furthermore, it may lead to discrimination between persons to whom religion means everything and those who may be merely followers of others who may suppose that it may perhaps mean something. It has often been an aid to the cause of religion to be stripped down to those to whom it was really a cause—the cause above all others. That process is today, in the absence of some artificialities, perhaps easier than it has been for some time.

Forms in which religion embodies itself, rites and ceremonies, traditions, teachings, which were originally personal views, and again, official doctrines in which some of these teachings have issued, with also priesthoods and organizations which make ceremonies and dogmas their care, these all do exercise directive influence, not merely upon communities, but also upon individual minds. The young and the less self-reliant among the mature are rather naturally moved in this way. The older and more self-reliant may, nevertheless, seek through the community to do their part to perpetuate that to which experience has taught them to attach significance. Modes of expression and manifestation may be a reliance and, in a deep sense, a necessity, even to the more highly developed religion of the inner life. They give form and bound to emotion, guidance to thought, fixity to purpose. They make possible co-operation in purposes. They provide continuity. They establish and maintain relations of the individual with his fellows. Even the most reflective forms of religious life, private and personal forms, do not leave behind them that aspect in which religion is a phase of community life. In societies for which these things are no longer true, religion stabilizes itself. It then declines and presently, for individuals, it may die out. The creation of new forms of expression of religion is sometimes cheerfully undertaken by those who have slight knowledge of the seriousness of the task. It is naturally futile for those who have no religion to try to find better form for it. The creation of new and real forms of expression of religion is not likely to be effective until need for change has been somewhat widely felt among those to whom religion is really significant. Conversely, however, unwillingness to change forms of religion, whether its rites, its teachings, its working organization, may be only an indication that the vital nature of religion is being unconsciously denied. Only its phenomena, possibly very ancient ones, are being held fast to. Such confusion as between forms and substance in religion is certainly one of the reasons for the decline of interest in religion. In periods of rapid advance of civilization in other regards as, for example, in our own time, this is true. On the other hand, it must be owned that tenaciousness of inherited forms appears to be greater in religion than in any other area of life.

Above all, religion deals with the great mysteries of life, with those which, therefore, many men are prone to leave to others to teach and administer on their behalf. For a like reason, those who teach and administer religion are sometimes prone to be aware of their influence and to defend their exercise of it. Furthermore, effects of the retardation of helpful change in the embodiments of religion are not likely to be so immediately obvious as in those phases of life of which no man escapes the constant pressure. The highest interests of mankind are not always the first to be considered. After all, religion is organic to the whole life of humanity and the whole life of humanity to it. It is, therefore, the more to be deplored that, on the one hand, religion, as many apprehend it, would seem to have so little to do with the great and necessary movements of the life of humanity. On the other hand, it is equally to be deplored that, by others, religion should be judged almost solely by its practical relation to immediately good and praiseworthy purposes —even to purposes which deeply religious persons think are hardly worthy of its support. It is a calamity that, in the midst of the welter of the modern world, religious men should by some be assumed to have little interest save in their own views and practices. It is, however, almost equally a calamity that the religious themselves, in the panic of this recognition, should give the impression that the whole of religion is in its practical, and perhaps novel and utilitarian applications. Surely there must be some religion to apply. It is simple to say that the applications will teach us religion. But this does not always happen, at least not to the unteachable. It is a pity that the Church as organization should make the impression that in a world of constant change, this is the one institution which never changes. More disastrous still would be that it should be so ready to change in order to be popular, that it should abandon its distinctive purpose and become only one among many of the means of bringing about the general secularization of life.

Considerations above alluded to are the familiar ones. They have for purpose to establish distinction between the forms which from age to age religion takes—and sometimes keeps—and that phase of the activity of the spirit which religion is. This distinction can hardly be absent from the minds of those who take a larger view of the present variety of modes of manifestation and, as well, of cultivation, of religion. How much more is this the case if one views the long history of his own religion, ponders the variations which it presents in its teachings, in its total apprehension of the relation of religion to life. More still must this be the case if one envisages the fact that even his own faith has, in its long history, commanded the allegiance of men of many different races. It has absorbed into itself traits of alien religious inheritances. In still greater degree, moreover, must this be true if one ponders the facts concerning other religions. He realizes the vast influence which these also have exerted through ages, the influence which they now exert, the truths which they embody, the modes of life which they exemplify, the contribution to human welfare which each of them has made. If, furthermore, one takes into account the unnumbered generations which must lie behind the short period which we can in any way trace, if we note the survival of earlier forms in the later ones, if our mode of approach puts us upon trying to find resemblances however small and seeking to understand differences however great, then first do we appreciate the significance of signs, even the most obscure, which the religious impulse has given of itself. Then first are we in a position to realize the unity of human experience in this regard. Then first do we appreciate the blinding effect upon ourselves of the assumption that forms which are familiar to us are the whole, even of our own religion, or still worse, that our own religion is the only religion. Then first do we realize how this assumption leads us to approach other religions with prejudice, or, at the most, with curiosity. Then perhaps do we realize how this tends to generate another prejudice, its very opposite. This is to the effect that no matured religion is real religion, that what is really decisive is that which we observe, or even only surmise that we observe, among primitive men, the most rudimentary form or formlessness. That such a view obtains with some learned men, and is supposed by some to be the issue of the theory of the evolution of religion, does not admit of doubt. The real problem is to arrive at some notion of the essence of the matter by comparison of all the phases and all the stages of its manifestation. This is the thing which makes a definition of religion of the sort which has been of late so often attempted, on the one hand, so difficult, and, on the other hand, so unnecessary. Edward Caird, the Master of Balliol, wrote a generation ago in his "Evolution of Religion,"—"The idea which we seek is not to be found in any element common to all the religions. Even if such an element could be detected, it would be too general to supply us with a clue to the facts of religious history. A definition so obtained would correspond, if to any, to the lowest only, to the most primitive form of religious life. It would not be a principle adequate to the explanation of the endless multiplicity of forms which religion takes in different ages and nations, or of the way in which they successively arise one out of another. Rather, in conformity with the idea of evolution, a definition of religion must be derived from a consideration of the whole course of its history viewed as a process of transition from the lowest to the highest form of it. In fact, if the different religions are to be regarded as successive stages in a development, what we have in that history is just religion progressively defining itself. The idea of religion would be most clearly expressed in the most mature form which it has reached as the result of the whole process. Reflection, therefore, would have to read that history backwards. It would have to view what is earliest in the light of ideas derived from the consideration of what is latest."[1]

MANIFESTATIONS OF RELIGION

1. WORSHIP

We turn now to speak more in detail concerning two manifestations of religion, namely, worship and organization. There is also a representation of religion in speech, namely, preaching. Concerning this last, we have already spoken in the previous part of this chapter. We chose to do that because it is primarily concerned with ideas of religion. As to preaching we shall never get beyond words which Chaucer wrote in his "Prologue" concerning the "pore persoun of a toun"—

This noble ensample unto his scheep he gaf,
That ferst he wroughte, and after that he taughte,

. . . .

But Cristes lore, and his apostles twelve,
He taught, and ferst he folwed it himselve.

In a brief paragraph introductory to the remainder of this second chapter, I beg to note one fact. I take all my

[1] Vol. I, pp. 60–61.

illustrations here from one religion, namely, Christianity. I do this with intent. It is a departure, indeed from a principle which we heartily acknowledge and which has guided us thus far, namely, that of instructive comparison with other religions. The principle will guide us again. Christianity, however, has dominated in almost overwhelming measure two millenniums of European civilization. Its decisive influence we in America inherit. And within the last two centuries the same influence has been widely spread in much of the rest of the world. This fact alone gives to its worship, its organization and the life which is lived under it, a preponderance which may justify for us the course which I here temporarily pursue. Comparisons with other religions we find natural. Hardly a century ago this was not the case. For most of us one religion was true, others false. Judaism had been persecuted. What of paganism survived in the Christianity of Europe, survived mainly because it was not recognized. Parallel claims for Mohammedanism simply sharpened Christian antagonism. Elements from the very structure of the Roman State were taken over into the Roman Church. Only in less degree was this the case also in the Eastern Church. For long ages, the Church dominated the chaos of the Western world. Just so, the classic mystery cults had made themselves felt in Christian worship, and classic traditions of philosophy were fundamental in scholasticism. We now see all this clearly. But in extraordinary degree the makers of the Middle Ages and even the proponents of the Reformation seem to have been unconscious of it. Both the advocates of vital change and those who resisted changes in the name of an inviolable tradition sought justification for their contentions, mutually exclusive as these often were, in apostolic tradition. Both carried their justification back to Christ and the apostles, Protestants almost as if the intervening ages had not been. This is one of the most interesting observations which one could make upon aspects of Christian history, especially in regard to worship and organization from, say, the fourth to the sixteenth century. Worship and organization were, of course, influenced, as all things human must be, by their environment. But men chose not to see it so. In the paragraph on life, on the other hand, particularly life in the post-Reformation world, I have undertaken to delineate the reversal of all this. Yet it has been rather slowly that recognition of racial traits and traces of other religions have been acknowledged. Such recognitions are more common in Protestant missions. But they are practical and very real in Roman missions as well.

Worship is more nearly perpetual and universal, when men's minds turn to religion at all. Certain great expressions of worship have been perennial. They are moulds into which every man lays his own desires and needs. They speak to us the more because they talk to us the less. The other thing which comes before us here is characteristic organization. The organization of the humble little body of believers came into being for purposes of sympathy and defense. The time came when, in a zeal for domination, it brought out many of the forces of the world against it. Few organizations have had so long and varied a history, few more benign and, occasionally, few more devastating influence. Even in its splitting up into the many forms of Protestantism, it still illustrates the same paradox. Worship is expression of religion as emotion. It is gratitude. It is contrition for the past, as also resolution and hope for the future. It is sympathy for others. It is self-dedication. It is outgoing, precisely because it is the inward and the upward look. One might make more such little phrases. These may suffice to point direction. It will accord with our general plan if we confine ourselves mainly to the history of Christian worship. Doctrine also has played its part in this. The long period of the conversion of the northern races brought accommodations with the worships of other faiths. Worship would have place in the guidance of converts with whom more elaborate instruction would perhaps have little meaning. Catholic tradition has always shown an imperious fidelity in this regard. One needed only to attend a service in the Cathedral in Peking in the years after the Boxer uprising to feel this. Losses among converts had been great. Similar remark might be made as to the amazing fidelity shown in the history of the Jesuit missions in Japan in the two hundred and more years between Nobunaga and the opening of Japan in 1869. It will be almost enough for us to speak of the beginnings of the grand tradition of worship in the Western world. This is the more true because one of the things which the Reformation sought was to bring worship back again to the simplicity which it had in the early Church. For some the example given in the Scriptures themselves sufficed. It would be difficult to say how much Protestantism—except, of course, in the Anglican Church—lost in this endeavor. Our main purpose is, however, to indicate the principle which lies at the back of this tradition.

The earliest things that we know about religion mark it as primarily manifest in feeling. That feeling was evidenced by men who lived the life of thought in but limited degree. Further expressions of religion were in the area of action. Action was influenced, if not determined, by actions and attitudes of others. Natural fear of the unknown was a chief motive. Force of the community was exerted to exact of the individual action comporting with those fears. Development of individuality was slow. Yet the individual in his awakening was often the source of influence for salutary change. We are probably right in thinking that changes in reference to religion would not be the earliest changes commending themselves to the group. Practical matters relating to development of communal interests would have natural precedence. Superstitions in reference to gods or to the dead would make changes in this area slower than in areas where facts were more obvious. One must say something of this sort as to the great empires of Western Asia, as also of Egypt. Progress in those civilizations was in some respects amazing. Understanding of religion remained for long periods relatively stationary. The images of deity show that. The Code of Khammurabbi, who is at present thought to have reigned in Babylon before 2250 B.C., impressed us, on its relatively recent publication, as the document of a civilization far in advance of anything that we had known of so early a date. Babylonia was a land of agriculturalists and merchants, presently of soldiers. Light thrown by the tablets upon government, social life, trade, brings to us surprise. Knowledge of the phenomena of the heavens amazes us. What is said of religion leaves the impression that this had made no corresponding progress. Images of the deity with the head and breast of a man and the body of a bull might have told us that. The Egyptian Book of the Dead also reveals a state of things more rudimentary than that which we know concerning Egyptian civilization of the time. I am not sure that we read all the symbols aright. But the birds and other animals which appear in the figures at the tombs arouse reflection. The Greek states, notably that of the Athenians, Socrates as pictured by Plato, Plato himself with Aristole, left upon the history of thought marks comparable with no others. It was such a little country. The period between the defeat of Xerxes and the ventures of Alexander was so short. The tragedians were certainly far above the level of anything that we know about the priesthood of their day. Socrates died under accusation of corrupting youth. One of us who reads the "Apology" must think that the populace in whose name the accusation was brought had not been much corrupted by the wisdom of Socrates. The rugged republicanism of Rome, disintegrating after the Punic Wars, the genius of Augustus, the moral character and true religion of Marcus Aurelius, and then again, the decline and fall of the Empire, point all the impressions which we have thus far received. The kingdom of Solomon, about the outward greatnesses of which it would seem that there must be some exaggeration, the amazing period of the prophets, the unknown authors of many Psalms, move us profoundly. So far as life is concerned, however, all this degenerates in the period of scribes and Pharisees and the apocalyptic.

Then comes Jesus. How should Jesus know of the world problems which we have tried in these few sentences to recall? Whether he knew much or little, his greatness lies in the fact that he took hold of the problem from the other end, the problem of the inner life, the realm of the spirit. His sovereign contribution may almost be summed up in those few words. If Jesus knew that all who ever came before him were, as he said, thieves and robbers—if we should say that he knew not only that they had failed, but knew also why they failed,—we should be saying a very great thing. If we say that he probably had but rudimentary knowledge of many efforts that had gone before his own, we should be saying a more probable, but a still greater thing. It is abundantly clear that he was a man of highest intelligence. His country was by then a crossroads of the known world. Yet what is cardinal in Jesus' teaching bears little or no relation to vast knowledge of such facts. What he knew even from the history of his own people was mainly that the effort to make men good by laws and ceremonies had failed. What he said might, however, as easily, have been the fruit of the reflection of a nature so simple and direct as was his own. Hear him say, "Out of the heart are the issues of life." Hear him denounce those who sought to make clean the outside of the cup and platter. One might respond that these things are so obvious that almost anybody could have said them. True perhaps. But few people have tried to build up a religion by saying them. Fewer still have sought to re-create a world by that conviction. The men whom he chose to be his disciples were certainly very simple people. One of them, Judas, went back. He was probably the least simple. What equipment did they have? One may say, at all events, pure hearts and teachable spirits. How much did they know about the issues of the course of things of which he and they were the beginners? One might almost ask how much do we know, except that we are sure—sometimes—of his principle. And we, too, when we are not at our best, depart from it.

What was Jesus' point of contact with these men of his choice? Outwardly one great point of contact, at the least, was the simple practice of worshipping, the regulation of life which the fellowship in the synagogue brought to them. And what did they do in the synagogue? They read the sacred book of their race, sang hymns, offered prayers, both individual and also under the leadership of others. Address was made, perhaps rather frequently by scribes and Pharisees. Of these we cannot really think that all were what some of them undoubtedly were. But there he with his disciples heard uplifting and exalting speech and gained support of hope and trust. They might also hear high debate. The synagogue permitted that. They would join with people of faith, their own faith. They would share in ministrations of mercy. The more ceremonial worship, that which thought itself the greater worship, was now all concentrated in one place, the temple in Jerusalem. This was likely, as often in such cases, to be administered by people with a varying sense of what the faith which they professed involved. The particular point for us is that, with all that was revolutionary in Jesus' teaching—he certainly was not so unintelligent as not to know how revolutionary he was—he never let himself be drawn or driven to live his own life quite by himself. He had joy in the fact that these simple followers trusted him. He never wanted them to live a life altogether by themselves. With all that was private and personal in religion as he apprehended it, it is just as sure that he apprehended a side of religious thought and feeling and life which could best be lived in company with others and to a certain extent, for the sake of others.

When he was gone, perhaps all the more because he was gone, they felt themselves bound to carry on the endeavor. Gautama also gathered a group of those who were to learn of him. What we learn of this group reminds us more, however, of the schools which Greek philosophers gathered. It will be recalled that these schools of philosophers at first implied a certain leisure on the part of those who constituted them. The very word school says that. Mohammed also, zealot, reformer, conqueror of those who resisted being reformed, drew to himself and welded to one another in blind enthusiasm those of a like mind. Nevertheless, it is not without reservations that we can speak either of a Buddhist or of a Moslem Church. The schools of Greek philosophers we could not speak of as having achieved the status of a church at all. For the matured, diversified and yet unified institution, protean, perpetual, at times almost omnipotent, which we know as the Christian Church, there is, strictly speaking, no parallel. Even when we speak of the Jewish Church, we mean a different thing. The Jewish Church was and has remained racial. From their fellow Jews the followers of Jesus soon felt themselves constrained to part. The Jews facilitated their departure. The fact of a great Christian Church of all ages, with all its evil and all its good, had its relation first to antagonisms on the part of the Jews. It then met antagonisms on the part of the Empire, rivalries on the part of schools of philosophers, as also of Oriental religious sects of many sorts, and finally, an inheritance almost forced upon it from the dying Roman world. Yet there are a few rudimentary things which characterize it in all the amazing permutations through which it passed. One of these was fellowship. Another was the maintenance and the privilege of a characteristic worship. The third was responsibility for the spread of the principles of Jesus in their application to the lives of men. There was still a fourth—or perhaps we should have put it first—the sustaining of their fellows in suffering and sorrow, and even in the face of sin, by an eternal hope. Something like this must, in sum, be conceded to have been the aim of the Church.

Of course the word church—*kyriake*—is an adjective. The noun which it implied was *ekklesia,* literally, the body of those called out of the world through allegiance to their Lord. When the word *church* occurs, at all events in the

Gospels, we may doubt whether the passages belong, just as they are, to the very earliest tradition concerning Jesus. Or, to put it the other way about, we may wonder whether the Gospels, as we have them, do not show the mark of a usage later in its associations. None of this, however, casts doubt upon the fact that Jesus from the first contemplated an association of those thus called. Paul, founder of the Gentile churches, who withstood the "pillar apostles" to their face, is only less touching than was his Master in his craving for fellowship in his lonely and laborious life. He thought of his converts literally as his children. "By the grace of God I begot you in the Gospel." The younger Pliny's letter to Trajan describes the Christian assemblages for worship. He makes plain that the accusation which had apparently called out the Emperor's inquiry—all secret assemblages were beginning to be under suspicion—had not good ground, at least not in the sense that the Christians were either politically significant or morally reprehensible. Modern studies of the life of the times of the Christian origins—studies for which we owe much to Hatch and Mommsen—reveal how numerous and how various were groups and societies for the prosecution of given purposes in the lives of simple people. The burial societies reveal strong bonds in the circles of the poor. But as the aging Empire grew jealous, the activities of these societies were closely watched lest they should become centers of political agitation. Indeed it may be believed that the Christian societies laid themselves open in this matter, for example, in their constant emphasis upon a coming kingdom.

Far and away, as we have said, the decisive influence in Jesus' own childhood and youth had been the synagogue. There were times also when the shores of the lake, fastnesses of the hills, the loneliness of the desert, came to be for him a sanctuary. One can hardly doubt that the temple took more hold of the boy of twelve than of the man of thirty. Yet this was not exactly because it was the temple, nor yet because he was now thirty. Rather it was because, as so easily happens in highly organized religion, the formalities had overgrown, suppressed, the spirit which they were intended to express. The symbols were no longer signs of something else. They were just facts of worship. Worship was those facts. To some priests it was clear that men could not come to God without those ceremonies. To Jesus it seems to have become a question whether men could come, or, at all events, did come to God through such manifestations. There was not much in his experience, or in their own, to make the disillusioned little group of followers after his death desire to remain in Jerusalem. Indeed he bade them go back to Galilee. There was still less, as they came, presently to dot the lands about the eastern end of the Mediterranean, to put them upon anything more elaborate than the familiar worship in the synagogues, which were everywhere. Efforts of zealous followers of Jesus at Jerusalem to bring along with them their rites, customs and restrictions which belonged to their Jewish heritage resulted only in driving out freer spirits such as Paul. Paul clearly left the organization and the worship of the little communities which he founded largely to themselves, save only that they were bound in allegiance to the Lord.

Nevertheless, there was something else in the immemorial background of the religion of the Hebrews and, as well, in different ways, of almost all other religions. We cannot pass over it in silence. This element of worship turns upon the idea of sacrifice, and this might remind us of the temple. There were no sacrifices in the synagogue. But there had been sacrifices in domestic and local worship long before there was any temple. Jesus had spoken of himself as a sacrifice. Letters of Paul are full of allusions to the sacrifice of Christ on our behalf. The Epistle to the Hebrews literally substitutes the offering of Christ himself for those other offerings under the old covenant. One of the narratives in the ancient record of the very earliest happenings declares Jahve's preference for animal sacrifice as over against offerings of the fruits of the field. The divine repugnance toward human sacrifice is set forth in connection with the "father of the faithful." To be sure, the forefathers of Israel were, and for many generations remained, a nomad, pastoral people. Their riches were in flocks. But offerings of fruits of the soil were adopted when the Israelites had a soil. Heads of families were at times the offerers. Later, priests and Levites assumed the function. Judges, kings and prophets, on occasion, took the part. After the exile, greater celebrations were esteemed to be warranted only at the central shrine in Jerusalem. By this custom, with the difficulty of going up to Jerusalem, small as Palestine was, some Jews even in the Holy Land, and still more Jews scattered in the Dispersion, came but seldom to the great feasts. Some never came at all.

It will need no divination to assure ourselves that sacrifice gathered to itself interpretations. The reward of the toil of men co-operating with the fecundity of nature calls out men's gratitude and rejoicing. The taking of life, the shedding of blood, had a different symbolism. It was the giving back to God of something mysteriously precious. Further, this giving was in view of something which men greatly desired of God. Somewhere in the background of the race, at all events, lay human sacrifice. It is obviously the sense of guilt, the fear of punishment, which here comes into play. It is reconciliation, recovery, which is sought. Atonement must be made. The very word atonement gathered to itself this dominant sense, not simply of honoring God, but of appeasing God. The famous passage in Micah almost runs the gamut. "Wherewithal shall I come before the Lord and bow myself before the High God?" The prophet brushes all this aside, "He hath showed thee, O man, what is good. And what doth the Lord require of thee but to do justly and to love mercy and to walk humbly with thy God." Many Psalms are in that key. "The sacrifices of God are a broken spirit." Such thoughts were the inheritance of Jesus. Nevertheless it is not altogether to be wondered at that in the slow lapse of men from their own better insight, and with the avarice of ecclesiastical organization, the old sense about sacrifice came back. Salvation was a thing which could be bought if only one could pay the price. Thus begins a long history in the Christian Church as well.

Some Jewish folk, whether at Jerusalem or in the Dispersion, followed the line of a prophecy in the book of Daniel. It is about a Son of Man who was to come down from heaven in power and glory and set up a kingdom over the Jews. Vengeance was to be taken upon their enemies. To men of this spirit the writing which we know as the second Isaiah presents a contrast—one might say, a contradiction. It is no wonder that it was not popular. What could a nation, or at all events rebellious minds, make of a leader who was only a sufferer? Surely the fact that the cardinal teaching of the second Isaiah was so far in advance of its time had something to do with its being relegated to a secondary place. It seems to have been of little influence until the son of a Galilean carpenter saw in it a new inspiration for a moral and spiritual deliverance of his people and of all the world. He saw in it something different from the deliverance for which priests and rebellious secularists, agitators and people of the military mind hoped, fought for, and were hopelessly defeated about a century after Jesus' death.

In this prophecy, as also in its fulfillment in Jesus, it is out of the common elements of every man's life that a salvation, universal, age-long, can be achieved. No wonder that Jesus, with that incomparable mingling of divine humility with divine confidence which was characteristic of him, quotes these passages so often of himself. His followers to this day quote them of him. We took at one point in the first chapter the doctrine of the atonement for an example of different interpretations which, with the lapse of centuries, the central teaching of Christianity has undergone. May we not revert to this identical point, the sacrifice of Christ, and illustrate again, with this one transcendent example, all that we have to say here concerning the central act of worship in the Christian Church. The Mass is the symbol of that central teaching. The Communion is the reminder of it in Protestant churches. It is presentation of the deepest thing in Christian feeling, exactly as the article of faith about the atonement is the central statement of it for the world of thought. And yet, just as we saw in that other case, the course of thought has had a long and varied history. So here, the course of thought about the sacrament has had a long and varied history. Yet the symbol itself, exactly because it is a symbol, because its appeal is to what men feel, its issue is in what they will and do, its consequence is in what they are, the symbol does not need to change. Its interpretation must change because men change. The bread and wine were the same that they had been during the Passover which Christ ate with his disciples. They were the same that were in everybody's Passover. But they were not the same for those men after Jesus had said to them, "This do in remembrance of me." "For as oft," said Paul, "as ye eat this bread and drink this cup, ye do show forth the Lord's death until he come."

The Eucharist

There is, I think, no clear mention of Jesus' having participated in sacrifices. It would seem probable that he did. He left no specific word to his disciples about such participation. The word which he used about the bread and wine at the Last Supper—"This is my blood which is shed for you for the remission of sins,"—has been thought by some to indicate that he meant to do away with sacrifices as these had been a part of the worship of his people from time immemorial. Obviously, the Epistle to the Hebrews so understood: "But Christ being come, an High Priest of good things to come—neither by the blood of goats and calves, but by his own blood he entered into the holy place." A great passage in Paul is to the same effect: "Take, eat, this is my body which is broken for you. This cup is the New Testament in my blood—for as oft as ye drink it, ye do show forth the Lord's death." Already in Paul's time, there were abuses. Of these he said, "Every one taketh before other his own supper—What, have ye not houses to eat and drink in, or despise ye the Church of God?" The names that are used for this memorial are significant:—agapé, the sign of love; sacramentum, perhaps this means the soldier's oath, renewal of allegiance; eucharist, the giving of thanks. Still later, the Lord's Supper, with also Baptism, were compared to the mysteries. Indeed, the word mystery came to be so applied by Christians themselves. In the religious life of the ancient world, and especially in the period of its decline, a characteristic feature was its craving after mysteries. There was hardly a deity in connection with whose service some subsidiary cult of this sort did not arise. There were guilds of those to whom secret documents were made known. Christians did not escape this influence. The word mystery occurs in first Timothy, in the passage in which Christ is spoken of as "the mystery of godliness." Instead of faith, the author speaks of "the mystery of faith." The Apocalypse is almost made up of mysteries. It is no wonder if in the end this came to be the Church's own view of the Sacrament. In primitive custom, at least, food was set apart for the deity as an act of hospitality. Again, the god demanded shedding of blood, but accepted the sacrifice of the totemic animal instead of guilty men. Participation in the rite bound worshippers in a close bond. Eleusinian mysteries were participated in by a religious brotherhood. Mystery cults held out also hope of immortal life. The sacrament brought the worshipper into the immediate presence of God. Such facts seem to show that these ideas are a part of an immemorial heritage.

It is no wonder, therefore, if in the Christian communities, shut in upon themselves and often in peril, some of these meanings transformed what seems to us, in light of the New Testament so simple and natural an act as that of the Master. Silence of Paul touching the priesthood would seem to show that abrogation of the old sacrificial procedure was understood. Allusions to the priesthood in the Epistle to the Hebrews are of purely ideal sort. It was, like the priesthood of Melchizedek, eternal. This very notion of the priesthood is a thing for which the author is arguing. In the Didaché, the Eucharist—this name for the rite signifies the giving of thanks—seems to have followed a common meal. There was a thank-offering, part of which was distributed to the poor. Part of it was also sacrificially eaten. Robertson Smith says that not until Cyprian do we find the teaching that the body and blood of Christ are offered "in sacrifice." There are few enough clues to follow. It is not surprising if the early Christians were anxious to preserve their most sacred ceremonies from profanation and ridicule. Nor was it wonderful if they invested the sacraments with an atmosphere of mystery. Nor, again, is it surprising if, with the great influx of former pagans into the Church which presently took place, the thought of boons conferred by participation in the solemn rites underwent deterioration. Dean Inge has said that so long as Christian philosophy remained predominantly Platonic the materialization of the eucharist could not be complete. But in the end, as Harnack says, "Sacerdotalism gathered up and secured all that the Church most prized, its dogma, its mystical relation to Christ, the fellowship of believers, the priests, the sacrifice, the miraculous powers which God had given to the Church." One of the noblest utterances of the "judicious" Hooker, still within the century of the English Reformation, runs thus: "In the holy communion, it is not the elements by themselves but a faithful participation in them which confers grace. And faithful participation includes the intention on our side to perform the acts in consideration of which we expect the promised graces, and to co-operate in working out our salvation so far as in us lies."

One turns to the classic statement of Roman Catholic dogma concerning the Eucharist, namely, that set forth by the Council of Trent in its thirteenth session, October 11, 1551. It is this statement (Chapter IV) which relates to transubstantiation. It is fair to feel that perhaps the struggle with Protestantism influenced the militant shaping of this paragraph. Yet the substance is not widely different from the phraseology of the Fourth Lateran Council in the year 1215. By the Greek Church and under circumstances substantially similar to those which moved the Fathers at Trent, the doctrine was proclaimed by a Synod of Jerusalem in 1672, as an essential element of the faith of the Church. The doctrine was repudiated categorically in the twenty-eighth of the Thirty-nine Articles of the Church of England, the Latin text of which was published in 1563, the English translation in 1571. This latter statement was adopted by the American Church in 1801. The other five sacraments of the Roman Church were Confirmation, Penance, Orders, Matrimony and Extreme Unction. These were repudiated by the Church of England, in their character as sacraments, in 1563. In what Matthew Arnold rather irascibly called "the dissidence of dissent," Protestants took a more austere view of the Eucharist. Some rejoiced to do away so far as possible with that with which the Roman Church had surrounded it. I recall the celebration of the Communion in a little church in the Scottish Highlands, which I long ago attended. The table was spread down the length of the aisle in the little church. The participants stood. No word was spoken save from Scripture. For the singing of a Psalm, the key note was given from a pitch-pipe.

Baptism

Older than the Eucharist is the other sacrament, that of Baptism. With the Jews the bathing of the whole body in a running stream had been recognized as symbol of restoration from ceremonial uncleanness. The pouring of water on the hands was Pharisaic observance before every meal. But Christian baptism was a symbol of purification not from ceremonial but from moral impurity. With

John the Baptist, the rite was symbolic of repentance and inward renewal. The baptism was "unto remission of sins." Jesus' first preaching of repentance was coupled, like John's, with baptism. The Christian baptism added, however, a forward look which perhaps John's baptism had lacked. In Jesus' teaching, change in the inner life was fundamental. His teaching demanded the cleansing of the heart. The rite signified a new direction of the life. From this point of view the Christian rite, when once it had taken place as symbol of inward renewal, was not one to be repeated. Peter, at the Pentecost, when men, stirred by his preaching, asked what they should do, said, "Repent ye, and be baptized, each one of you, in the name of Jesus Christ for the remission of your sins, and ye shall receive the gift of the Holy Spirit."

Baptism was thus recognized as sign of entrance upon the new life. There is as yet no clear index of the method of baptism. The Didaché, which, by the way, is strongly anti-Jewish in its temper, speaks of "living water," by which is probably meant a running stream. Quite naturally, the earliest formula is "In the name of Jesus Christ," or again, "In the name of the Lord Jesus." In Matthew 28:19, the full later formula occurs, "In the name of the Father and of the Son and of the Holy Ghost." But we have no synoptic parallel on this point. Justin Martyr gives the full formula. Tertullian with Ignatius and Cyprian combat the shorter formula. Probably baptism took among Christians the place of circumcision among the Jews. Circumcision was administered on the eighth day. It had signified the inclusion of male children as members of the holy people. It would be natural, therefore, that children should be baptized. Paul speaks of baptism as effecting a union with the death of Christ. Yet in Jesus' conversation with Nicodemus in the Fourth

Gospel, even a man who had been a teacher in Israel and of the strictest ceremonial purity is enjoined, "Except a man be born of water and of the spirit, he cannot enter into the Kingdom of God." But it is to be remembered that the Gospel of John is late. Already with Tertullian and Cyprian in the West, and with Cyril of Jerusalem, at all events, in the East, the water of baptism was thought of as itself the means of conveying a divine power to those to whom it was applied. Constantine is said to have postponed his baptism until the very end of his life. Augustine gave baptism a dogmatic interpretation, in that inherited guilt also was washed away in baptism. To Protestants in their early dogmatic utterances, baptism was symbol of forgiveness of sins and of the imparting of the Holy Spirit. It was, therefore, if it had been rightly performed, not to be repeated. With the Lutherans baptism with water, joined with the Word, assured forgiveness of sins and freedom of the will to do good. The Anabaptists, holding that children were not competent to the act of faith, demanded baptism again in maturity. Baptists rejected infant baptism and, esteeming that they followed more strictly the Scripture, held to immersion. Quakers rejected baptism altogether, as also the Eucharist, following their feeling of the inwardness of everything in the spiritual life. There seems to be good ground to think that until the twelfth century in Europe, immersion was the usual form of baptism. This is still the case in the Orient. In the Western Church, sprinkling became practically universal. Baptisteries were erected for the special purpose in the great days of Gothic building. Early in the seventeenth century those dissenters in England who later came to be called Baptists returned to the ancient manner, administering the rite by immersion. In practically all other respects their contention was identical with that of those who later were called Congregationalists, from the form of government which alone they esteemed to be warranted by the Scripture.

Prayer

It will hardly be denied that in the first *élan* of the freedom which the men of the Reformation took to reform the public services of worship, they went beyond the necessities of the case. There was weight in the argument that these services should be in a language "understanded by the people." The languages of western Europe had passed out of the inchoate state in which they had long been. They began to be the vehicles of epoch-making literature like the poems of Chaucer, or Mallory's translation of the Arthurian legends into English, or the poems of Dante in Italian; like the poetry of the Troubadours and the Trouvères in French and the sources, at all events, of the poem of the Cid in Spanish. The Bible had been "done into English" by Wycklif almost one hundred and fifty years before Luther and his rendering into German, or Beza's translation into French. Indeed, there were five translations into English before the King James. There was quite as good reason why the service of worship should be translated out of Latin into living tongues of Europe. The lands which became Protestant pressed for such translation. The process was completed in England before the adoption of the Prayer Book of Edward VI. Almost simultaneously similar steps were taken in Germany and France. Of course, fewer men read then than now. The fewest private persons possessed books. The feeling about prayers went further still among Puritans and the more radical reforming groups.

It was that in the personal participation of the leader in the act of prayer lay guarantee of the immediacy and sincerity of his praying. In this lay also the possibility of his voicing the very desires and petitions of those on whose behalf he prayed. And, finally, it was one of his duties to teach men to pray for themselves. One cannot but feel the force of all this. Yet in retrospect one is fain to think that it resulted, often, in the substitution of immediate personal solicitudes for the grandeur of expression of universal needs and wants in the life of the spirit. At least public services of worship should have place for these as well. Also by association with them, private supplications attain a dignity of universal expression. And, what is perhaps of even greater moment, the demand of what is rather direfully called extempore prayer laid upon the leader of such devotions a burden to which the powers of the greatest are not at all moments equally adequate, and to which the powers of some are not adequate at all.

It is indeed fairly sure that a man will never pray well "by the book" who does not sometimes pray well without the book. But it is equally true that, especially in the universal terms which are precisely those needed in public prayer, a man will not always rise to the greatness of his privilege who has not communed often and long with the greatness of other praying spirits, and lost himself at times in the spirit of age-long and universal prayer. This is the only road of avoidance of the occasional, the petty and personal, of the obtrusion of one's self, of the patronage of others, in a matter in which either obtrusion or patronage is more odious than in any other imaginable thing. Occasionally, such prayer seems little short of unseemly familiarity with men and unwarranted assurance before Almighty God. It is the laying bare of things which should, indeed, be laid bare to the Infinite Sympathy, but some of them would be best laid bare by the souls concerned, even if they did not do it very well. The sympathy of God might cover the deficit. No one who knows will deny that in schools for the ministry the teaching men how to lead others in prayer is, indeed, the thing most deeply to be desired. It is also the thing which is almost utterly impossible to achieve. It is, at all events, most naturally done—I had almost said most tolerably approached—when two spirits, seeking nothing but reality, accept the task by the aid, at least, of the great literature of prayer which for more than three thousand years our two inherited faiths have accumulated. We might even trust to the aid of the God, to whom alone "All hearts are open and all desires known and from whom no secrets are hid," but "from whom also cometh down the spirit of prayer and supplication." One thing in this effort should be ever remembered, and is sometimes forgotten. There is a literature of prayer which is in its own way one of the greatest literatures of the whole world, a literature almost literally in every language which has ever achieved any cultivation at all and of every age and of almost every faith. And finally, there is much to say for prayers of which the worshipper knows every word by heart—has known their every word since childhood, his parents knew them before him. They seem to him like the voice of the Church Universal in its confessions, its petitions, its words of trust and hope in the God and Father of us all, and of all men in mankind's belief in the life everlasting. Not to have known that there is such a literature, not to have some parts of it under one's hand and more of it written on one's heart, would seem almost like living one's religious life in vain.

Hymns

The custom of singing in connection with acts of worship is ancient. It is not certain that the Vedic hymns were sung, or whether they were merely odes in praise, to be recited. Certainly the hymns of Hesiod were of this latter sort. And to take a modern instance, of this latter sort is surely Milton's "Hymn on the Nativity." But in the book of the Psalms, there are a number which bear in our King James version the curious title "Songs of Degrees." These are now thought to have been pilgrims' songs of the "going up" to Jerusalem. The Greek titles of certain Psalms in the Septuagint mark them as "Hymns of David, the son of Jesse." The famous chapter in the book of Ecclesiasticus, "Let us now praise famous men" is entitled "Hymn of the Fathers." It is certain that there was singing in the synagogue service. After the Last Supper, Jesus and his disciples "sang an hymn," before they went out into the Mount of Olives. Paul and Silas sang in the jail at Philippi. What were later called the canticles, the Magnificat, the Benedictus and the Nunc dimittis, follow the form of Hebrew poetry. They seem to have been in immemorial use in the Christian Church. Very early appear morning and evening hymns, both Greek and Latin, translations of many of which have place in modern hymn books. One of these is thought to be the origin of the Gloria in Excelsis, still said or sung in almost all our churches. It was not until the fourth century that Greek hymnody was imitated in the West. Its introduction seems to have been due to two great figures in the Latin Church, Hilary of Poitiers, and Ambrose, Bishop of Milan. Augustine speaks of himself as "moved to tears by the sweetness of Ambrose's hymns and canticles." To Ambrose is ascribed the composition of the Te Deum—whether rightly or not is uncertain.

Benedict is supposed to have prescribed hymns of Ambrose to be used at the canonical hours in his newly founded Order. But the Ambrosian usage gave way after the time of Gregory the Great. This was all the more the case as the monastic influence was carried to the missions of the North and West. Northern impulse in hymn writing and Church music in general began to make itself felt. This was the time when legends about the authorship of immortal hymns began, like that, for example, which attributed the "Veni Creator Spiritus" to Charlemagne. Famous hymns were not uncommonly assigned to famous people—not all of them famous for their piety. So also the "Veni Sancte Spiritus" was attributed to Robert II, King of France. Later, the same hymn was attributed to the greatest of all the popes, Innocent III. Certainly the group or school of Aidan of St. Victor, who died after 1173, brought the production of such hymns to greatest perfection. There was noble hymn writing also about a century later in the time of Thomas Aquinas. It would appear that the "Adoro te devote, latens Deitas" was written by Aquinas for the then new festival of Corpus Christi. There have been various revisions of the body of hymns in use in the Roman Church, the first of them apparently in the time of Leo X. The French Church, at times, went its own way in this regard. The Paris Breviary of 1735 remained optional until a comparatively recent date. There was a period of revival of hymn writing, especially among the Jesuits in Germany, even so late as the end of the eighteenth century.

Luther was himself a musician. He wrote hymns and also made translations of Psalms. Perhaps best known are a Christmas hymn "Von Himmel hoch da komm' ich her," and the greatest of all his hymns "Ein' feste Burg." Almost as famous is the battle hymn, "Verzage nicht du

Häuflein klein." This is said to have been sung by the army as they went into the battle of Lützen in which Gustav Adolf fell. Gerhardt was perhaps the great German hymn writer of the seventeenth century. The world at large has somewhat lost a feeling which it once had about the Pietist hymnology. In England, Cranmer's first instinct is said to have been to follow Luther's course. The Reformed in France and Switzerland had set the fashion of metrical translations of the Old Testament Psalms. Clement Marot had made some such translations. The influence of Calvin was decisive that his churches should use only Psalms. Knox carried this conviction to Scotland. The Sternhold and Hopkins Psalter, the first part of which was published in England already under Edward VI, long held sway in the English Church. Of course, the Te Deum and the Benedictus and the Gloria in Excelsis in English, came with the Edward VI Prayer Book. The Scotch clung rigorously to the Psalms. The Puritan regime in England supported them. This first established the usage in the American Colonies, at least, so far as related to New England. It is sad to say that Milton, who wrote several superb paraphrases for Psalms, never wrote a hymn for Church use. The Old Version gave way to the New Version. But progress, even after the time of Bishop Ken, who wrote exquisite hymns, was slow. One can hardly speak of a Church Hymn Book in the sense in which we use that word until the time of editions of the Prayer Book which date about 1791 and thereafter. Yet before that time had come the great movement of hymn writing by Charles Wesley and, at least of hymn translating, by John Wesley. Besides, there was a wealth of hymns all the way from the time of Elizabeth and Charles, but these found their way into Church usage only slowly. Dryden, Addison, Doddridge and Watts might be named in evidence for this assertion. The reign of psalmody was not broken in America, at least not in New England, until the end of the eighteenth century. Then came in this country also the era of a revivalist movement which produced hymns just as the Wesleyan revival had done. The period of the rise of the Oxford Movement in England produced many noble hymns, two of them by Newman himself, as also by Keble, John Mason Neale and Christopher Wordsworth. Approximately the same period in America brought forth hymns of Whittier and Sears, of Ray Palmer and Oliver Wendell Holmes. It may seem strange to one of us that the use of pipes, which were gradually assembled into what we call an organ, was so much associated with secular uses, and even worse, that these were forbidden in churches for almost a thousand years. The organ as we now know it began to be developed about the year 1100.

2. ORGANIZATION

The personal religion of Jesus was no contravention of the observances of faith and practices of piety of his people. Ordinances and institutions of religion are natural and necessary. He observed those which were natural to him. He frequented the synagogue and studied the sacred book of his people. He did not contemplate the withdrawal of religious men from the normal world of human affairs. On the contrary, he thought of the amelioration of the world of human affairs by the spirit of God working through such men. Without casting undue reproach upon the reforming temper, it is clear that Jesus was not a reformer. It was not that he did not see the evils of his day. He proposed, however, to take hold of those evils from the end opposite to that by which the reformer usually lays hold of them. He proposed to change the spirit of men and thus to send out men of a changed spirit to change the world. He was not a social theorist. He saw the evils of his time—and they were great enough—primarily from the point of view of religion. Need we say that he even knew all the evils of his time? Can we say that he foresaw the particular evils of our time? What he did know was the hearts of men. Programs were not enough for him, or again, they were too much for him. He was not a maker of programs. What he wished was to touch the heart and so to change the life. For that he must begin with a single man. Natures so changed would do the rest. It is easy to say that he was a vague idealist. But has not the history of two thousand years proved that he was right?

For the very reason, however, that he was a man of the spirit he knew the need of institutions of religion. He did attack some attitudes and organizations of religion, some modes of guidance of the men of his day. He frequented the temple as he had opportunity. It was his high sense about the temple that made him drive the money-changers from it. One may, indeed, wonder how much of the pomp of worship—for even in Herod's day there was pomp—was congenial to his simple soul. It is not easy to think, if the beauty of nature so moved him, that he was not sensitive also to the grandeur of a place of worship with its exalting rites. He attacked priests, but not for being priests, only for being unworthy ones. There were worthy ones. Priests from whom one must withhold respect were rather in evidence in the crisis of Jesus' life. They naturally would be so. Good priests in high station must have been either few or quiet under the Roman domination. The temple which Herod built must have been a bid for favor on the part of a man who needed it. The fact that there were two high priests at the time of Jesus' death is significant. The Idumaeans had sovereign rights of a sort. The Procurator represented the overlordship of Rome. Priests who could find their way between the fear of the Procurator and, as well, that of the King, who could enjoy the favor of two high priests, listen to the clamor of the populace, keep on good terms with Pharisees and Sadducees, can hardly have belonged, all of them, exactly to the number of the pure in heart. The synagogue, on the other hand, had come to be a place, at least of the regular worship and instruction, among the simple-minded and sincere. Synagogues were everywhere. The scattering of the Jewish community over the world which followed the conquests of Alexander had made of these Jews the most energetic and prosperous of their race. For these also the synagogue worship was the common bond. The religion of the household in Egypt or Asia Minor seems to have been mainly a matter of domestic tradition. The religion of the City States, like those in Greece, was the tradition of a priesthood charged with the public cultus. So far as we know, it was hardly more. The situation of the Jews was different. They possessed a sacred literature covering the principles of their religion, as also of their ritual. There was something also for the household and the individual. Furthermore, this Scripture had come to be viewed not merely as a sacred inheritance, but as the very oracle of God. The formulation among Jews of an ever stricter belief in the nature of revelation, ending in the tenet of verbal inspiration, falls in the period of the development of the synagogue.

A similar view came to be held by Christians in their difficult times, not alone of the book which they took over from the Jews, but of their own New Testament as well, when that canon was gradually closed. Palestine is so small a land that we might wonder how the devout dispensed themselves from the "going up" to Jerusalem which had been enjoined. Galilee, however, contained many foreign elements even in its sparse population. Moreover, between Galilee and Jerusalem lay the hostile Samaritans. For Jews of the Dispersion frequent journeys to Jerusalem were impossible. For all these reasons, the gathering of devout Jews in a synagogue need not be thought of as from the first, or in intention, as a substitute for the temple worship. That for many and with the lapse of time it became such is quite clear. Pharisees were probably the natural leaders of the movement. Schools came to be attached to the synagogue. The only salaried officer of the synagogue was the attendant who also kept the sacred books. The building belonged to the community. The synagogue is perhaps unique among all the things that we know about the religions of the ancient world. The type is, moreover, characteristic, at intervals, at all events, in all the long history of the Christian Church. Protestantism in breaking away from the Roman Church largely reverted to it. The mystical sects long before the Reformation observed something like it. We might wonder whether Jesus was never in the temple from the time of the ceremonies about his birth to his twelfth year, and, as well, that he was in the temple so few times that we can be sure of during his ministry. The synagogue he loved and frequented all his life. His disciples frequented it with him.

The reassembling of the frightened disciples in Galilee or elsewhere after the death of Jesus would, in so far as any forms were necessary, naturally have taken forms reminiscent of the synagogue. Those concerned were Jews. Among disciples, discourse might naturally take direction of reminiscences of Jesus. Presently, there was at Jerusalem, as also in the regions round about, bold proclaiming that in Jesus prophecies had been fulfilled. Such is in fact the substance of the speech of Stephen, for which he paid with his life, Saul of Tarsus standing by. Guidance rather than rule was needed. Precedence was accorded to those whom Paul later called "pillar apostles." At the head of these was apparently James, the brother of the Lord. Naturally there was continuance of rites like fasts and abstinence from certain meats. Ceremonialism, however, would be questioned when teaching concerning Jesus began to be spread among Gentiles. This was, in fact, the matter of a difference of opinion which presently showed itself in the Jerusalem Church. Saul of Tarsus, Pharisee, disciple of Gamaliel, says that after his vision on the Damascus road, he "took not counsel with flesh and blood." However, the things which he did, the gospel he proclaimed, stirred the disciples at Jerusalem. In his view not too much of the yoke of things specifically Jewish was to be laid upon Gentile converts. Not without a struggle a concordat was reached at Jerusalem which was, in the end, not satisfactory to either party. The missionary journeys of Paul, first in Asia Minor, and then in Greece, ranged more and more of his converts on the side of his contention. His own thought had been, at first, that in going to a new place he must seek out the synagogue. He soon gave that up. Often rejected, sometimes with contumely, in his own dramatic phrase he "turned to the Gentiles." There came an interval of which he writes that the Jerusalem Church glorified God in him. But the "pillar apostles" did not change their views. Paul's own passionate rejection of the law, which once he had adhered to with fanaticism and which he now condemned as bondage, no doubt confirmed the direction which his spirit took. He was ready to go far in committing details of worship to the new organizations, as, for example, to the Corinthians. The issue brought him a heartache. It was not that he did not know how crude the Corinthians were. But the only way to build up the characters of the men was through their own experience. This was the principle of his mission. The Gospel was for all men. Those who believed in the Lord Jesus need not and, indeed, could not, enter into the Christian life by way of the Jews.

There was already a church in Rome when Paul came thither. Paul was a prisoner sent by Felix upon his own appeal to Caesar, on the ground of his right of Roman citizenship, inherited, at all events, from his father. His letter to the Romans, in some ways his greatest epistle, written we do not know how long before he met the Romans, deals more than does any other of his epistles with doctrinal questions. It begins with a comparison of Jewish teaching with his doctrine of salvation by faith in Christ. It postulates, of course, that Judaism was known to the Roman Christian community. Everything came to Rome, as one of the satirists had already said. Paul's argument is not a statement of the rudiments of Christianity. On the contrary, it is a classic setting forth of his own interpretation of truths already in a general way familiar. And this was less than three decades after the death of Jesus. If Peter had been the actual founder of the church at Rome, it might seem strange that Paul's letter contains no allusion to him. On the other hand, his breach with Peter might have been just such a reason. It may well be true that Peter died in Rome, certainly Paul did. The sea-borne commerce of the Mediterranean, the network of post and military roads, even as these were then developed, made Rome the center of the word. Men of commerce, military men, servants of the State, travellers of every sort, idlers in pursuit of sensation or amusement, continually brought news of the Christian movement thither. At Antioch believers were first called Christians. But Rome came, presently, by a sort of genius of the place, to put its stamp upon an organization which proved necessary and, in the end, supremely influential.

For obvious reasons, the organization and authority of the Church was one of the subjects ardently discussed in the time of the Reformation. To us it seems clear that in the earlier stages there was very little government within the little local groups of adherents of the new faith. Beyond these there was as good as none at all among them as a whole. They spread swiftly over a good part of the ancient world. No inconsiderable part of the evangelization in the earliest days may have been by what we should call lay persons, merchants, soldiers, travellers of every sort. More specific Jewish influence faded rather rapidly for reasons which can easily be surmised. Deacons are mentioned in the book of the Acts, but in a connection which shows that their service was practical, "serving tables" it was called. The earliest mention of religious functionaries, if we may call them such, in these early Christian groups, is that of apostles, prophets and teachers. Of course, great weight was accorded to apostles. At first, no doubt, these may have been actually of those who had companied with Jesus, or at least, of those who had companied with those first companions of Jesus. Paul, however, was not for a moment in doubt as to his right to rank himself with the apostles, although it seems quite clear that he had never seen Jesus. He was, in fact, the outstanding, if not for a time the only, apostle to the Gentiles as such. The word *apostle* is no doubt used in a wider sense of persons who came with a particular message or who spoke out of some special experience, or again, who had ancient and honored association with the cause. The word means "one sent." Such apostles were probably only visitors. Prophets might be either visitors or residents. The synagogue tradition gave such men their place. The word means "one who spoke for God." Teachers were almost surely resident. The word suggests that the task was that of making known the Master and his teaching. The Old Testament was a book of oracles. Paul calls it by that name. Letters of apostles, especially of Paul, had been sent to some communities in default of visits which he would probably have preferred to make. There are also letters to individuals. In less degree the like may have been the case also of other men who might be called apostolic. Some of these letters were sent from one community to another. The so-called Pastoral Epistles of Paul present problems from which modern New Testament criticism took its departure. There is something in them, or at least in two of them, which is rather obviously of the spirit of the great apostle. It is, however, difficult to think of the office of bishop as having been so far developed anywhere before the time of the death of Paul. One is inclined to think that the letters may have been re-written perhaps to meet a particular need.

Later—one does not know how early, but certainly not with uniformity in every place—officers necessary to the organization were declared to be bishops, presbyters and deacons. The word *presbyter* preserves for us the sense of the weight accorded to older men, both in their testimony to the Gospel and also most probably in matters practical. This was the case already in the synagogue. The word *episcopus* betrays a different origin. The *episcopus* was a high, and perhaps the highest officer in groups like the mutual benefit associations, workers' organizations, burial societies, widespread among the plain people in the Empire of the time. It connoted one who has oversight. Superintendent would seem to be a fit translation, guardian of common interests, representative of the body when it needed representation. The word *episcopus* appears among us as bishop. Just so presbyter has come down to us as priest. The bearer of this title came to be thought of as at least the ordinary functionary in acts of worship. Thus with time, the order, bishops, priests and deacons took the place of the earlier order, apostles, prophets and teachers. Administration and representation were taking the place of the purely devotional or hortatory leadership. Relations of the Christian communities to the outside world came to be more and more essential. Ignatius, Bishop of Antioch, who died a martyr in Rome, probably in 138, is the first to set forth this form of organization as being of the inner and essential nature of Christianity and as binding upon all true churches everywhere. It is evident, however, that in Ignatius' time the acceptance of this order, and more especially his theory of it, was by no means universal among the widespread and often racially oriented communities. It was, however, workable. It was, indeed, in principle so obvious that in the stern times which presently came upon the Christian organizations it did go far toward becoming the accepted type. It went further, until, in the combining of bishoprics—there was apparently, at first, a bishop in every church—the bishop came to have power over cities and even provinces. It was impossible that the bishop of the Imperial City, Rome, should not at some time take the place of all in his representation of the Christian cause to rulers, or more likely, at first, to the courts. The like happened for provincial bishops before governors and magistrates. Then, also, there was the matter of defending the faith against heresy and the churches against schism. Presently it became one of their corporate responsibilities to define the faith which was to be defended.

The time was passing when the Christians were all simple people. Intellectual movements of the time took hold upon the Christian cause. The so-called apologists—men who "spoke for" the cause—had defended, each one of them, his own view of the Christian cause, and each in his own way. That would not do for long. Christianity was not the only religion of the Orient which had invaded the Empire of the West. Movements religious, ethical, social, of every sort were rife. Men were the more prone to give themselves to these movements of discussion and philosophizing, just as men of another sort might give themselves over to their lusts, because, for the time, and often during the reign of the best emperors, there was little else for them to do. Participation in public life was denied them. Nor were all the troubles of the Christians with those outside their own circle. Already in the second century one can speak of two dangers, parallel one with the other and yet, in a way, of opposing sorts, which Christianity had to confront. The one was what was called the Gnostic movement, the other Montanism. Gnosticism has been called the rationalism of the second century. It would have substituted for Christianity a philosophical religion supposed to be more in accord with enlightened reason. It was founded upon supposed knowledge of relations and forces of the universe. In reality it was based upon ideas borrowed from the philosophers, mingled sometimes with the old pagan worship of heaven and earth. The god of the Gnostics was the Abyss, the Silence, the Incomprehensible, the Unapproachable. Christianity ran the risk of being transformed into another of the many mystery cults. At the opposite extreme was a fanatically ascetic movement known as Montanism, which began as a prediction of the coming of the promised Paraclete who had revealed himself to two Phrygian women. The movement declared the perfectability of Christian men and women under the guidance of the Holy Ghost, as also the return of Christ and a thousand years of bliss. The center of the movement was the little city, Pepuza, in Phrygia. To Pepuza the returning Christ was to come. It was a crude mysticism of a sort which recurred again and again in the Middle Age. One reads of it not without a sense of the pathos of it. Irenaeus, bishop of Lyons, was sent to Rome to try to dissuade the Roman bishop from too severe procedure against the Montanists. Tertullian was perhaps their most famous convert.

The Neronian persecution seems to us like the freak of a madman. The time came, however, when the increase of the numbers of the Christians everywhere, with their rise to places of influence, caused the movement to appear to the government an ever increasing evil, and presently, a peril. Everyone knows the severity with which secret societies were hunted down. Christian societies could be so interpreted. What should the Empire do with people who refused homage to the statues of the emperors? This demand was made especially of soldiers. Their punishment was severe. Of course, demands like these were but a sign that the Empire was already in decadence. Yet what could one do with people who said that they were subjects of another king, who defied local authorities and did everything in secret, just when the government was growing suspicious of all secret organizations? Moreover, the Christian community laid itself open, by report at least, to accusations which may have arisen out of its sacraments, the drinking of blood, as the phrase went, the eating of the body of their Lord, the accusation of

tion of Christ to God. Paul of Antioch had contended that Jesus was true man, although distinguished by gift of miraculous powers and by holiness of character. Paul had been degraded and was later excommunicated. Some inferred that God the Son and God the Holy Spirit were only different revelations of the same one God. Those who thus held were called Monarchians. Others held Christ to be indeed a spiritual being, created before the world but subordinate to God. Arius, a presbyter at Alexandria sometime after 313, had declared for this subordinationist view. Athanasius, after 328 bishop of Alexandria, took the opposite side. The Council of Nicaca declared for the unity of God and Christ with the Holy Spirit, the familiar trinitarian formula. Constantine had indeed inclined to Arius' position, but yielded. Controversy was wide and bitter. A second oecumenical Synod of Constantinople, in 381, declared the Nicene deliverance to be creed of the whole Church. Origen and Clement, a near contemporary, already in the third century had offered, long before, a solution more in line with the tradition of Hellenic thought. But Hellenic thought was dying. The view prevailed that man's salvation was the work of God. It came to be thought of as exclusively the work of God. The greatest of Latin theologians, Augustine, gloried in the thought of man's salvation as the work of God alone.

The Council of Nicaea dealt also with the questions with which we are here primarily concerned, those, namely, of organization. It confirmed traditional privileges of the churches. Those mentioned by name were the churches of Rome, of Alexandria and of Antioch. Constantinople was Constantine's capital, the second capital of the world. A bishop of Constantinople now appeared as a new power in the constitution of the Church. At the Council of Chalcedon, 451, the bishop of Jerusalem was elevated to the rank of Patriarch of Palestine. By this time also the question was already raised of a monarchical head of the whole Church. Who among the bishops should be that head? The see of Constantinople had come already to be of supreme importance. Rome was going toward its decline. Invasions of the barbarians, among whom the Goths were mostly Aryans, had diminished its prestige. Rome actually fell before Alaric in 476. The Emperor at Constantinople was now the Emperor of the whole world, at least he claimed to be such. What wonder if, after the fall of Rome, it was felt in the East that the bishop of Constantinople should be the supreme head of the Church? The bishop of Rome took up this conflict. After all, it was Rome which had created the Empire. The fact also of the apostolic origin of the Church at Rome began anew to be urged. The presence of apostles, Paul and, as it was claimed, of Peter also, within a few years after the death of Jesus, was set forth. The death by martyrdom of one or both of these in Rome was newly emphasized. After the fall of Rome, it was indeed unavoidable that much of the secular power should be transferred to Constantinople. Transfer of the spiritual power the Western world disputed. This was the feud which later led the two churches of Rome and Constantinople mutually to excommunicate one another. The remnant of secular sovereignty of Constantinople upon Italian soil, mainly the region about Ravenna, was saved for a short time by Byzantine generals and the victories of Theodoric. Wonderful churches in Ravenna, with also the tomb of Theodoric, are today memorials of this time. But the proceeds of Theodoric's victory were nil. There was still to be a long night in which, in the West at least, the Church was to be the only general influence. Often it was a power as of a State in dealing with the petty states about it.

This was true even far beyond the confines of Italy. The House of Pepin in what is now eastern France, had worked hand in hand with the Roman Church. It maintained order in an empire which some day would include the most of France and of western Germany, as we now know this. On Christmas Day in the year 800, Charlemagne was crowned by the Pope in the old St. Peter's at Rome as Emperor of the West. The Frankish Empire thus became the precursor of what presently was called the Holy Roman Empire, which surrendered its name to Napoleon only in 1806. It went, this Holy Roman Empire, hand in hand with the papacy as guide and stay of Europe. Its history is celebrated in notable fashion in Lord Bryce's first book. The decline of Constantinople, the wreck of its empire, was occasioned in the end by the perpetual advances of Islam, as also by the internecine wars of the Crusades, but this was consummated only in 1456 at the hands of Mohammed II. The decline of the Greek Church into somnolence and ineptitude in this long period did the rest. Meantime, the Empire of the West was growing apace by the energies of all the new races. The Republic of Venice sacked Constantinople already in 1204, in the name indeed of the Fourth Crusade but with little evidence of any Christian sentiment in the intrigue. Meantime, Russia was, some part of it, being slowly converted. The work began with two Constantinopolitan monks, Cyril and Methodius. But this was for long but a meager compensation to the Christian cause. The futile suggestion of Cyril Lucar, Patriarch of Constantinople, for a reunion of the Roman and Eastern Churches, was made more than a hundred years after the Reformation had separated nations of the north and west of Europe from the Church of Rome itself.

Certainly no one can wonder at the access of power

which the earlier events just recorded brought to the Roman papacy. The Church may be said to have been the one great source of light and power, the one advocate of peace and grace, the one unifying influence in Europe in all the changes which Europe underwent from the sixth to perhaps the fourteenth century. Its language was the universal language. Its learning was the one typical and constructive learning. By the Church were founded almost all the universities of the Western world. What wonder if its colossal power, so often beneficently exerted, came to seem to be the one transcendent influence in all the ages which we still describe as Dark. Only the great evils which had grown up in this same long period of unlimited power made it possible for men to think that they might, and in the end, that they must, break away from the influence to which their whole world owed so much. The mediaeval world toward its end was undermined with intellectual and religious and, as well, with political and social rebellions. What we call the revival of learning turned the minds of some men back to the ancients for a light which they felt that the Church no longer gave them. The feudal system was outworn. What were to become democratic tendencies made themselves felt. The Reformation was only one more, and the most portentous, of these rebellions against the Church which had been so long in power. Discoveries of America, and later, discoveries in the Far East, made the world seem larger than men had dreamed. They opened opportunities which the Middle Ages had never known. We do not wonder that Protestants, held together at first by common antagonisms to the Church of Rome, presently developed antagonisms among themselves. The initial of the movement was, however, that the reformers felt that only by breach with the Church could they maintain liberty of thought, with the right of private judgment, which we all accord to be one of the distinctive traits of the modern world. Meantime, successors of the reformers, some of them at least, are able to look upon the Roman Church and feel an inexpressible debt to it for its influence upon the thousand years which lie back of all the modern nations. Without that influence modern Europe with America would be inexplicable, no matter how true it may be also that they would be inexplicable without the fact of the final rebellion.

By the year 800, as we have said, what have been called the invasions of the barbarians were, at least for western Europe, mainly over. The chaos which followed, at first, the division of the Empire of the West from the East, was also to some extent a thing of the past. There were those who thought that something of its unity and prestige, at least in the West, could be recovered under the old name. The so-called Holy Roman Empire merited, in some respects, the gibe attributed to Gibbon, that it was so called because it was neither holy nor Roman nor quite an empire. It had, for nearly a thousand years, a checkered career. Sometimes it was in alliance with the Church, more times in conflict with the Church, occasionally even in open warfare. Bishops and abbots were often also landed proprietors, great feudal lords, in person at the head of their troops. Popes were able to marshal one part of Christendom against another. The Empire stood, as time went on, in the more or less dim consciousness of the autonomy of the State as over against the omnipotence of the Church, with its appeal to heaven and its hearty promises of hell. Not everyone even now reflects how new is that which seems to us an axiomatic truth. I mean, the assertion of the complete independence the one of the other, of both State and Church. As might be expected, results of this confusion of ideas were both bad and good, perhaps preponderantly bad. There was a time at the end of the tenth century when the morality of some of the popes would hardly bear speaking about. There was a time in the fourteenth century, the days of the Great Schism and the so-called Babylonian captivity, when the policy of popes would have done credit to political adventurers. There was a time just before the Reformation when the morals, say of Alexander VI, the military policies of Julius II and the very incarnation of the spirit of the Renaissance in Leo X, sometimes make one wonder whether these men could have been the heads of a Church. And these three reigned in succession. This phase of the life of the papacy did something to precipitate the Reformation which had, however, been long, in any case, preparing. Despite the fact that some describe the Middle Age as the Age of Faith, and despite the fact that ecclesiastical institutions of one sort or another were much in evidence, one of us, if he were to wander back into it would find it, I think, an evil world and realize that to some extent ecclesiastical institutions contributed to the evil. Of course, the more learned and quietly influential of the mystics were clerical. The state of learning would bring that with it. There were few, and in some times and places practically no, learned men except those who were educated for the Church. Most noteworthy among them were mystics who escaped being exactly clerically minded, for example, Suzo and Thomas à Kempis. Eckhart, Tauler, Berthold of Regensburg, preachers of the three half centuries between 1220 and 1360 are much read by Protestants, perhaps because we seem to hear in them already the Protestant note. On the other hand, the Brethren of the Free Spirit, the Brethren of the Common Life, with also Lollards, were in large part lay. Reformers before the Reformation, men of this sort have been called. Persecuted, of course, they were. The affair of the Albigenses looks to us like the conflict of the very extremes of the two contentions. But the tragedy of it will never be forgotten. Others, however, through their secret conventicles and their hidden communications, over almost the whole of western Europe, prepared in quiet the masses upon whom, in the end, the success of the Reformation rested. Men like Pascal and the Jansenists, with their renewal of the cloistral life for both men and women at Port Royal, and again, men like Fox and the Society of Friends who hardly admitted the validity of any church at all, and certainly not of the cloister, show the same trait under circumstances widely different. Pascal had no thought but to remain a Catholic. Fox could hardly remain a Protestant as Protestantism was then understood. But their contention was salutary in their own time and for the world at large in later times.

It is not easy to see how some of the Protestant churches could have survived without the support of their respective states. Think of Luther and the Electorate of Saxony. There is, to be sure, in this case and in some others, no evidence that they desired to live without this support. Yet perhaps even simple facts like these should be seen in a longer perspective. The rise of nationalities made the expression of the impulse to national churches inevitable as these would not have seemed to their forbears and they have seemed less inevitable to their descendants. The rise of national literatures was only a little more than a century before the Reformation age. The Renaissance affected the different peoples in very different ways. Social institutions were forming on diverse lines. A whole movement which was an intermediary stage between the unity of mediaeval Europe and the diversity of modern Europe had been in progress for perhaps three generations. That these differences should have registered themselves in the ways in which the various peoples met the emergency of the religious reformation was quite to be expected. Certainly the diverse forms which Protestantism took in one land and another were closely related to the national temperaments which formed them. They were, some of them, portentously impressed with the necessity of preaching. Against the background of the neglect of preaching which seems in general to have prevailed at the end of the Middle Age, this new emphasis may have been fitting. Wycklif in his banishment to his little parish at Lutterworth obviously thought so. Furthermore, there were great divergences among Protestants themselves as to the degree in which they desired to separate themselves from the mother Church. The Anglican Church is apparently divided within itself to this day, as to how far it did separate itself from Catholicism—more divided perhaps than it was two hundred years ago. Perhaps one of the reasons for the great service of this church is the fact that it did not so radically as did others separate itself from the continuity of a great and ancient institutional life. French Protestantism after untold agonies received the Edict. It then suffered the revocation of the Edict. Most of the Huguenots were banished—to the enrichment of the rest of the world Geneva, and likewise the Scotch, were never in doubt as to their separation from the mother Church —or at least, they expelled those who were in doubt. They fearlessly set up a new government in one place and governed the government in the other. Something of the same sort may be said of Holland. There the issue was fought out, partly under the guidance of William of Orange, which led to the founding of the Dutch Republic. The rift in English Protestantism widened at last into the Puritan Rebellion, which was both religious and political in its nature. It spread to the northern colonies of America. Here it had hardly played out its role until the end of the eighteenth century. Perhaps it was the good fortune of the American colonies that, when they had won the War of the Revolution and came to draw up a constitution which transformed them into a nation, they well knew, by that time, that their population was of so many racial and also religious types that there was nothing for them to do except to make absolute separation between Church and State. In a measure this has become typical for many, one might say almost all, modern States. Of course, the movements of thought of the eighteenth century, Deism and Rationalism, had helped to this issue. But the logic was inherent in any case. The Wesleys held fast to the Anglican Church so long as they could and separated themselves from it not without reluctance. Many Anglicans felt the same regret when it was too late. Fox and the Quakers were, in the English inheritance, the only ones who drew the ultimate conclusion that the religious community needed as nearly as possible no organization at all. It was a group of worshippers in the spirit. Religion was spirit. There were no clergy, no ceremonies, no ritual. The function of common worship was reduced to its lowest terms—the intercourse of like-minded men and women waiting for the moving of the Spirit of God. One cannot, however, escape a reflection like this, that with all the wonder of the protest of the Friends in their original prophetic outburst, it seems to remain true that a spirit, to do its work in the world, must have some sort of embodiment. Conversely, it is true also that an embodiment to remain true to its idea must have and trust the spirit, or rather, it must advance to ever truer embodiments exactly because it is itself a spirit.

The antitheses within the Reformation itself to which

we have just alluded had strange consequences in our particular matter, that of organization. Some Protestant churches remained state churches and were at times exposed to evils only less formidable than those which had been imposed through centuries by the hierarchy which they rejected. On the other hand, those who declared for dependence on the Scripture alone to guide them in matters of organization and worship, showed, in the first place, astonishing divergences among themselves as to what they thought the Scriptures did teach. In some imprudent moments, they showed determination even to subject the State to themselves, as did the Puritans of the Long Parliament in England, and for a much longer period in New England. Most of them gave a place only second to that of Scripture to profound and elaborate systems of theology, like those of Calvin in Geneva or of the Scotch after Knox. In general, we may say that Protestants cherished the dream—some cherish it still—that they had set themselves free from this coil of circumstance which we have endeavored to describe. Sober reflection upon history is likely to lead us to conclude that the coil of circumstance is life itself. More radical reformers believed that they carried back the form of government of their churches with its ceremonies, to the simplicity of the apostolic model. And yet here, too, one would think that the radical differences of the models which all alike proclaimed to be apostolic might have given them cause for reflection. Above all, with their view of an externally miraculous inspiration of the Scriptures, and of the supreme authority of these, they bound themselves fast, without knowing it, to a theory of the nature of authority not different in principle from the view of the nature of the authority of the Church which they had left behind them. It was an external authority over man's reason, all the time that they were proclaiming the right of reason and exemplifying the results of the exercise of the right of private judgment, even, as it often proved, on the part of some who had no fitness for such judgment. Here, too, we have to look facts in the face. And then again, we have to ask whether, as things then were, their contention would have survived at all had they not had recourse, without fully realizing it, to an authority beyond that of either Scripture or Church, in the soul within and the God above. The defined and determinative view of the Roman Church as to its authority is also only an interpretation, made somewhat more stringent in these later days by recourse to the open claim of infallibility. One might wonder why infallibility had not been claimed centuries before. In truth, it was claimed, only not in the way of formulated conciliar decision. But we should remind ourselves that Protestants also claimed their Scripture to be infallible.

Only a generation ago, it seemed in some quarters at least, as if those who could no longer adhere to the doctrine of miraculously inspired and equally miraculously transmitted Scripture, might have to seek some new church or perhaps no church at all. Romanists, after all, have learned to live with the infallibility decree. They do so by interpreting it. The divisions of Protestantism make it easier for one with new convictions, if persecuted in one city, to flee to another. There is not exactly another city to which a Catholic might flee, but there are interpretations. No one can fail to be profoundly grateful to the great Church for exercising authority as it did, and does. There are those for whom our question here of the nature of authority does not yet arise. No one can fail to see that some of those who reject the outward authority, whether of Scripture or of Church, end in having no authority at all. In truth with some the beginning may have been in the desire to have no authority. The authority of inward control by conviction and purpose, the fashioning of one's life to an ideal, is indeed the goal. Yet stepping stones to that are often, perhaps always, outward things. They are like the loving discipline of our homes, the contact with Christian institutions from our youth, which make us, almost without knowing it, to choose, and, afterward, when knowing it, to confirm the choice. One sometimes thinks that for want of homes which, at their best, are also religious institutions, for want of churches which are places of profoundly affectionate association and not merely a roof over an empty space for oratory, or again, for want of a book like the one which our spiritual ancestors—I mean both Christians and Jews—have held to be in some sense an oracle of God, liberty, as many of our generation grasp it, is likely to prove exactly what it is not. Such liberty is obviously proving, to many, not the pathway to self-realization which loud libertarians proclaim it. To some it is but the path of aimlessness—if aimlessness can be called a path. If that grows, we shall have to go round once more the same old circle which the race has already travelled more times than once. That may not be so bad for the race, because it would appear that, even so, we do go up a little. But what about the individual? And after all, the two problems of the individual and of society can hardly be separated.

Certainly the lack of unity in the Protestant world may almost be said to be incomprehensible to men of Catholic faith. It sometimes seems distressing even to indurated Protestants. Mere manoeuvring does not reach it. Perhaps only a real crisis will bring unification. What Matthew Arnold described as the "dissidence of dissent," and elsewhere spoke of as "every man for himself in religion" has indeed been a grave handicap. If men were so fundamentally dissenters before they left home, what more natural than that they should have continued to dissent from one another after they had arrived. Nowhere has this been more evident than in America. There was a time when the resourcefulness of individuals was the very key to the opening up of vast regions of unsettled country across the continent. Some took with them the religion which they had before, but were perhaps too busy to do much with it after they arrived. We might acknowledge, with perhaps an unfitting tinge of humor, that the lack of what Mr. Arnold called culture was one of the keys to influence in some places. In the sequence, however, these causes established, or perpetuated, denominations which grew even more diversified in their isolation. They still render difficult unifications of bodies from which the real meaning of their separateness has already long since disappeared. Loyalties to a short history may make difficult a real amalgamation for the creation of a longer and better history. Time is, however, long. And results which today seem remote may yet be brought about. Perhaps only times of stress for the whole cause of religion, like that upon which it is quite possible we have now entered, will convince men. It is certainly to be deplored that the great expansion of Christendom through missions—the greatest in all history—has come at a time when this division and sub-division of Protestantism into sects was, one might say, almost at its very worst. Missions, being so largely under denominational auspices, must present to those whom they would reach a spectacle rather difficult to comprehend. Perhaps, on the other hand, it is quite logical that attempts at Protestant unification should promise, as they seem just now to do, speedier success in missions than they do in the home lands. What of denominationalism the indigenous races may have with docility taken on, they may find it almost a relief in maturity to lay off. It was to them artificial in any case, in a sense in which the original divisions of Protestantism were certainly not that. And yet some of these, too, have largely outlived their influence.

3. LIFE

I have written in vain if I have not made the impression that the whole of life is the area of the manifestation of religion. We should never think of describing certain hours of the day in Jesus' life as set apart for his religious work. He lived a very natural life in his time and place, devoted to varied duties, minor obligations, real enjoyments, sober reflections, solicitude about all sorts of people. All of these were as truly expression of his religion as were his prayers or his hours in the synagogue. One of the impressive things about him is that he never had, and obviously did not seek, any kind of religious station. That is not to say but that the highest station needs just such a man. But he was too far ahead of his age that there should have been any station waiting for him. We have known men and women of whom it would be true to say that nothing was conventionally religious about them because everything about them was really religious. The crown of it all, for some people whom we have known, is that they never thought of themselves as being religious. Perhaps we might say that one of the crowning things was that they thought very little about themselves at all. One cannot read of St. Francis in his glorious maturer years without thinking of him as a man of that sort. With him, the fact is quite wonderful because the contrast is heightened by things which, on his own confession, we know about him when he was a very different sort of a man. Some phases of religious life and work can be singled out for description. Our illustrations must, however, be but few. Even those selected must be brief. Religion is never a fragment, although some religious people give the impression that it is. In light of this our choice becomes difficult. Such choice is, moreover, not made easier by the fact that the history of Christianity is not merely long, but that it is also very wide. And always at the back of one's mind is the sense that, after all, Christianity itself is only one of the religions which have commanded the allegiance of mankind and made, some of them, great history. Of Christian history, however, we have more distinct impressions.

With this for apology, it will not seem strange if I choose for my first illustration of Christian life, monasticism. All of itself this is a vast and influential bit of history. Most Protestants have regarded it as a great movement which it is well to have over. But as one thinks what inadequate work we are making in our Protestant era, and especially just now, of our fundamental conviction that Christianity is a spirit for literally every aspect of life, one is fain to think that sane things said about monasticism might be impressive in our time. While we set out to make the Christian spirit the inner motive force of every aspect of human life, what we see all about us is that the very spread and intensity of these boasted applications have, for some of us, largely submerged the Christian spirit, until not all people seem to know what the Christian spirit is. One sometimes wonders whether history may not lead some earnest souls back again over a part of the same road which we may have thought was forever behind us. Perhaps we may come again—and need to come—to some new phase of what we used to call renunciation, in order that we may have enough religion left to deal with the phases of life which will remain.

Monasticism

It is commonly assumed that a mystical mode of thought, together with convictions concerning an ascetic practice of life, were the antecedents of the monasticism which, from about the time of the Imperial recognition of Christianity, began to play so great a part among Christians in both East and West. To be sure, both of these elements had made themselves felt among the ancient Greeks. Yet they never led larger groups to isolate themselves from their fellows. Still less did they occasion the development of great and long-lived international institutions which had for their purpose the cultivation of such a life. What we read of monks, especially among the followers of Buddha, goes indeed far back of the maturity of Greece. We do not know, however, that there ever grew up in the earlier period vast central institutions devoted to the cultivation of such a life. What we read of such a movement among Jews about and after the time of Christ is not very impressive. Ascetic practices, however, asserted themselves rather early among Christians. Men and women abstained from marriage, from eating of meat, from the use of wine, devoting themselves to prayer, to religious exercises and to works of charity. They did not at first withdraw altogether from their families or vocations. In time, however, the tendency toward the giving themselves up wholly to practices of religion set in. We are accustomed to say that this phase of the movement had to do with the corruption of the world in which they lived. After the recognition of their faith by the Empire, this corruption no doubt spread among the Christians themselves. Ambition, desire to take on the traits of a worldly life became evident. In Egypt by the middle of the third century, it was the custom of some ascetics to live in solitary retirement, although often in the neighborhood of towns and villages. It was such a life upon which Anthony entered about the year 270. He withdrew to the east bank of the Nile near Fayum. It became the tradition that Anthony was the father of monasticism. Others came and took up their abode amongst the rocks surrounding his retreat. They called upon him to guide them in the path of life which they had chosen. Farther to the south, in the neighborhood of Dendera, Pachomius established, before 350, communities in which life was regulated by rules. Through Eustathius of Sebasté, a monastic life was introduced about 340 within the confines of Greek Christianity in Asia Minor. It was Basil who adapted this to Greek, as also to eastern European needs and ideas. Laws laid down by Basil continue to this day to be the laws on which Greek and Slavonic monasticism have developed. The element of work was discarded. Slavonic monks, especially, gave themselves up for the most part to devotional contemplation.

In the West it was Benedict of Nursia who established monasticism in 530. He opposed the tendency to extreme bodily austerity. The life was to be one of self-denial, but not of an uprooting of qualities of both mind and body. The monk was, moreover, a unit in a community whose corporate life, stringently regulated, he had to live. The day was divided between public services of worship, with also hours of private devotion, this on the one hand, and on the other, a strict assignment of labor, generally agricultural, and equally strict hours of study. The monks were vowed to poverty, to abstention from marriage and to obedience. As one reads the Benedictine rule, one is impressed with its amazing simplicity. The

Benedictine rule became the model, less and more, for all subsequent foundations in the West. Similar foundations for women came into being under the leadership of Scholastica. In time the Irish-Scottish Church, which also had founded monasteries at Iona on the west coast of Scotland and Landisfarne on the east coast, declined and was ultimately absorbed in the Roman Church. It will be remembered however, that even in the time of Boniface monks of that tradition took memorable part in missions, more particularly to Germany. They entered from the north while the Benedictines approached the same work from the south. One walks the terrace at Monte Cassino, viewing the peaks and plains of the Apennines, and reflects that here for something like fourteen hundred years men have worshipped and worked and studied. Hence went out monks to every portion of western Europe in missionary labor, in the founding of cloisters under their rule, and to the learned life, upon which, before the rise of the universities, no institution exerted so great an influence as did Monte Cassino. In my student days, one could still see here, on Good Friday, the ceremony of the foot-washing which, until a few years ago, was continued also in the Chapel of the Burg in Vienna. One reads the tablets, reminders of popes who, in the great days of the Church, were called from among these monks, of missionaries for something like a thousand years, of great scholars of the Order of Benedict in many walks of life. There is hardly a place in the whole world where the services of the Church to all the world are more impressively called to mind than in this home of the Order of St. Benedict. One is led to think of the outposts of the Christianization of the north and west of Europe after the order and safety for which the Empire had stood had failed, and before its semblance had been restored in the Empire of Charlemagne and the Frankish civilization which followed. In spite of pillage and destruction of monasteries by Northmen and Saracens, and in spite of occasional widespread abuses, the Benedictine institution continued and progressed. Throughout the whole early Middle Age, Benedictine monasteries continued to perform with substantial fidelity the religious, as also the industrial, social and intellectual functions for which the rule had been created. They anticipated the founding of the universities, as well, with also the organization of charities. In spite of reforms which monastic institutions themselves underwent, their original debt to the Benedictines could never be forgotten.

The first Order in the stricter sense of that word was that of Cluny, founded in 910. It was substantially Benedictine in rule but wielded extraordinary power, secular as well as religious, up to the middle of the twelfth century. The greatness of the Order was in part due to an extraordinary succession of its Generals. These were in the rule of noble families, educated at the highest level of the culture of their times and of signal ability in the conduct of affairs. The world is drawn to the ideal of the Franciscans—the Minorites, the Seraphic Order. Both of these latter names were taken from the founder's own declaration of the purposes of the Order. Francis of Assisi, revolting from a life of self-indulgence, gave himself to the service of the poor, the sick, and, especially, of lepers. When eleven others joined him, he proceeded to Rome to secure papal sanction for their endeavor. The greatest of the popes, Innocent III, had his misgivings. He accorded provisional approval, but only by word of mouth. The formal inauguration of the institution came in 1209. Francis himself had no taste, and possibly no talent, for the government of a world-wide Order. This fell to Elias who became his vicar. Francis died in 1226, not without forecast of the fate which would attend his beloved venture, but leaving, one might say, a very image of the love of men and, for that matter, of birds and animals and flowers, which has never faded from the hearts of men. Yet in spite of the evils which were, one might say, the evils of the time, some Minorites have in every age been faithful to the mission which Francis, in the pure spirit of a child, with also the strange forecast of a most reasonable man accepted, of ministry to the spiritual needs of the poor, the neglected and the outcast. No nobler tribute could be paid to Francis than was paid a generation ago by Paul Sabatier, a Protestant.

The Society of Jesus received the papal authorization in 1539. It is related that just before Ignatius Loyola, a soldier wounded at Pampeluna and undergoing tedious recovery, experienced conversion, Luther had burned the papal bull which proclaimed his excommunication, in December 1520. Development of Ignatius' idea was slow. He conceived the Church as in a state of war. Two things which he laid before Pope Pius III indicate that fact. It was demanded that the obligation of worship customary in all the Orders might be fulfilled privately and separately. Furthermore, the founder placed the General, for life, in a position of almost unexampled authority. Military obedience was demanded. The papacy had misgiving about granting such a charter. No Jesuit would deny that it was a military Order in a sense in which none of its predecessors had been that. Francis Xavier was second only to Loyola in the service of the ideals of the Order. It was in the generation immediately following that voyages of discovery opened up both the Far East and America. They drew a completely new map of the world. Xavier went as a missionary to the

Malabar Coast of India, feeling the call of what we describe as foreign missions, as no Protestant felt it for another hundred and fifty years. There was ground for this latter fact, of course, in what proved to be an almost mortal struggle for the establishment of Protestantism in Europe itself. Xavier, who, like Loyola, was by birth a Spaniard, went out first to India, then to Japan, and died on the little island of Saurian, in the harbor of Macao in 1552. He was preparing to enter China. He was only forty-six years old. We know indeed that Franciscans had gone to China long before the time when Xavier planned the mission which was cut short by his death. But that was to evangelization just what Marco Polo's journey to China had been in the history of discovery and trade. Descendants of the first converts of the Roman Catholic missions in Japan had, under the rule of the Shoguns, been obliged, under terrific persecution, to renounce their Christianity. They did, in fact, continue their worship in strictest secrecy. They were, again and again, subjected to persecution and martyrdom. Yet, in 1854, toleration was extended to them, at the time of the opening of Japan to the influence of the Western world. It was then estimated that there were some thirty thousand Japanese whose forbears had tried to keep alive the Christian faith through more than two centuries in which the death penalty had been attached to the confession of that faith.

We must add the history of the Jesuit missions, mainly in Canada in the early years of the seventeenth century, with the journeys of their missionaries down the Mississippi to the Gulf of Mexico. We must recur to the fact that Louisiana, with old New Orleans, recalls to this day a French and Roman Catholic civilization only less than does Quebec. Franciscans were in Mexico and California. We have the record of an achievement of the very greatest significance a hundred years before Protestant missions were begun at all. We are only too apt to dwell upon other activities of the Society of Jesus, such as were, it is fair to assume, mainly in the mind of Loyola when he asked for the recognition of his Order. These were again much in evidence in the history of the Thirty Years War and after. We have to remember that Elizabeth dealt with a heavy hand with the Jesuits. But so she did with the Brownists. She was not her father's daughter for nothing. We think also of discussions of great bitterness which marked the era of the controversies of Jansen and Pascal. We are likely to think of the long and severe persecutions in Spain. It was opposition to the establishment of freer secular government which led to the suppression of the Order by action of the Crown of Portugal in 1769. We remember that this was often the attitude of the founders of the republics in South America after the Napoleonic times. But if we are looking for the evidence of Christian life and the acknowledgement of a worship not exactly our own, it is true these things should be recalled. The Society of the Jesuits remains to this day a great power in the Roman Church. And again, the Orders of consecrated women have given for many generations, and still give, scope for a life and work of women in almost every nation of the world. While the admission of women to almost every phase of active life in the modern world is one of the achievements mainly of the last half century, it remains that the religious Orders for women gave, fifteen hundred years ago, and still give, a communal life whose scope and influence it would be impossible to overestimate. In ages in which ordered and open access to courses of great public and private service was not guaranteed to women as in the modern world, the orders for women gave place and scope for them in both. They afforded opportunity for careers of greatest influence and distinction. It may be doubted whether the opening of almost every thinkable career to women in the modern world is an unmixed good, if it leads to forgetfulness of avenues of usefulness and self-realization in which, for forty generations, women have found their place and done their work and showed the very highest qualities in the service of mankind, which was also their service and worship of God.

The Reformation—and After

It should be recalled that we are in this chapter dealing with a few very significant manifestations of religion. We have confined ourselves to illustrations taken from the Christian religion and the life which has been lived under its convictions. We have limited ourselves, perhaps in a measure unconsciously, to the life of this religion as it has been lived in the West, our own inheritance. Even here we can take examples only to illustrate our general proposition. Moreover, the life with which we deal was for more than a thousand years practically limited to the continent of Europe with Great Britain. After the Great Schism, the contact of Western Christianity with even the Eastern Church was relatively slight, and sometimes hostile. The Kingdom of Jerusalem, despite the touch of devout idealism which it had, was short-lived and hardly more than a military occupation. The Crusades themselves were scarcely more than a series of wars against the rising power of Mohammedans, although they were undertaken under a sentiment about the recovery of the Holy Sepulchre. The Fourth Crusade, in 1204, under the leadership of Venice, actually turned against Constantinople. The conquest of Constantinople by the Turks in 1453 might perhaps have been averted if the West had co-operated with Byzantium at that time. But wars of Moorish pirates upon all shores of the Mediterranean were brought to an end only by Don Juan of Austria in the time of Charles V. Vienna itself narrowly escaped capture by the Turks as late as 1683. In European Christendom itself there was, toward the end of the tenth century, a time when the level of morality fell very low, if we may judge from testimony concerning the papacy itself. Then there was the period of the Great Schism and the so-called Babylonian captivity of the popes at Avignon, a period in which, in the struggle of parties, in the ambition of candidates for the papacy, and in the efforts of reforming councils, there were at one time three popes. Then came the revival of learning. With all the unmeasured benefits which this brought, there was bound to be in some sense a resurgence of paganism. Then came the Reformation which can hardly be understood as a rebellion in religion alone. It was also a great moral indignation. It was, as well, a reflection of the rise of the nationalities and of their languages, to which we alluded in the last chapter.

An Augustinian monk said, "If ever a man had been saved by monk-righteousness, I had been that man." His visit to Rome may have opened his eyes. To him Staupitz said, "But, Brother Martin, it is written that 'The just shall live by faith.' " Luther was excommunicated in 1520. He burned the bull when he received it. He translated the Bible into German while protected in the Wartburg in 1521. Henry VIII had been called by the Pope "defender of the faith," for his refutation of Luther. By dint, however, of his divorce from Catherine of Aragon—and much else—he left to his little son Edward a realm already well on the way toward the

Reformation. Edward VI, under the guidance of leaders, Cranmer and the rest, inaugurated that movement. Mary, Catherine of Aragon's daughter, a pathetic figure, sought on the death of her brother, to turn back the clock. Elizabeth, perhaps more for political than religious reasons, took the other side. James, the son of Mary Stuart, Queen of Scots, was glad to be rid of the presbyters who had brought him up, but possibly not altogether willing, and certainly not able, to return to the ancestral church. Charles played with the thought of an absolutism in State and Church for which it was now too late. He merely brought on the Civil War, made way for the Long Parliament and Cromwell, and was beheaded. The return of Charles II to the throne, and then James II, merely confirmed the purpose of the people. It was thus the fortune, and in some sense the glory of the Church of England and, one might add, of the realm as well, that it took almost a century and a half to establish a Reformation which, after William and Mary, made England truly and conservatively a Protestant land. The Reformation here preserved some best things in the Catholic faith and administration—more than did any other church which the Reformation brought forth. It broke definitively with the Pope but maintained an episcopal organization with a world of sacred tradition. It preserved much of the service of worship, only this was now in English. It brought forth a revival of preaching which made its pulpit famous far into the eighteenth century. It conserved also a relation of the Church to rulers and leaders in the land which was to prove highly salutary. This was true almost without reservation until, at all events, the time of Wesley.

In Germany which had led in the rebellion against the Church, the movement was less fortunate. The lands, and with them the churches, were divided. The Protestant cause itself was divided. The Emperor, Charles V, remained a devout Catholic. He understood, however, that he held his crown as Emperor by election. Of the Electors three were indeed bishops. The other four were virtually independent sovereigns. One, Frederick the Wise of Saxony, was the foremost Protestant in high position in his age. Another, Philip of Hesse, loyally upheld him. These States, with also others, were minor sovereignties. The word *Protestant* has a curious history. It was applied to a party in the Diet of Speyer in 1529 whose initial protest had been against a more radical element in their own party. It gathered to itself, however, in the end, the allegiance of the more reasonable elements which took up the struggle against, be it said, both the ancestral Church and the Empire of which Charles was the titular head. It was under these circumstances that the component States either joined in the Reformation or else adhered to the ancestral Church in accord, to be sure, with the disposition of their peoples but also by the concession of their own particular sovereigns. In general, the whole north went to the Protestants. The south, particularly Bavaria, remained with the ancient Church. Charles was also by right of inheritance sovereign of the Low Countries, a considerable part of which sympathized with the revolt. A part might have remained with the old Church save for the mistakes of his regents and the truculence of the Duke of Alba, who drove the inhabitants almost unanimously into furious warfare. The result was the formation of the Dutch Republic which remained a republic until the general revision of the map of Europe after the fall of Napoleon. The great Protestant leader was, of course, William the Silent. Of this area, at present Belgium is practically uniformly Catholic while Holland is almost solidly Protestant.

The Swiss Confederation as it existed at the time of the Reformation also became in part Protestant and, in part, especially in the east, remained Roman Catholic. Here in this little area there were, as now, three languages, marking the diverse descent of the peoples. The Canton of Geneva had as its religious leader, Calvin, born at Noyon, in France, who had indeed entered the priesthood, but was later summoned by Protestants to Geneva. He never held political office, but became perhaps only the more truly the dictator of the policies of the republic. He greatly influenced the course of events in France. Through Knox, one of Mary Tudor's exiles to Geneva, he determined, one might say, the course of events in Scotland, which, it should be recalled, was an independent kingdom at the time. In France, although it had been in some sense a cradle of the Reformation, as it was also a cradle of the Renaissance, the history of Protestantism was less fortunate. Marguerite d'Angoulème, the sister of Francis I, fostered the Reformation. She gathered scholars and leaders of the movement about her, Beza among others, poets and men of letters as well. Possibly it was just because of this humanist cast in the earlier years when some of the other peoples were deciding their fate in this regard, the movement made no great progress. Leading spirits of French extraction like Calvin made themselves necessary in other lands. More and more as the House of Valois declined, the Guises came to ascendancy. Catherine de Medici, wife of Francis II, ruled under the names of all three of her impotent sons. Before the death of the last of them the times had brought about the massacre of St. Bartholomew in which Coligny perished with the flower of the Protestant nobility. By the time that Henry IV of Navarre, the son of Jeanne d'Albret, upon whom the Protestants had set their hopes, had come to the throne, he was able to say that "The unity of France was worth a mass." He did, however, grant in 1598 the Edict of Nantes, giving large liberties to Protestants, but was assassinated in 1610. The Bourbons succeeded him in the person of Louis XIII. By this time the age of discovery had advanced so far that the Huguenots who could get out of France went, some of them to England, others to Holland of course. Louis XIV in 1685 rescinded the Edict. They migrated also to Prussia under the Great Elector. They came to America, both to the colonies which were to become the United States, as also to Canada and to South America, presently also to South Africa. They enriched every Protestant church in the world, but they built no permanent church or state of their own.

One would gather from that which we have thus far said that England was the country in which, in a gradual and gracious evolution, Christianity passed from the Catholic to a unified Protestant national Church. This was fairly true for, let us say, the earlier years of Elizabeth. Then dissent began, or perhaps we should say emerged. Brownists argued that there was no warrant in Scripture for the episcopal form of government. The reference of every question to the very word of Scripture carried men much further than had at first been thought. The form of government, as of worship also, was to be reduced to that which could be vindicated by example of the apostolic community. There was to be no authority above the congregation and no authority in this, except in the consensus of the believers themselves. This marks the emergence of the contention which led to the formation of a little community at Scrooby in Yorkshire, which presently transferred itself to Leyden and ultimately came to Plymouth in Massachusetts. The local church was the administrative unit. Groups might combine for common purposes but no one of them had authority over any other. Elizabeth was as hostile to this view on the one hand as to that of the Roman Catholics on the other. Punishment of emissaries of the Catholic faith was severe. Some high personages in the realm clung to the old cause, holding Mary Queen of Scots, to be in some sense their representative. Elizabeth had long imprisoned her and finally caused her to be beheaded in Fotheringay Castle in 1587. It is but fair to say that a political element had also to be reckoned with. Punishments were meted out to some representatives of more extreme Protestant views. Men were executed in connection with the Gunpowder Plot in the early days of James, which was laid to the Catholics. In the second decade of the reign of James, Baptists, who were Congregationalists as to the form of government, put forth views as to the sacrament of baptism. Then there were also followers of George Fox who were subsequently called Quakers. These went nearer than did any of the others to the abolition of all forms of worship as well as of church government, even if we should not say of the Church itself as institution. The most interesting thing about George Fox, their founder, a cattle drover, is that with something like divination of the modern theory of knowledge, he dissented from the view of the authority of Scripture which had, with Protestants, so largely taken the place of the authority of the Church. All these phases of Protestantism in England made themselves felt in the earliest years in the English colonies on the coast of North America.

Presently also, differences of continental Protestantism entered here with immigrants from those lands. This prepared the way for a sectarianism which was characteristic of these colonies. The evils of this sectarianism conferred, however, one great and lasting benefit, already alluded to. The Constitution of the United States provided that the function of government in religious matters was confined to its guarantee of "liberty to all."

Among the Scotchmen in England in the time of Mary Tudor was John Knox who fled ultimately to Geneva. He consorted with Calvin, preaching for some time to Scottish and English exiles assembled there. He arrived again in Scotland no long time after the return of Mary Stuart on the death of her young husband, Henry III, King of France. Knox in his fervor and, indeed, with great ability, carried through the Reformation of the northern kingdom in defiance of the young queen and her Scottish husband, Darnley, of the House of Stuart. When Darnley was murdered, Mary later fled to England, as she thought, for the protection of Elizabeth. Her child, James VI of Scotland, later James I of England, came under the guardianship of the Earl of Moray. Knox thus gained a free hand for his reforming work. The Scots adopted the Presbyterian form of government. This might be described as a kind of mean between the Church of England on the one hand and Congregationalism, on the other, to which latter Baptists and many others of the religious bodies in that destructive and creative era bound themselves. Presbyterianism is thus a representative government throughout, as compared with the aristocratic government of the Episcopal Church, and again, with the more purely democratic quality of Congregationalism in all its forms.

The eighteenth century in England brought forth a

movement which has had great influence both in England and America and, indeed, among English-speaking peoples throughout the world. John and Charles Wesley, sons of a Church of England clergyman at Epworth in Lancashire, who was indeed of the High Church party, gathered, first in Oxford, a company of kindred spirits for the cultivation of the religious life. They adopted a *method* as they called it. They inaugurated what later came to be called a revival, a preaching to the neglected, deliberately calling out more pronounced acknowledgement of experience on the part of the converted. Charles Wesley wrote hymns for these meetings, which were often held in the open, at first because no church would have them and then because no church could hold them. They separated themselves with reluctance from the Church of England. Many in the Church of England have since regretted that separation. It will need no saying that the Methodist body has been one of the great forces for the evangelization of America, the Baptist Church only in less measure. The Presbyterian and Reformed and Congregational bodies have in the main appealed to their own constituencies, at first to those of the same national inheritance. All have signally shared in the religious development of the maturer life of this country. One principle was dear to the hearts of believers from the earliest days of the Reformation, the principle so often proclaimed as the "priesthood of all believers." This has worked throughout the history of Protestantism for the sharing of the laity in church government. More and more as time has gone on, the laity have taken share in religious responsibility. George Fox and the Quaker movement, from its inception, took the ultimate logic of this contention. They never had a clergy at all, or even an approach to it. They were all "friends of God." There is scarcely anything more touching in literature than is the account in George Fox's diary of an interview between Fox and Cromwell in the later days of the Protectorate. The Protector already foresaw the issue of his too early effort to establish a Christian commonwealth. Cromwell was too great a statesman, and, incidentally, he was too old a soldier, not to know that Fox's views were not then practical. But he also knew that from the point of view of the ultimate Christian verity, Fox had much right on his side.

The active period of the settlement of the coast-wise colonies of North America, which ultimately formed the United States, coincided approximately with the period of the dire conflict between Catholic and Protestant powers on the continent in the Thirty Years War. It coincided also with the equally portentous division of Protestantism into sects. The hostility of these among themselves was at times checked only by the necessity which was upon them to meet the hostility of the Catholic powers. The same century and a half was marked in a general way by the decline of the motive of mere discovery and adventure which had preceded in the history of commerce. Men substituted ventures of trade and, in the end, of colonization. The goal of these rivalries was still largely the Atlantic seaboard of America. Virginia was first settled under the impulse of trade. Among the supporters were representatives of the aristocracy. Religious initiative was on the side of the Church of England. On the contrary, the group which had, in 1606, left England for Holland, and in 1620 landed at Plymouth, was made up of middle-class Englishmen who represented no government connection and, unhappily, no satisfactory financial backing. They were of the more advanced type of Puritan conviction. In the first winter they narrowly escaped total failure. Ten years later, Puritans of more moderate view, and in far larger numbers, came to Massachusetts Bay. They represented considerable capital and some financial experience. They also exacted far better terms from their Company at home. They received a royal charter in 1629. They had practically given up hope of such issues as the Civil War was presently to promise. There was also an extraordinary proportion of university men among them. From these sprang in 1636 Harvard College. They were, like the Plymouth men, as we should now say, Congregationalists. The Dutch came to New Amsterdam representing the faith and order of the Netherlands Republic. But the Duke of York seized the Dutch settlement, in the time of Charles II, and it became New York, although retaining to this day some qualities of the Dutch settlement. Quakers came to Rhode Island and, after Penn's purchase, to Philadelphia. Lord Baltimore, a Roman Catholic, signalized himself—perhaps also he had a sense of humor—by the proclamation of religious liberty in Maryland. By that time, however, commercial motives in the Colonies had become evident. To a certain extent these supplanted both racial and religious expectations. Huguenot refugees were at New Rochelle close to the Dutch in New Amsterdam, and in many other places as far south as Beaufort in what later became South Carolina. John Wesley spent unhappy years in Georgia, but that was while he was still meditating, not without aid of German Pietists, his reform in the Church of England which was to become Methodism. Scotch Presbyterians, many of them originally Argyleshire men, who had fled to Londonderry and, in turn, fled thence to the shores of Delaware and Chesapeake Bays, added themselves to this picturesque variety of types.

After the tragic end of the Thirty Years War, when Louis XIV had annexed a considerable part of Germany, German Lutherans came to Pennsylvania. By and by there were Moravians in North Carolina and Pennsylvania. What wonder if the very origins of Christianity in the United States predisposed us, one might say, to sectarianism. And sectarianism was then far from being a drawing-room difference of opinion. There was, moreover, plenty of wilderness in those days to give room to all for the continuance of their characteristic differences. Later in the eighteenth century came the Methodists, themselves the church of evangelism, which, in a sense has remained their strongest trait. Descendants of all these groups topped the Appalachians and had the whole West before them. Christianity spread under the forms of the varied denominations of its advocates. Of course, the Roman Catholic Church was already long since in its various settlements in the valley of the St. Lawrence and down the valley of the Mississippi and, again, in Mexico and along the California coast. The growth of the Roman Catholic Church in the eastern coastwise States came largely when there was a definite bidding for man power in the manufacturing interests of those States. The famine in Ireland in the decade of the forties in the nineteenth century added its quota to the number of these immigrants. It would be safe to say that no small part of the work of Protestant evangelization of the vast western and northwestern territory was at the first the work of men of little education. The importation of negro slaves to the southern States had begun much earlier and was later to be the occasion of the tragedy of the Civil War. Before, say, 1830, the rapidly increasing number of African slaves in the southern States were under some sort of religious influence of the churches of the master class. After the threat which the Nat Turner rebellion constituted, in 1833, the negroes were cut off not alone from the rudimentary education which their children had sometimes received along with the little children of the master class, but also from attendance at the churches of the masters. They were thus delivered over to a ministry of their own race who could, for the most part, by no possibility have had even so much of training as some of the clergy in either West or South among the whites.

One thinks of the evangelization of northern and western Europe by the monks, mostly Benedictines, twelve centuries earlier. One makes vivid to himself extraordinary resemblances and, again, amazing contrasts between these two disseminations of the faith. One might say that even with the denominations, as we now call them, which we mentioned on the seaboard in the seventeenth and eighteenth centuries, we had varieties enough of religious experience to meet all preferences. What we now see is that almost every one of these denominations was to proliferate into several or many varieties of religious profession until the Religious Census for the United States for 1926 shows only just less than one hundred ecclesiastical organizations. The differences between the minor members of the list, at all events, few except their adherents understand, and perhaps not all even of these. That is only a consequence of the kind of movement which the "religious winning of the West" has been. The number of groups diminishes a little from census to census. Bewildering details find their place within certain great types. Even among these there is a growing sense, if not an outward fact, of unity which sometimes at least, makes us feel that unity of spirit may, after all, exist despite diversity of form. But such unity of spirit ought to put an end to some of this diversity. In fact some part of it stands for very little which is any longer real, while yet it constitutes a hindrance to the best of Christian life and work. It offers opportunity, at times, to ascendancy of unfit persons. It hinders co-operation of Christian bodies in respect of what are the true needs of Christian life in our time. Perhaps religious and moral difficulties which lie ahead of us may in the end aid us in this regard.

Expansion of Christendom

We should not begin a paragraph upon this theme without recalling that we are ourselves, the overwhelming majority of us, in the inheritance of peoples of the north and west of Europe who, rather more than a thousand years ago, received the Gospel from the emissaries of an older Christendom of southern and southeastern Europe. The ancestors of these emissaries had, in turn, received the Gospel, probably from the varied peoples of the eastern end of the Mediterranean and thus, ultimately, from Palestine itself. In a general way, the process and progress had been much the same. In the earliest period the emissaries were probably largely lay, tradesmen and travellers and soldiers. The means of travel had been the network of Roman post and military roads and, as well, the routes of sea-borne commerce. I once made a map of the spread of Christianity before the Council of Nicaea. I found something like five hundred and ten places mentioned in the literature of the period which could be located by the aid of the Peutinger Table. Then came a decline in the movement of deliberate propaganda. The energy of Christian men spent itself largely upon other problems. This was the period of the great theological strifes and of the consolidation of such gains as the Christian church had thus far made. In the large, it was perhaps four hundred years before the work of the spreading of the Gospel to include peoples in the west and north of Europe was deliberately taken up again. Tennyson described our forbears as "the godless host of heathen swarming o'er the northern sea." Tacitus in his Germania had given, long before that, a more complimentary description of the qualities of the Saxons of his time. Perhaps at the back of his mind was a comparison of those people of the forest with the degenerate proletariat of the Rome with which he was familiar. But the point to be seized is that Christianity did ultimately make those peoples its own, not, however, without leaving deposit of myth and legend upon the Christianity which these new peoples came to hold. Modern books on the history of religions deal with the faiths which these peoples, with also those of Great Britain, had formerly held. The emissaries of this period were largely monks, Benedictines from the south, with presently also monks of Irish-Scottish connections from the far north. It is to this second great missionary movement that we ascribe the Christianization of the Europe which we are likely to have in mind when we speak of our own ancestors. Something of the same sort was happening, at least in a measure, in the Balkans and southern Russia at the hands of monks and missionaries, not now of the Roman Church but of the Greek Church whose center was Constantinople. This movement also presently suffered an arrest. It is thus obviously a mistake to suppose that the zeal for Christian propaganda has been continuous. Far from it. Perhaps we might describe the longer intervals as periods of consolidation of gains thus far made, periods, that is, of development of the respective peoples upon substantial Christian principles, in contact with the growingly powerful influences of the Church, with also, we might add, the perpetual development of the Church itself.

The great modern period of voyaging and adventure, of the expansion of trade, of which Columbus, Vasco da Gama and the Cabots may be taken as typical, felt little that we could describe as the impulse of missions. There was competition of peoples vigorous and often unscrupulous. There were in many places beginnings of the slave trade on the part of nations which had never thus far known it. Perhaps slaves were to take the place of serfs who were growing less submissive and also were more useful in war. In the period of the great breach between the Protestant lands and the ancestral Church, Xavier had made an heroic beginning in India, and then in Japan. For that matter, Franciscans had made themselves felt in China already two centuries earlier, having gone almost surely by the land route, just as the first of all great modern travellers, Marco Polo, had done. For Protestants who were presently to have so great a share in the work, the time had not yet arrived. The reformers had not time or mind for missions as we understand them. They had enough to do at home. It was Pietists, originally from Austria but settled in Saxony, who, under the impulse of Zinzendorff, inaugurated the first typical Protestant mission from Europe at the end of the first third of the eighteenth century. It was, however, well toward the end of the eighteenth century that what we know as the Protestant movement of missions began. The period of new zeal for this effort may be said to have set in when conflicts about dogma, not alone with the ancient Church but between the sects of Protestants themselves, had begun to wane. But this other situation brought with it beginnings of missions not upon the basis of a united Church, as with the Catholics, but upon many and various denominational bases which must sometimes have given recipients of the Gospel much to think about. This was the more true because few of the subdivisions of Protestantism were, in the long run, willing to be without witness of their zeal in this matter of the Christian propaganda along their own denominational lines. And still another thing—largely within the nineteenth century—the spread not merely of western trade and of this phase of religious propaganda were doing their part to change the face of the world. Beyond these, the impact of western civilization in every thinkable aspect of it, with also awakened desire of remote peoples to enter into the western heritage in civilization, in matters of education, and in forms of government, modes of life, complicated the situation. There were no longer lands on the earth which were completely outside the influences above described. There were no peoples who were unknown and, for that matter, there were no more peoples who were unknowing, of much of the evil, with some of the good, which Christendom itself contains. Barriers which once seemed insurmountable had vanished. But new barriers, inward rather than outward, jealousies, ambitions, rightful self-assertions, had taken their place. We say that nothing but the spirit of Christianity can solve problems which these last two generations have conjured up for us. But then, a still soberer reflection might be that nothing save the Christian spirit can solve the problem of the old nations of Christendom under the new conditions which they, too, now face. It appears that the world will have to settle these questions all together or not at all.

We took occasion to speak of the foreign missionary

activity of the Society of Jesus in India and Japan forever connected with the name of Francis Xavier. An era of great distinction in Roman Catholic missions in North China bears the name of Matteo Ricci, who came to China, indeed, in the year 1582 and died in Peking in 1610. With his name should be associated those of his successors, Verbiest and Schall. They were men, especially Ricci, of high intellectual attainment. They made approach to the learned of the land. There were those who distinguished themselves in astronomical work and teaching. One of Ricci's followers was a tutor of Kang-Hsi, the greatest of all the Manchu emperors. The work of these men survived a bitter persecution on the part of those who resented the presence of foreigners in China. But rivalries of other Orders of their own communion undermined their influence. After the death of Kang-Hsi in 1723, the influence of this great mission of truly learned men to highest circles of China declined. The attitude of exclusion of all foreigners was resumed. This dominated the contact of China with the Western world until the Opium Wars and the treaties which followed them after 1830. The temper which sought to exclude all foreign influence again took possession of China. This spirit dominated the period of the opening of trade relations, even down to the epoch of the foreign wars and the forcible opening of ports. Then came the grand disaster of the Tai Ping Rebellion to complete the prostration of half of the Celestial Empire. The Roman missions, when they were resumed in China, had to meet the same situation with the Protestant missions, and have been compelled to begin their work at the same level. Only perhaps since the capture of Peking by the Allies in 1900 was influence upon education of the ruling classes opened to both Roman and Protestant missions alike. Since the death of the Dowager, and in part under foreign influences, China has been gravely disoriented within itself.

As to the Protestant churches, if it is true that Luther said that he did not feel the call to foreign missionary work, it might be alleged on his behalf that what with the strife with the Roman Church, with the development of Protestantism, not to say also the presence of Anabaptists in his own land, he was preoccupied. The period of the Thirty Years War was not calculated to call out what was later to be known as foreign missionary endeavor. John Eliot, pastor in Roxbury, formed centers of "praying Indians" at Nonantum and Natick and translated the Bible for them. But that work was broken up in King Philip's War. The first wider impulse came in the wake of Pietism and to the body known as Moravians, who, indeed, traced their Protestantism to Huss but, driven from Poland and then from Austria, had found refuge in Saxony under Count Zinzendorff. They signalized their piety by missionary work among the Eskimos, and in the West Indies, for North American Indians and as well, in India. Their work was what we should call purely evangelistic. They were called to counsel by representatives of the British East India Company, and therewith, we may say, we have a small beginning of modern phases of the work. When Hyder Ali, the Nawab of Mysore, refused to receive an embassy of the British, he said, "Send me the Christian, Schwartz, he will not deceive me." Trade and the interest of civilization, the wide range of European influence and, for that matter, of European force and diplomacy, with also education, were beginning to go side by side with religious influence. This is the thing which more and more distinguishes the modern era of missions. This represents the impact of all aspects of our civilization and, as well, it must be added, the rivalries and the vices of some of the civilizers. These were to accompany the zeal of the missionaries in all time to come. The relation of these two factors in the opening up of the world to Western influence has been by no means always good. It was, however, at the end of the eighteenth century and in the early decades of the nineteenth century that the international outburst of feeling as to the foreign missionary problem made itself felt. It was after the second era of the great discoveries, after the taking possession on the part of Europeans of Australia, after New Zealand had been re-discovered by the British, having been discovered by the Dutch a century before. Then also all the islands of the southern seas came within the sphere of European or American influence, and, it might be added, greed. The British East India Company had been for the first time brought to book. The trial of Warren Hastings inaugurated the era of reform. British feeling about African slavery had begun to be aroused. American minds in the North were turning against it. It was a period of enthusiasm touching many moral and social questions. The rights of man had been much discussed. There were those who contended that those rights were the same wherever man was found. There were, on the other hand, those who felt that the stronger peoples might make a good use of the weakness of others until these latter were awakened to their rights. Treaties of trade, including the opium traffic, practically forced upon the Chinese, illustrate these views.

There had been in the Church of England since 1701 a Society for the Propagation of the Gospel. It was in the founding of the Church Missionary Society, however, in 1799, that the new spirit more fully manifested itself. Also this Society, at first, contained representatives of other denominations besides those of the Church of England. I might here add that the American Board of Commissioners for Foreign Missions was founded in 1810 and also, in its earlier years, included representatives of denominations other than the Congregationalists who were interested in missionary work. English dissenters, particularly Baptists, even before this time had given characteristic impulse to the cause. The dissenting churches gradually formed their own societies. At this time also the necessity of a system of education was first really envisaged by these societies. Such a system was actually inaugurated by the British government in India before the Mutiny of 1857. Sanitation had become in most densely settled regions an obligation of government. The long series of Governors-general, occasionally men of greatest distinction, with also beginnings of the evolution of representative government, has been an index of the same advance. This latter, the evolution of representative government, is by no means yet complete, nor are the issues all as yet clear. But it is a piece of history, on the whole, incomparable with anything which has ever been done by any other State. Both on the good side and on the bad side, it thus illustrates the thing which we were saying about nineteenth century international contacts and contests. Colonization and trade, European influence and, for that matter, European interests and occasionally force, have come to go side by side with denominational and religious influences. Diplomacy, trade, colonization, all have had their share in the movement. The number of missions representing different denominations of Christians and holding more or less different views, with also differences of form of government and worship, is still formidable. But efforts are being made for unifying these bodies in their work. A United Christian Church exists in southern India which is an example to all of the rest of Christendom.

If the mission of Xavier had been made possible by the expansion of Portuguese trade, if Dutch trade with Japan had been carried on without any appreciable missionary activity, those were, at all events, the first signs of a new time. French trade with the Orient or with Africa was, before the French Revolution, not important. English voyages of discovery went everywhere in the eighteenth century. Missions followed the discoverers. Other things also followed. Botany Bay in Australia was a penal colony. Materials for manufacture were brought to Europe from all quarters of the world. Manufactured goods were sold in all quarters of the world, and this by no means by England only. Colonial empires large and small were developing everywhere. There was hardly a portion of the new world which was not owned, or at least claimed, in the old world, save only the United States, which had, indeed, declared their freedom in 1776, but their claims had not yet been made good beyond the Appalachians. The rest of the continent belonged to, or its possession was disputed by, the English, the French, the Spanish, or again, it had not yet been given up by the American Indians. Relations between missionaries and those who were identified with commerce were not always amicable. What those connected with trade thought about missionaries could be heard in the smoking room of every ship. In fact, in somewhat ameliorated condition, this situation exists down to the present time. There was, moreover, a humanitarian and reforming spirit abroad in the decades about 1790 which was different from either the purely commercial spirit on the one hand or the specific religious endeavor on the other. Transformation in the attitudes of governments in Europe followed. The British abolition, at first of the slave trade and then of slavery itself in British dominions, was in strong contrast with that which then obtained in a large part of the United States. Yet it was to England that for a time the Confederacy looked for support against the northern States in the Civil War, and this supposedly because of the necessity of cotton to English manufacturers. Political ideas made propaganda everywhere. Witness the rise of the South American Republics, more especially in the period following the fall of Napoleon.

In and under and through all this was the commercial motive. There were opportunities to be embraced. Careers were made possible. The wealth of those who gained the advantage was of a magnitude never before dreamed. It would be foolish to say that this did not, some of it, redound to the advantage of missions—some of it also not. But it put a different face on all questions. No example is more salient than that of Japan. After the opening of the country and in reversal of an age-long attitude, in touching confidence in the whole world, there was, for a time, the utmost friendliness to all things foreign. Of much that Japan is in the world of today foundations were then laid. But by equally good right, and perhaps of even greater significance, was the fact that, presently, came a period of distrust of all things foreign, of natural eagerness to regain the mastery in their own house, which had once been perhaps too lightly given away. The history of the Doshisha, the college, now one of the national universities, at Kyoto, founded by Neesima in imitation of his college, Amherst, and which had been helped by the American Board of Foreign Missions and by philanthropic American friends, presently underwent strong reaction. Only after a generation has it entirely regained its confidence in its earlier friends. The case is quite typical. One is haunted across the interval of half a lifetime by the recollection of a saintly old Scottish clergyman and what had once been his little island paradise in the South Seas. His people were to him like children. In the old days, disease and cannibalism had kept the population reasonably small. Now it had grown to such proportions that young men, also young women, were going off as contract laborers to the cities of Australia. There they died, some of them in vice, and for some of them, if they were good laborers, the time never arrived when their contracts ran out. The old man came to this country for friends and money. He went to England to gain government intervention, if he could, in the grave injustice which grew with the lapse of years. The history of the Sandwich Islands is much like that. There are representatives of a third of the greater races of the world on these small islands. There is much wealth. There is high education to be had. But there are almost no Kanakas left. You hear the same sort of stories—with differences—about workers in Johannesburg and the Rand. The difference is that with the breaking up of tribal allegiance new negroes come constantly to the Rand to begin again the same old round. Livingstone had some foresight of this already in his day. The world's best and the world's worst is there to behold. Perhaps the moral of the whole movement is the moral for all Christendom as well. There seems to be no reason why the Gospel should not be attended by all the gifts of civilization. It is, however, rather evident that it is by the Gospel alone that men are able to stand up against the gifts of civilization. That is a lesson which we do not need to go to foreign missionary lands to learn. But it is particularly tragic for those who, for the first time, are seeing the generation of their friends learning it in all of its intensity and fatality.

The problem among the peoples which we once thought we could take under our tutelage in the manner, mainly, of a propaganda for our faith, has expanded under our hand into the necessity of teaching also many lessons in the civilization which goes with the Gospel, educational, political, social, even sanitary. We can hardly be said to have had any clear idea to what all this would lead. Certainly we had little forecast of the situation which the Great War produced, a situation in which whole peoples arose in desire to appropriate many of the benefits of a civilization which we had thought our own. In the interval since the Great War many states, like the one which inherits the old Ottoman Empire, have reacted in hostility not merely against the religion of foreigners, but also against their own, in efforts for progress and enlightenment which they esteem, for the moment at least, more necessary. A great wave of secularism passed over a very composite nation in which Christian educational and philanthropic work had been for a century devoted to subject populations, Armenians and others, whom the Ottoman State hardly more than endured. The same wave of secularization is, however, passing over many nationalists besides the Turks. It has effect upon missions in the nations also which had been regarded as the source of missions.

The Africa of the real Africans, with languages whose number still puzzles the philologists and whose dialectal variations cannot all be traced, is probably peopled by men of a more or less common descent and of the antiquity of whose race we have no measure. Even in the youth of men now living, the center of the continent was marked in huge letters with the word "Unknown." It was probably just as much unknown to Herodotus. There was an immense and, in modern times, ever increasing trade of all the world with Africa, or rather, not trade at all, but just plunder—and plunder not only of the property of men, but of the men, women and children themselves. The Dutch were at Capetown in 1652. Their charter mentioned the duty of instructing the natives in the Christian religion. But, in the long run, no one has been harder on the black than some of the Afrikanders. The American Colonization Society in 1817 transferred certain freed negroes to Liberia, which, in 1847, was declared an independent State. But Liberia also shows that liberty is not the only thing necessary. Great Britain declared the African slave trade illegal in 1807. We in this Republic declared it illegal in 1864, and only at the end of four years of almost suicidal war. There was an era of exploration at the end of the eighteenth century. Livingstone had been accepted by the London Missionary Society in 1838. Later, he gave himself to the work of exploration. He reached Quilimane on the Indian Ocean in 1856, four years after his departure from Capetown, having travelled twelve thousand miles on foot through wilderness never before, so far as we know, traversed by civilized man. He died in Bangweolo in 1873. He was buried in Westminster Abbey. Great work had been done in Uganda under the Church Missionary Society after 1885. In the Congo Free State, missions had been largely Roman Catholic under a Belgian Society. Upon their work supervened the Leopoldine debauch. The Paris Society, representing the old Huguenot Church, took a place beside them in the French Congo. Here worked and still works one of the most famous scholars of our generation, Albert Schweitzer. South Africa, especially Johannesburg and the surrounding country, represents the hardest problem. On top of it all came the Boer War in the last year of the nineteenth century. When the Great War came, many thought that the Dutch, with whom their old defeat still rankled, might join with the Germans. Some did. It was easy, at times, for those of us interested mainly in the "Western Front," to forget a war in southeast Africa, as also a war in the valley of the Euphrates, not to speak of a war presently in Siberia, and a war on all seas in both hemispheres. It is exactly in Africa that, in a time of the decline of Moslem power, at all events in its old seats, Mohammedanism is apparently making new and great conquests. Certainly Moslems have had their share in seizing and holding African slaves. But the violence which slavery offers to the faith of the great Arabian is not so great as that which we now feel that it represents to the religion of Christ. The inexpressible wrong done both to the black man's body and the white man's soul which slavery was and entailed, might easily lead the black man to feel that, after all, the Moslem was his nearest kin. Zealots may come to think that the great field for the recovery of the faith of the great Arabian is in Africa.

I published just after the Great War, under the title "West and East," certain lectures which had been delivered in Oxford just before the War. How far have we come! Those lectures dealt with effects of the Christian movement, an expansion which had characterized mainly the nineteenth century. No one could have forecast in 1913 the perspective in which that history must be viewed in 1935. Some imagined that a third period of suspension of propagandist activity like the two to which we have above referred, say, from the fifth to the eight century, and again, like that from, say, the tenth to the sixteenth century, had come upon us. I should say that that depends exactly upon what it is that Christendom proposes to do. For mere propaganda, for mere setting forth of the distinctive principles of faith, I sometimes think that that may be true. For the setting forth in all its fullness of the life which is lived and to be lived under our religion in all its manifold exemplifications, I do not think that that is true. This last is our opportunity. It is a haunting reflection that it is exactly in this most modern period of missions that the effect of true religion in all areas of life, intellectual and social, economic and political, has come more and more to be emphasized in the main aspects of our endeavor to make our religion known. From that we should take heart. But we certainly shall not have—and should not desire—success in this endeavor unless we, as individuals and churches and nations, can illustrate our contention that religion is, after all, nothing but the secret of the good, of the better and the best life, best not alone for us but for all men. And it will require the best of men of all sorts to be the emissaries of that propaganda. And some of them will not even know that that is what they are. And it will take time.

PART III

THE TRANSCENDENT

PART III

THE TRANSCENDENT

I. THE RELATIVITY OF THE TEACHING

IN the ancient volcanic country to the east of Volterra a mounting drear from either distance or height, lies the strangely desolate pile of San Gimignano, with its five square black towers and its ancient Augustinian monastery. In the chapel of this ancient house is a fresco of Benozzo Gozzoli painted after 1460, celebrating the life of the patron saint. The walls are almost covered with the frescoes of the legends of the saint, even more numerous than the shades. In several of the frescoes the figure occurs two or three times. In the lower corner of the picture which I have in mind is depicted the wandering child with the faith of the Fathers, who is trying—with a shell, to empty the sea into a pool in the sand which he has made. The legend had represented him saying to the great theologian: "My effort is not more futile than yours—to express in the finite realm the doctrine of the Trinity." Somewhat thus I feel as I approach the question of the relation of Jesus to God.

It will be remembered that Luther was an Augustinian monk. Some time before he began his epoch-making work he had visited Rome. Whether it is historically true that, halfway up the Scala Santa, he had risen from his knees and walked down, the tale is at all events typical. It was not upon the point of the doctrine of the

Part III

THE TRANSCENDENT

1. OF THE RELATION OF JESUS TO GOD

In the ancient volcanic country to the east of Volterra, a morning's drive from either Florence or Siena, lies the strangely desolate town of San Gimignano, with its five square brick towers and its Augustinian monastery. In the chapel of this last are frescoes of Benozzo Gozzoli, painted after 1460, celebrating the life of the patron saint. The walls are almost covered with the frescoes, in fact, legends of the saint were more numerous than the spaces. In several of the frescoes his figure occurs two or even three times. In the foreground of the picture which I have in mind is depicted an enchanting child with the halo of the Christ. He seeks, shell in hand, to empty the sea into a pool in the sand which he has made. The legend had represented him saying to the great theologian:— "My effort is not more futile than yours—to express in the language of men the doctrine of the Trinity." Somewhat thus I feel as I approach the question of the relation of Jesus to God.

It will be remembered that Luther was an Augustinian monk. Some time before he began his epoch-making work, he had visited Rome. Whether it is historically true that, halfway up the Scala Santa, he had risen from his knees and walked down, the tale is, at all events, typical. It was not upon the point of the doctrine of the person of Christ that Luther broke with the Church. It was, as everybody knows, upon the doctrine of justification. Staupitz had found him on his knees grovelling on the floor in his monastery at Erfurt, crying, "Oh, my sins!" He said to him, "But, Brother Martin, it is written, 'The just shall live by faith.' " Years afterward Luther wrote in retrospect:— "If ever a monk had earned salvation by work-righteousness, I had been that monk." Calvin became the head of the other great doctrinal tradition of Protestantism. Calvin's view, borne by Knox, became the foundation of the Church of Scotland. Perhaps Calvin was more truly steeped in Augustinianism than was Luther. Zwingli made stand against Luther in the discussion at Marburg concerning the doctrine of the Sacrament. He was more truly in the humanist tradition than either Luther or Calvin. Possibly he was too truly a humanist to approach the power of the others in that confusing and difficult time. He had not the firmness nor, again, the emotional appeal of Luther. He did not approach the amazing intellectual force or the truly French gift of systematization which belonged to Calvin.

Perhaps one question at a time was enough. The question of overwhelming significance for the moment was, Does salvation come by faith or by works? Luther was by temperament a mystic. Calvin was one of the least mystical of men. He was a systematizer, a theologian, in a sense in which Luther was not that. He brought to the ordering of the Protestant contentions, as over against the scholastic inheritance of half a thousand years, intellectual gifts of the very first order. It was characteristic of the man, and perhaps of the then current phase of the movement, to be eager to exclude that which the reformers esteemed irrelevant, as compared with that upon which they set so great a price.

"What shall I do to be saved? Is it by faith or by works?" One looks at the so-called Formula of Concord of the German Protestants of the generation after the death of Luther. One can understand how, in its effort at inclusiveness and, at the same time, its purpose to exclude some questions which had meantime been raised, it came to be called, by some in ridicule and by others in bitterness, the Formula of Discord. Yet it is significant, and perhaps also characteristic of Calvin's generation, that a Spaniard, a physician by training, a theologian by interest, Servedi, with two Italians, uncle and nephew, the Sozzini, should have brought a very different question to debate, namely, that of the person of Christ. Servetus strayed into Calvin's city to debate it. He met there a fate which seems to us only the more tragic in proportion as we sympathize with the general aim of the Reformation. The three, and particularly Servetus, had raised a question which was still far down the horizon. He paid with his life in Geneva, a thing for which, even if Calvin did not exactly order it, he has hardly been forgiven. The Socini wandered to what was then Poland, modern Transylvania. Perhaps the best that can be said for their opponents is that these had insufficient sympathy with men who raised other questions than those with which they themselves were struggling. They may have thought that they already had difficulties enough. It may also be true that supreme questions concerning the person of Christ are not even now soluble, in the sense in which working solutions were then urged for some other questions, for example, that of the authority of Scripture and that of the meaning of faith. Conviction upon these points brought something like half of western Christendom into one solid and determined following. Perhaps we might use the colloquial phrase,

The other question was not yet ripe. Is it yet ripe? Hardly, in Servetus' sense. It is, however, as good as certain that no solution that could then have been reached would be a satisfactory solution now. Not all of the solutions of other questions which were then reached are now satisfactory. But the assumption of freedom of discussion is now among Protestants as good as guaranteed. Perhaps that is one of the best of the gains of the Reformation. And yet it took the reformers and their successors some generations to learn that.

That for which we are primarily indebted to the Reformation is a proposition which the reformers, almost to the last man of them, first asserted for themselves and then denied to others—the right of private judgment. That is the old phrase. It described a feeling which, after all, was fundamental to Protestantism. Of all our convictions the most living and potent ones are those which we have arrived at for ourselves. But is that true, even now, of all Protestants, and especially of the combative among them? And had that tenet of the Reformation been, at the moment, so widely emphasized as we are disposed to emphasize it, there might have been no unity of Protestant men in making a stand against the authority of the Roman Church, entrenched as this had been for something like a thousand years. Indeed, some of us might go one step further. We might say that the judgments which we really hold are not merely the ones which we have reasoned out for ourselves. They are convictions concerning which we claim—and use—the right to change our opinions if we see cogent reasons for so doing. Very few Protestants held that conviction then. Not all hold it now. Some now do battle for what were private judgments of the reformers four hundred and fifty years ago. These can hardly now be called private judgments of all who do battle for them today. They have become tradition and inheritance. They may be as truly a bondage as was the bondage from which reformers gave their labors and not a few of them their lives, to set us free. Yet, after all, history is not made by extremists who would solve all questions at once or last questions first. Real history, solid progress, is made by men and causes which solve necessary questions now and trust to others, or even to the future, to solve other question in the order in which they may arise. Certainly the city of Geneva honored itself when it set up, some years ago, a memorial to Servetus, not far from the noble monument of the Genevan reformers themselves. Even a passing stranger may share the regret that it was not given to the generation of the reformers to see all the problems which their own claims involved. The question of the relation of Jesus to God was, as we have said, not one of those about which, primarily, the struggle of the Reformation turned. That it was raised by Servetus, even in his manner and measure, is all the more noteworthy. That a small number of men of like conviction should have built up communities in what was then the freer atmosphere of Poland, is perhaps more noteworthy still. For, within two generations, the Roman Church had reasserted itself with almost unexampled power in Poland. A few generations more and the unity of Poland itself was lost. Its identity as one of the kingdoms of the world was sacrificed to the joint ambitions of Prussians, Austrians and Russians, to be regained only through the Treaty of Versailles. The little community which then gathered to the thought of Servetus and the influence of the Socini dwindled. The bitterness of the struggle which Protestants had to wage until long after the Thirty Years War, may have obscured other issues than those already formulated. If Protestants had not been able to unite, even in the partial and jealous way in which they did unite, Protestant Europe might have been annihilated. The Thirty Years War showed that.

The later years of the eighteenth century in England, with also the earlier years of the nineteenth century in New England, saw an awakening again to the issue which so long ago Servetus had precipitated. From Priestley to Martineau in the mother country, as it truly was in Priestley's time, and in America—because Priestley later came to this country—under the leadership of Channing and his compeers, the old contention took shape again, or rather, it took new shape. It combined much for which the eighteenth century, meantime, had been struggling. In this country it is not untrue to say that the movement was aided by the rigidity into which New England theology had settled after the Great Awakening. Even those of us whose inheritance for ten generations has been in New England orthodoxy, with a mingling at certain points of Scotch Calvinism, can now see new approaches. The rise of the sciences of nature, with also wider studies of man, have given fresh impulse to a survey of the question which Servetus and the Sienese precipitated. Studies of the nature of the Scripture and of the history of doctrine furnish new angles of approach. But, once for all, if there is a mystery in the Christian religion, it must be this one of the relation of Jesus to God. It is the mystery of all true religion—the mystery of the relation of souls to God and of God to souls. It must be this which the relation of Jesus to God illuminates. At the same time, the relation of men, even such as we are, to God might well now prove our point of departure. If we begin at the other end, that is to say, with God, we certainly run great risk of assumptions as to

God, which are not wholly, or not at all, derived from the specific religious experience of men. Still less are they derived from the indefinitely more complex views of nature which obtain among us, and of which our own fathers had only slight idea. Perhaps, after all, some play of feeling—our own real feeling—in the matter is safer, at all events, than is abstraction and speculation. We do not attain the God of our quest in this matter by reasoning from the abstractions of philosophy. You may test that assertion by thinking of Aristotle or even of Aquinas, or of those of our own day whose favorite assertion is that God is the Absolute. We might know beforehand that the absolute is no place to seek for response to religion. Again, you do not get the God of religion by reasoning upon the achievements of the physical sciences and thinking what sort of a being God must be who manifests himself in the phenomena with which the sciences of nature deal. We can feel after the God of religion, "if haply we may find him," only in the experiences of the inner life, most significantly, our own inner life. And when we do thus find him, we find that he is "not far from every one of us." I assume that God may be any one of several things that the philosophers have said about him. That depends upon the mood of our quest. But we find that aspect of God which is turned toward religion when we feel the needs which the religious mind and heart reveal.

We were familiar only a few years ago with a form of the production, on every street corner, of electric light—a form which seems now largely to have disappeared. This old apparatus, however, furnished Percy Gardiner with one of the aptest of his famous illustrations. In one of his books, and in an essay touching our topic of Christology, he uses this image:—When we approach two carbon points the one to the other, there flashes at last between them a blinding light, by the power of which we see other objects, far and near. But into that light itself, because of its very intensity, we cannot see. Just so—I paraphrase for the sake of brevity—in our thought of the person of Christ, the Church has immemorially dealt with the question of the "Light of the world." Just so, two opposite poles of thought, two worlds, that of the divine and that of the human, have been drawn one toward the other. In the radiance of the mysterious relation consummated in Christ, men have viewed life and man and God. But when we try to fix our eyes upon precisely that relation itself, it is as if we gazed into a blinding abyss of light. In the whole history of Christian thought, I take it, this is exactly what men have done. With variations indefinite, according to changing modes of thought of ages, men have sought to see Jesus in the light of God. But what they really have seen has been a man's life as illuminated by that great light. The Man of Nazareth, no one disputes, is a concrete historical magnitude, an empirical fact. Whatever else he was, he was real man, "very man" as the creeds say. He was set in actual and definite relations to the great stream of the life of the world. He had his place in the movement of humanity. He was a Jew, born under Augustus, dying under Tiberius. He lived out his little span of years in a Roman province. He said such and such things. He did recorded deeds. He was a man of distinct traits of character and personality, of exalting influence upon the world about him and of unequalled influence upon the world after him, even down to our own day. He lived and worked within certain great antitheses which his age and race and national faith created. He is, I say, for our reflection a concrete historical fact, a personage in whom, for purposes of this discussion, one of our poles of thought, humanity, is represented. Men have sought, however, to bring together here, for once, the two greatest of our ideas, namely, that of man and that of God. They have aimed to think of one person in whom these orders of being coexisted, coalesced. In doing this, however, they have met one of the inescapable conditions of thought. They have been subject to a law of the mind which they could by no possibility elude, but of which they have been, for the most part, unaware. They have compared, or, one might almost say, compounded, things which differ, without adequate reckoning with those respects in which they differ. They have treated as if they were logically comparable two things which stand differently within the mind itself.

One pole of our thought is the true humanity of Jesus. That is obviously the pole from which we must start. The other pole is our thought of God. God himself, however, is no empirical fact, no concrete historical magnitude, no personage in the sense in which we have claimed that for Jesus. Quite the contrary. Just in being transcendent, in belonging as we should say, to the other world, in being, as we believe, the life of this world, and yet not all manifest in it or identifiable with it, God is a magnitude of a different sort for our thought. Let us give over for the moment the abstractions of theologians and philosophers. God is to you and me, to our deepest thought concerning him, life of our life, soul of our souls. God is the object of our aspirations, the source of our inspirations, revealer of something of his sacred will in our consciences, comfort in our distresses, power in our weakness, wisdom in our ignorance, guide in our darkness, forgiver of our sins. God it is who purifies and uplifts and ennobles our souls. God it is who gives us the sense that we are not alone in the world and that we shall not be put to confusion. God it is who gives us the sense of victory, not perhaps in this world, certainly not wholly in this world, but victory over the world, even when all things in the world have gone against us. God it is through whom we feel that nothing in heaven or earth is of consequence so only that we have hold on him and he has hold on us. God it is who is revealed in the love and faithfulness of men and women, in the purity of little children, in the grand strife of men on behalf of an ideal in life, in the joy of sacrifice which brave souls have had, in the heroism of death and in the confidence of immortal life. God it is whom we feel to have dwelt among us full of grace and truth in the spirit of Jesus. God it is who, indwelling in transcendent measure in Jesus, has revealed to us in greater measure what life means, what man is for, and how we have to think of the just and loving, the holy and compassionate, the invisible and ineffable God himself. But there are other senses in which Jesus does not reveal to us what God is like. We have to ask the world of nature some of these questions. And we now ask these questions out of a knowledge of nature which men have only recently learned and are still learning, a kind of knowledge, which, if we think of Jesus' humanity as in any sense a true humanity, Jesus simply did not have. Rather, what he said on these subjects was at the plane of the knowledge of his time. The same must be said if we are thinking of knowledge of history, of much of history before his time, of history other than that of his own nation. And most of all is this true of the history subsequent to his time, of which we cannot ascribe to him any knowledge whatsoever, except the insight and the forecast of the principles of the life of man as he saw and taught us to see those principles. That word concerning Jesus, that he was *"God manifest in the flesh,"* needs to be taken far more literally than it has often been taken. The phrase, "In him dwelt all the fullness of the Godhead bodily, full of grace and truth," rings true if what we are thinking of is Jesus' moral excellence, his spiritual majesty, his compelling grace, the spell which he cast over men, the redeeming power over the personalities of men which his personality from of old exerts. If we ask him philosophical questions, we might say that he has no answers at all, save in the sense in which his surpassing knowledge of man furnished him insight, rather than knowledge, in the sense in which we use that word.

But we realize that these are not the terms in which men have, for the most part, in time past sought to define either God or Jesus. These are not the distinctions which men in their questions have for long ages so much as even had in mind. This is not even the angle from which they endeavored to approach a definition of God. Quite the contrary. From the very childhood of the world, in poetry and symbolism, that is to say in the language of imagination, and again, in maturer ages, in that of metaphysical reflection, men have sought to do an altogether different thing. They have taken, let us say, the image of a king, and, of course, among Orientals, of an Oriental potentate. They have forgotten, or, in fact, never thought, that it was an image. Or, they took the phrase, "Shall not the Judge of all the earth do right?" and hastened to conclude that what they in their time and circumstance thought to be right is that which the Judge of all the earth has done and does and will do. And even Jesus' own words, "My Father, your Father, our Father," has, as we have already said, been often used to call up images of the character and purposes of God which we cannot for a moment think that Jesus meant to imply. The softness, weakness, the mistaken quality of the purposes and conduct of a human father which have sometimes had place in the genuine purposc of his life, these all belong among the things which could never by any possibility be alleged of God. And these are only some examples of how men have used the language of earthly experience to describe the unearthly greatness of God, the heavenly quality of his purposes of love. One might say, "What other language could the writers have used?" To be sure. But they might have remained aware—or at least, we might be aware—that that was what they were doing. The earthly image cannot be pushed too far. Or rather, perhaps it would be more just to say that they failed to realize that the language of feeling and imagination, which is by far the best language that we have with which to attempt reaches toward our notion of God, can never by any possibility give us a definition which we can throw around God and the things of the kingdom of heaven. Rather, as was long ago beautifully said, such language "is not a measuring rod. It is only a telescope by which we might kneel down and look up into heaven." We realize that God and God's dealings with men submit to no such definitions as we are able to make of them.

Or again, when this appeal to the imagination, this poetical interpretation, came to seem to other minds and other ages too naïve, then men proceeded to describe God by a method practically just the opposite of this transference of familiar human qualities to him. Maturer men and generations gave themselves to reasoning and ended, though perhaps often unconsciously, in metaphysic, which is, one might say, the polar opposite of poetry. They reflected upon the misery of men and sprang to the conclusion that God, at all events, must be wholly blissful, unapproached by pain. But would that be a God for men and women to cry to, when in mortal pain? They thought of the weakness of man and declared God to be omnipotent. They thought of the ignorance of man and alleged the omniscience of God. They felt man's limitation in being banned to a spot and asserted the omnipresence of God. In truth, the mind of man would seem, at times, almost to have revelled in thus depicting God in terms which, when we scrutinize them, would seem to represent the effort to ascribe to God all that man lacks and to deny to God all that man is and has. On that basis alone, if we really made earnest with it, could we draw near to God, or believe that he could draw near to us? And, frankly, we must ask ourselves the question, did Jesus manifest those qualities of omnipotence, of omniscience, of omnipresence? And what do we gain by ascribing to God all that man is not, and then saying that once in history one man illustrated all of that? But men have gone still further, and more consciously to metaphysical extremes. They have described God as the Absolute, the Universal, the Ground and Substance of all, the First Cause, the Unknowable. These are just a few of the words of this sort which might be gathered if one were to try to follow out this clue. There is something which might almost touch one's sense of humor—perhaps I had better say, one's sense of tragedy—in this enthusiastic heaping up of such declarations concerning God, as if the very purpose were to put him far from us. He is far from us, but it is the purpose of religion to bring him near. The pith and purpose of all this effort which we are trying to describe was to say that God is as much unlike man as possible—that God and man are mutually opposite conceptions. And then, in the doctrine of the person of Christ, as it has sometimes been framed by the theologians, we are supposed to bring them together. At the end of the road in this direction is some kind of an abstraction for God and a completely unhistorical personage for Jesus. However much or however little this line of thought may have to say to us in our abstractionist moods, it has something less than nothing to say to us in the way of religion. And yet we had always supposed—Jesus himself taught us to suppose—that the great aim of religion is to help men to know God. Surely that is the simplest meaning of the incarnation. And could we say that what I have just described was a true incarnation?

A Christian writer once wrote the beautiful phrase, "that they might know God and Jesus Christ whom he has sent." Manifestly, and indeed in our own experience, some do know God who would be only bewildered by these abstractions. That is not to say that abstractions do not serve a purpose. They do, in a scheme of thought, or rather, in the perpetually changing schemes of thought which the widening and deepening of human knowledge bring. All of that, however, simply goes back to the discrimination which we tried to make in the first chapter between intuitive knowledge and the rationalizing knowledge which we are rather more likely to call by that name. And, as we then said, there is no reason why the two should not be combined. In fact, there is every reason why they should be combined. They should serve as complements or supplements the one to the other. Reflective knowledge keeps our intuitions sane, and our intuitions serve to keep at least the feet of our speculations on the ground. But there is every reason in the world why the one which belongs clearly to the intellectual life should not be insisted upon in the area of the emotional life. Of course, the reverse is equally true, that the things which seem true to our emotional life should not refuse the aid which an enlarging intellectual life brings to most men and, in still larger degree, to the ages in their succession. And it is also true that no one of us lives two lives, intellectual and emotional. We live one life of which those words try to describe two phases. They are two phases of our own normal life. Jointly they contribute to our knowledge of ourselves and of the world and of God.

But surely here comes to evidence the thing which we alleged a moment ago. What we may find in some famous definitions of God is not God at all. It is at best a definition of God in such terms as devout men, in a crisis of their own inner life, or in crises in the life of mankind, have been able to supply. It was a definition with such apparatus as the intellectual life of the race of that particular time, with the course of events, had furnished and emphasized. It was a definition, or rather, such moderate success in defining, as men have, either then or at any other time, been able in varying manners to achieve. But what we have in that language is not God. It is a conception of God, the conception of the particular man or men who made it. And almost surely it would illuminate the crisis, if we knew it, in the life of faith at which the men then stood. This is only to say that what we have in such formulae is not God. It is an idea of God, less or more adequate, always more or less relative to the needs and experiences of those who make the definition. That is the fact which you have to read off the long series of definitions of God which different men and movements, even in our own religion, have brought forth, which different religions have brought forth, which varying emergencies in the religious life of our successors will bring forth. These, too, will demand different definitions because men must meet different situations. But we have God, and God has us, in those inward experiences of him which I tried in my previous paragraph to hint. That inward experience of God, that actual possession of God,

God's possession of us, has existed, no one can deny, in men who have had the greatest variety of conceptions concerning God. It has existed in us individually when our conceptions of God were quite different from the conceptions which we now hold. Pray God it will continue when our conceptions as to God may be still different from what they now are—as they will be, if we live and grow in mind as well as in religious experience. Of what use is it to be alive if we do not alter our conceptions of so fundamental a matter? Of what use is it to have experience if experience does not lead us to ever nobler conceptions? The experience of God excludes, one might fairly say, no humble and reverent definition of God. But the most learned definition of God does not necessarily contain, or even necessarily imply, any deeper experience of God. It is certainly identifiable with none. I should go so far as to say, that life changing as it does, experience deepening as it should, if our conceptions as to God did not change at all, that might prove only that our reflection, at all events upon this experience, had been allowed to stagnate or was long since dead. That would prove only that, intellectually, we were substituting some definition, our own or that of somebody else, for real, living, growing reflection on the great theme of God. None of us will claim that, if we are living Christians, we do not grow in our conception of God. The experience of God existed in us when we were children, when our ideas of God were most naïve and inadequate. It exists in us now, as I hope, in our maturer years, when our ideas of God differ widely from our past ideas, and differ widely from other people's ideas, people with whom we are quite aware of being at one in the religious life. My ideas of God may differ widely from yours. Shall I say you have no experience of God because you do not accept my definition? Or would you say the converse of me? I do not see how if we have any living ideas we can help differing from one another. We should certainly be insufficiently alive to religion if we did not differ from one another. It will exist, this our hold on God, or rather—and what is far more important —God's hold on us,—this will exist when, as I hope, our life ripens, our experience deepens, our participation in the lives of others enlarges and our conceptions of all things relating to the religious life are far nobler than they are today. One may have the experience of God and very little definition, or, as perhaps I ought to put it, a constantly changing definition. And, conversely, one may have an indefinite amount of definition, evolved for ourselves or, more likely, borrowed from others, and with all that, we may have little or none of the fresh and constant experience of God.

But in the age-long struggle of mankind to understand Christ, men's minds, for the most part, at least, have not traversed the distinction with which we have just dealt. They have not endeavored to bring together the historical magnitude which Jesus of Nazareth unquestionably was with the God who is given in our own inner experience, and which we read off the soul of Jesus in his experience. For with all that we say concerning God in history, God is not an historical magnitude in the sense that Jesus was. Men have not always even conceived that this was the problem. Rather, the contrary. They have endeavored to bring together in the creeds, and in their theologies, an historical magnitude with an abstraction, a metaphysical magnitude whose definition was approached mainly by the process of dwelling upon all the things in respect of which God has been thought of as unlike man. Such definitions rested for ages upon a dualistic theory of the universe. Its very postulate was that

God and man are two mutually exclusive conceptions. Whatever was divine was *ipso facto* not human. Whatever was human was not divine. What was natural was not supernatural. Whatever was natural to man was, in Augustine's teaching, hostile to the grace of God. Whatever was of the grace of God was contrary to the nature of man. Man must have a new nature bestowed upon him in the miracle of grace in order so much as to begin the life in God. Until then, "all his righteousness was as filthy rags,"—a quotation which was often devoutly made, while completely ignoring the connection in Scripture in which it stands. By such language the youth of some of us—I include myself—was darkened. These are, of course, the well-known propositions of a dualistic theory of the universe. Such were the issues, or at least some of the issues within the field of theology, of such a philosophy. The issues for the souls of some men and women and children were often tragic in the extreme.

The concrete figure of the Nazarene is, indeed, sufficiently indescribable in his moral elevation and his spiritual loveliness, but altogether undeniable in his human experience and influence. What wonder, I say, if men sought to bring together this figure with a definition of God gathered from every area of human reasoning except the one which would seem to us to be the relevant one, namely, that of valid experience of men's souls—what wonder that they met difficulties? There is something pathetic in the struggle of one and another of the great Christian minds of the centuries to see how in the person of Jesus Christ, God and man could be one. The very definitions from which they set out declared that the two could by no possibility be one. Either was by conception the polar opposite of the other. Exactly in proportion as one felt the real and true humanity of Jesus, it was difficult for men to assert his deity. Conversely, in that proportion in which one felt in Jesus that in which he transcended any humanity which we have known, just in that measure did his real humanity become difficult to maintain. Down the course of history, believers might be divided into two opposing camps. The one contained, indeed, at all times the overwhelming majority. These were they who felt the divinity of Jesus, or, as they were apt to say, for full measure, the deity of Jesus. These, however, made of his humanity, at times, more or less of a semblance, but not quite a fact which one could take hold of with certainty. The other represented the line of protest. It was a very thin line in the days when, for ages, almost the only learned people in all Christendom were the clergy. It contained some who felt for something like its full force the real humanity of Jesus. But these were, and not merely on the terms of the others, but even on their own terms, fain to wonder about his diety. For ages, the Church gave itself to a dogma, officially declared orthodox, of two natures yet one person forever. It eliminated from its communion those who thought to find an actual fusion of the two natures into one nature, those, namely, who were then called Monophysites, or again, those who declared that this person with two natures had, nevertheless, one will. These were called Monothelites. What wonder if the Christ of dogma became a mysterious figure before whom, indeed, men's souls bowed in adoration. They felt that only thus could the full truth and power of the Christian religion be maintained. Perhaps, and this most commonly, they felt that this was a mystery about which the clergy only could know anything. What wonder if in the liberty of thought which, indeed, in later generations has been claimed by many, but by no means availed of by all, the Christ became a wholly mysterious figure, to whom functions and attributes were assigned and of whom deeds were asserted which yet lifted him out of any possible historic connection. Or else, and this especially in the sequence of the age of rationalism, this benign and sublime figure, shorn practically of all transcendent meaning, was reduced to the stature of a good teacher and a worthy example for men.

In simple truth, it is not so much that we are, all of us now, I suppose, more or less instinctively inclined in our philosophy to a monistic view instead, at all events, of the old stark dualism which so long prevailed. It is not so much this, I should say, which leads us to review in our minds the statement of the relation of Jesus to God. And yet it must be owned that the holding of a view under which the universe is a unity, and God and man, in the highest aspect of man's nature are obviously one, has rendered our escape from the ancient dilemma somewhat easier. A philosophical review, however, does not go to the root of the matter. Christianity is not a philosophy. Religion is not a metaphysic. The real reason lies deeper than that. It lies, rather, in the fact that our whole conception of salvation is altered. Therewith are altered our conceptions both of the Saviour and the saved. We do not now think of salvation in terms which once prevailed in the Greek Church, a sense which is quite obvious in some of the most famous of the Fathers. This was the sense of some sort of union in essence—that was the phrase—of the redeemed man with God, which union in essence was to be fulfilled when life is over. "Man's becoming God," the ancient phrase ran. This phrase some of the Fathers used, I suppose, in some mystical sense, "God became man in order that man might become God." Or, again, we do not think of salvation, as often in the mediaeval Church, as a conferment, a benefit, almost externally bestowed, a reward, or, with others, a consequence of election in the inscrutable goodness of God. It was the alteration of our relation to God, or, at all events, the change of God's disposition toward us, in view of the merit and satisfaction of our Redeemer Jesus Christ. It was like an acquittal—only not like an acquittal, in that it was conferred upon those who had been guilty, but whose guilt God in his mercy passed over. It was imputing to us, even now, of Christ's righteousness—a phrase which some Protestants almost down to our own time have gloried in using. And then, by consequence, it was also our entrance into a heaven of bliss by and by. We no longer think of salvation as something so simply wrought out on our behalf. It is not a favor granted to us in view of something which someone else has done. And, frankly, we are simply unable to think of righteousness as imputed to anybody. Whatever else might be imputed, it could not be rightness in ourselves. We feel that this is a contradiction in terms.

We cannot think of blessedness as simply prepared for us. We have to think of ourselves as prepared for blessedness, and this by a measure of blessedness which we now actually share. We cannot think of our being supremely and eternally blessed, unless we are in ourselves prepared in some slight measure, or at least preparing, to be blessed. When we put it in these words, we see how far an interpretation inherited from the mediaeval Church and descending to us from classical Protestantism no longer avails. For some of us still living and writing, precisely such language, I might justly say, was used in unforgettable moments of our bewildered experience. I withdraw the word bewildered, because in our perfect love and trust of our parents, we were not bewildered.

We trusted their superior wisdom for that which we owned we did not understand. We were quite sure that they understood. But we should long since have been hopelessly bewildered, perhaps brought to the rejection of the high matter concerned, if we had not in the meantime, in sad struggle maybe, or in the serener process of our own maturing, found ourselves able to revise those terms. I speak from experience. I understand that the rudiment, the bare point of departure of my religious life had been conferred upon me. But just so, the point of departure of my physical life was conferred upon me by my parents. Just so, my mental life was, not quite so obviously, and yet in large measure, conferred upon me by my teachers. I am not in error when I say that my religious life at its beginnings was in some measure conferred upon me by others—again, I should say, by my parents. But at these levels, it is not once and for all that such conferments take place. It is a process continuous, ever repeated, by the good and wise of all ages, by the saints and Christ, through the spirit of God given to them, and even to us. The grand phrase "father in God" carries the image still further. Yet in all of these respects, it has been, it is, and it will be, not a mere conferment. It must be, and more and more it has been, my life. It is I who live it, physically, mentally, spiritually. I live, and in those great words of Paul, if I may take them to myself, "I live by the faith of him who loved me and gave himself for me." But it is I who live. We cannot think of inward and spiritual life as conferred on us in any other terms than those. I think with unspeakable gratitude of all the varied and good impulses which have come to me. I think that this recognition should have been far greater than it ever has been. But I am able to think of no reward, and least of all a reward from the all-knowing God, for what I have not tried to be and do. In fact, I do not like to think of it as reward, at all. It is just living recognition of a life which is my life.

We think of Jesus as of one in whom all of this which we strive rather vainly to describe, toward which we struggle in a far off way, was more complete, more truly realized, more effective both for himself and other men. But just so, men and women whom we have known have been in their measure effective in such transfusion of their life into us, such translation of our life into the life of others. We think of Jesus as the one among men in whom God, as the secret of character and power, as the soul of life, lived in a fullness in which he does not live in us, and in which we may be ready to believe that he has lived in none other. We think of him as one who also has called us in God, or, if you choose, through whom God calls us, to know for ourselves, as best we can, the kind of life which he has lived. We think of him in the direction in which that phrase of the Epistle to the Hebrews points when it says, "God, having of old time . . . by divers portions"—note the words, "divers portions"—"spoken unto the fathers in the prophets . . . hath at the end of these days spoken to us in his Son." We think of him as one who prayed that his disciples might be one in God even as he himself was "one with the Father." We think of him as one who, without stepping for one instant outside the loved, the familiar, touching, glorious relations of the normal human life, yet incarnated God—if we can loose ourselves from an inherited interpretation of that word —realized in his own time and place an ideal of man, demonstrated the unity of the spirit of man with God, in a measure that none of mankind whom we have known has done. He called men to the realization of themselves in God. He makes us believe in God as, primarily, and for the needs of our souls, the infinite reach of that holiness and love, that spiritual power of which we have intimation, example in the best of men. These have been prophetic spirits, sacrificers of themselves on behalf of others, servants of great ideals, advocates of eternal purposes of good, at all times and everywhere.

And, after all, is not this exactly what most of us now actually do? We think of God in the concrete terms of Jesus Christ, his life, his character, his purposes, his death, which, after all, was only the inevitable fulfillment of his life. This he himself surely came to see as his life went on, although we can almost see, at one moment in the Gospels, the struggle which that recognition cost him. We do not any longer think of Jesus in terms of an abstract view of God. If we substract the real man Jesus from this vision of God, nothing remains except perhaps preconceived notions of God or, at the best, abstractions which may be philosophy but are certainly not religion. This is perhaps one reason why not all philosophers are religious men, and why some very simple people, not philosophers at all, are religious men. We seek to establish a definition of God—if we must have a definition—in terms of what Jesus has been to the world, and more intimately still, of what he is to our own souls. We seek to make earnest with the proposition that it is through Jesus that we best know God. We can approach an understanding of Jesus because he is so eminently human. Beyond a certain point, we do not wholly understand him, because he laid hold of something which men do not themselves attain. When gods of the Greeks for a time became men, it was often for very problematical purposes. But even of Bodhisattvas, it is related that they deferred their entrance upon bliss in order that they might preach the saving gospel to men. Pascal said in words which are positively startling in the great mystic, "Christ is the God of men." Glover, in a passage quoted, by the way, by Archbishop Söderblöm, and in language quite colloquial said, "God could not do better than to be like Christ." Certainly a whole trend of modern theology has for its unconscious impulse, and sometimes for its explicit mission, to emphasize that we have to think of God in terms of Christ, reversing the age-long effort to think of Christ in terms of God. It was perhaps Schleiermacher who marked out the path which we here tread as we approach the spiritual magnitude of the person of Christ and, may I not add, as we approach through Christ the immeasurably greater mystery of God. All personality is mysterious. The influence of one man upon another, the influence of a woman upon a man, of a child upon them both, is at bottom a great mystery. "The secret things"—which are the determinant things—"belong unto the Lord our God," as the Scriptures long ago said. Into them, even as they enter into man's life here upon earth, the vision of man does not penetrate very far. How much more must that be true of God's possession of a soul and a soul's possession of God. Most of all would this be true of God's possession of the soul of Jesus and of Jesus' possession of God. Surely that is clear about which alone we are concerned, or, for that matter, that which alone we are able to allege. This oneness of Christ with God lies out upon a line along which we can see at least a little way. It lies out upon a line along which we can certainly say of some men and women whom we have known that they were at one with God, and this without ceasing for a moment to be men and women, blessing us through their lives and spirit here upon the earth. It lies out along the line of small salvations which our souls have already experienced, or are, at least, in process of experiencing. We own the depths of the mystery. But are not all of these things mysterious?

And now what have we done? If we were right in that which we said above, there is scarcely anything more wonderful in the history of thought than is the way in which the great body of Christian men have held, all these ages, to the conviction that Jesus was in some sense one with God. And yet the whole apparatus of reflection—and the theory of the universe within which we moderns move much more than did ever any of our predecessors—not merely gave them, but also gives us, no rational interpretation of that assumption. On the contrary, it made a rational interpretation extremely difficult, and to some, impossible. It is the most magnificent example of what I have in another place called the prophetic quality of real religion. It is the power of forecast from out the deep places of men's souls of that which men do not yet rationally think, but some day in the progress of the life of humanity they will think. So here, at our most crucial point, that, namely, of the conception of salvation, and with that, the conception of a Saviour, both old philosophies and our inherited theologies have made for us the approach to the problem of Christ, as we now see it, supremely difficult. "As we now see it" is, however, the saving clause for the reasonableness of our argument. Because, to our own ancestors, these arguments of ours would not have seemed conclusive. And, conversely, arguments advanced against the traditional position in the spirit of the age of rationalism were felt to be destructive. In some cases they really were that. The slow modification of views concerning the nature of Scripture itself, the prevalence of historical feeling as to dogma, the new orientation of philosophy since Kant, the rise of the sciences of nature, all make for us approach to the Christological problem different from that which was natural to our ancestors. It is one of the qualifications of a quiet mind to be able to put one's self back into a state of things in which, in a given discussion, certain factors essential for us had not yet even emerged. One needs, if he would be just to men with whom he no longer agrees, but who were in some cases more widely learned than most of us, to be conscious of this fact. That remark is certainly true of some of the greatest of the divines of the seventeenth century. The spectacle is not altogether edifying now, the reproaching of great men of their own time on the basis of an advance in the intellectual life of the race for which we ought not to be boastful, and are certainly in but small degree responsible.

The spectacle is still less edifying if one feels that, even with a theological view which we can no longer share, there was combined a zeal for God and religion which opponents, either then or now, do not always share. It is a pity to have an assortment of most modern views and to lose the sense of what religion is through being too ardent to refute old views of it. It is not that we have set aside the earlier effort of the ages of Christian men to combine these two polar conceptions of the universe, the thought of God, on the one hand, and of man on the other —to approach these, I say, until in the person of Jesus, the Light of the world, it flashes upon us and blinds us while it shines. It is not, I say, that we have desisted, or can desist from this effort. Too much that is vital depends upon it. It is only that we have marked out for ourselves with decision a new approach to it. It is mainly that we now clearly see that what we have to deal with in one, the major one, of our terms is not an abstraction. It is not a definition of God. It is God himself who can be known to men in this relation only as he gives himself to men, and as he gave himself, for aught that we can see, in incomparable fashion to Jesus. It is only that our minds rest, primarily at least, upon those things in God in which he is and must be comparable to man, and not upon those things in him whereof one might truly say with the prophet, "To whom will ye liken God, or with what likeness will ye compare him?" It is only that we do say with confidence that into this mystery of the transcendent God as he is in himself, Jesus of Nazareth gives us, or rather, Jesus of Nazareth is, the farthest reach of which we know. He gives us the truest clue. He is the best guide whom men have. When we bring the two magnitudes together, God is in our comparison not the abstraction with which men have struggled in the hopeless endeavor to make it match with the human traits of the Man of Nazareth. Quite the contrary. God is that toward which the soul of Jesus went out in a measure which surpassed, we may suppose, the measure of any other man. That leaves it open to us to say that God is the soul to which our souls go out, to be sure, in a far off way, but it is the same God to whom the soul of Jesus went out, and found, in a measure which transcends anything we know of other men. It is the God which he discloses whom we, too, can find in our feebler way and, finding, shall be saved—from ourselves. We must truthfully say that there is much, very much, concerning God, which we should like to know which Jesus does not tell us. But in the light of his character, and for the needs of our own souls in our struggle for character, for our entrance upon a different life, begun here and now, Jesus with his life and word and work are enough. These things are as sure as such things can ever be. There is much else that we do not now need to know.

I have made no secret of saying that the terms of

much of traditional doctrine which we, some of us, inherited seem to me now remote. The truth is that for the mode of our approach to the problem many other things that have been said and believed by devoted Christian men seem now unnecessary for us to believe. We do not disguise from ourselves the consequences which this new approach to the problem may have for some parts of the traditional dogma. But was not the traditional dogma, built up in ancient times, and repaired in modern times, worked out in defense against ancient and also modern views which we share even less than we share the views with which our fathers' faith identified itself? We are not blind to the fact that from this new center, if it proves to be such, a reconstruction of theology may proceed. The only response to that, which I know to make, is that reconstruction is, in any case, proceeding, and has been proceeding for some time. It is for us only to say whether we will aid that work or resist it. We realize with every generous impulse that in this effort we are not separated from some from whom, in our inheritance, we should once have thought ourselves separated. We are not unaware of contributions to this reconstruction which are now being made from every side, and of the prophecy which is therein contained of unifications in Christendom, with the forgetting of controversies about which nothing is so obvious as this, that on their own terms they are already obsolete. For all of this we may give thanks. I think, however, that we may say in all good conscience that we are contending for the same truth concerning the relation of Jesus to God for which, in ways which to us seem no longer feasible, our fathers in Christendom for unnumbered generations have stood. Even that, however, is of no great consequence, except perhaps to people who still linger in a more or less controversial and, perhaps I might add, to those who still linger in a more or less dependent state of mind. What is of far greater consequence is that we may feel that we have conserved for ourselves that which is characteristic of the Christian faith, that which has in it the power of God for the salvation of men, through the revelation of God which Jesus was, and is.

2. OF THE INTUITION OF IMMORTALITY

The fulfillment of the spiritual life of man presents, in some respects, a rather obvious contradiction to some of the laws of life in this world. The fulfillment of the intellectual life presents in another way the same contrast. It is perhaps these contrasts and contradictions which furnish the basis for the age-long and world-wide intuition concerning a further life which it seems to be open to humanity alone to choose. It is, therefore, of reasoned conviction that we speak, at this point, of the faith of immortality. In light of the nature of our knowledge, what we have to say falls between what we have said concerning Jesus, as manifestation of the spirit of God, and that which we have still to say concerning God, the Eternal Spirit of all good. We approached the figure of Jesus, so far as possible, from the human side. It is clear that he was true man, "very man," as the creeds say. Yet in him dwelt in fullness a spirit which is not of man alone. It is clear to us that the Gospels are narrative as this would have been written by men of approximately his own time. The testimony upon which they rest is that of men of his own race, and mainly of companions of his ministry. What they narrate is in the light of a Messianic expectation which was the background of their inheritance, as also of his. There are also intuitions of theirs concerning the Master, and amazing intuitions of the Master himself. These grew upon his fellows in their converse with him. There were also intuitions which grew upon him in the course of his career, quite evidently transforming his expectations. They caused natural hopes of the success of his endeavor to deepen into the conviction that the achievement of it would involve the supreme sacrifice. There are moments which appear to reveal the inner life of the Master himself which hint such an interpretation. It is not beyond question that some such revulsion took place in the minds of those who loved him. It is true that in the last moments of his presence with them it was asked of him, almost naïvely, "Wilt thou at this time restore the kingdom unto Israel?" And yet, the proclamation which they courageously took up, of the Gospel as for all mankind, rests upon the apprehension that the kingdom was to be something widely different from that which they themselves had earlier thought. It would be a realm of men of the Master's Spirit.

It seems quite clear that we can speak of immortality upon the basis of intuition only. Intuition is that which goes beyond our reasoning in the direction in which our reasoning has gone furthest. Frankly, for myself at least, I interpret the resurrection narratives as the visualization in terms natural to the disciples, as indeed to others of their time, of the intuition that the spirit of Jesus could not die. The work in the spirit which he had begun in the flesh could not end. Rather, it would take new beginning. In the great word of the apostle, death had "no more dominion over him." But whether the words of the Gospels are to be interpreted in this way or in some other way makes no great difference. It is interpretation in any case. Naturally no man among us will feel that his faith in immortality rests solely upon the testimony of the Gospels as to apparitions of Jesus in the flesh. Rather, this is probably true, that his belief in this testimony, if he has it, rests upon the faith of immortality. For many among us in whom that faith lives at the present day, it is fairly sure that they hold it as an intuition. It is a part of their interpretation of what is best in life. It seems to imply that which is still better. At the risk of a momentary repetition, let me say that I regard intuition as a perfectly natural functioning of the human mind. It is quite obviously the normal functioning in children who sometimes amaze us by their insight into people or situations. It is also the manner of judgment of many adults who have not had much of what we rather conventionally call education. Wider training of the rational sort, preoccupation with areas of learning and experience in provinces of life to which rational activity is the proper approach, alter the proportions in significant ways. It is quite proper, even necessary, that they should. But there are relations of a wide and, in the large sense, most reasonable life in which it is a tragedy, and sometimes even a comedy, if a self-conscious and perhaps destructive rationality completely takes the place of instinct and intuition. This is because in the higher areas of the affections, and in the areas of moral perception, intuition reasserts itself. It is no wonder that men almost universally in past ages, and occasionally even now, think of these intuitions as no part of the normal functioning of mind. They have asserted that intuitions of this sort came directly from God. They were inspirations in the sense in which that word has frequently been used almost down to our own times. Yet, in our sense of intuition, oracles, soothsaying, were not always a mere pretense. They were sometimes extraordinarily wise fetches into the truth, only that they were assumed to be of supernatural origin. Instead, they were, as we view them, perfectly natural functioning of the mind in areas where such functioning may be more farseeing than men's usual rationality. The traditional view of the inspiration of the Bible is a classic example of this sort. Mutual exclusiveness of the thought of the rational, on the one hand, and of the spiritual on the other, has been one of the unhappy consequences of this error of judgment.

It is true that the claims for the rational were at one time rather strident. But it is by some people overlooked that the claims of the supernatural have been also at times rather strident. What is important for us to recognize is that in the history of the individual, as also, manifestly, in the history of the race, the intuitional precedes the rational. But it also takes up the thread again. It seconds and succeeds the rational, confirming highest hopes and supporting noblest endeavors, long after the clear sense of demonstrability has passed. This is part of the history of a normal mind. In a new and large sense, perhaps a strange sense, we do take hold of the divine. Or rather, in a sense which is quite plain to us, the divine takes hold upon us. Intuition is the manner in which a balanced, teachable reason itself lays hold upon the transcendent. It is useless to appeal to intuition unless one takes intuition to be the "equivalent of the larger reason," forecast of that which for noblest reasons we find it necessary to believe. Intuition is not the flight into vague desires. Rather, it is sober intimation of that which has, indeed, yet to be proved, but to which the best of our reasoning points. It is something which transcends our present reasoning, based as this must be either upon experience or else upon abstract principles. But it is a faith which our present reasoning sustains so far as this can go. The supreme evidence for God is the sense in which our souls, at their best, demand something which goes beyond ourselves, and the glorifying influence upon life which that now confers, is the rational evidence.

Jesus died, as we have said, in utter trust of immortality. His life-long teaching, his whole living, had implied that conviction. He assumed that faith in his disciples. Yet it is not as if his own race had always held that view. Quite the contrary. The feeling for the tribe, as people of God, would seem to have been for ages preponderant with the Jews. The conviction of the perpetuity of the people, with the sense of having been chosen of God for a great mission, had sufficed. This view held its own apparently for ages along with, in later time, the growing faith as to the future of the individual soul. Perhaps it is to this priority of the race consciousness, with the relatively slow emergence of faith in individual immortality, that we may refer the prominence in Jesus' own time of the Sadducean party. Sadducees are constantly mentioned in the New Testament along with Pharisees. These last were certainly a religious party in the sense in which we understand those words. But Sadducees also debated with Jesus. In the Gospels they are explicitly said to have denied the resurrection of the dead. Schürer amplifies that statement into denial of personal immortality, and with this, of course, of retribution in a future life. Jesus' own argument, "God is not the God of the dead but of the living," is quite clearly an appeal to intuition. But it is not argument at all. Intuition is of the individual. Those would believe it—who believed it. Moreover, this intuition touched mainly the present and the future of the individual. It would not be likely to have great weight with those whose thought was upon the past, and that preponderantly the past, proud and also sad, of the nation as such. When we look into the prophets, especially the later ones, what we find is intuition, which yet, if we may so say, "reasoned of righteousness and of judgment to come." It is the awakening of the moral consciousness. It is the arraignment of the individual. It is the demand of repentance and renewal of the soul, as the primary condition of the recovery of character of the nation, and so, of the fulfillment of its mission in the world. This was the conviction in which Jesus lived. It is sometimes, in his preaching, as if it dawned upon him with inexpressible pain that his people, in failing to advance beyond their proud sense of the divine call of their nation, had rendered that call itself impossible of fulfillment. "Behold, your house is left unto you desolate." This it was which became one of the sources of his ever-deepening sense of mission to the whole world. It was the ground of his hope for the whole world, if men would hear his word. His injunction was that his gospel was to be preached to all the world. And more resolutely than all the rest, Paul took that thought of mission to himself, and more or less separated himself from the pillar apostles in so doing.

It may be interesting at this point to compare this faith in personal immortality, of the dominance of which, in the period of the prophets, we have just spoken, with speculative approaches to the same problem of the continued life of the soul, which have come down to us from the Greeks. Both Plato and Aristotle reasoned, each in characteristic fashion, upon this problem. Both belonged to a period not widely remote from the time of the flowering of prophecy among the spiritually-minded of the Jews, in other words, the growing currency of convictions which became the inheritance of Jesus. The period of the emergence in confidence of these prophecies of immortal hope for the individual man was also, approximately, the period of loftiest speculation on this same subject on the part of the Greeks. The Greeks were a race greatly gifted in directions in which Jews were not characteristically gifted at all. We realize how relatively small was the interval of time between, let us say, the second Isaiah and Socrates. And, for us modern men, the interval of space would have seemed to be almost nothing at all. Those two sentences bring home to us, however, how different was the ancient world from the world of our time. Races had pursued, in the main, the lines of their own development until, in fleeting way, the empire of Alexander began the work which, under the Roman Empire, made the Near East with the Western world and all its races permanently one. We go back to Plato and Aristotle for the first great discussion, at all events for the Western world, of the continued life of the spirit, and this viewed as a philosophical problem. Plato assumed pre-existence of the soul, its heavenly origin. He links this with the eternal or divine life of reason. To a certain extent the mystical and aesthetic element dominates in Plato. The disinterestedness of virtue is one of his favorite themes. The serenity of his outlook is characteristic. Everybody knows how Plato uses Socrates as the speaker in many of his profoundest reflections. Few can read them without wondering how much of what is said is Socrates and how much is Plato. But one of the most famous passages bearing upon our theme is this. After the elaborate myth of judgment at the close of the "Gorgias," Plato turns at once to the practical lesson, putting the words upon the lips of Socrates: — "I, then, Callicles, am persuaded of the truth of these things, and I consider how I shall present my soul whole and undefiled before the Judge in that day. Renouncing the honors at which the world aims, I desire only to know the truth and to live as well as I can, and when I die, to die as well as I can." With

Aristotle, we are positively amazed to find that he takes his departure from what we should call biological facts—of course, in his own apprehension of those facts. The soul is the life principle. It is the fulfillment of the body. Whether of all bodies, he does not say. But he distinguishes different levels of function. The function of reason is found in man alone. He says there are many things visible to the mind alone. And some are felt by the soul alone. But it must be owned that the full meaning of Aristotle's doctrine has divided his commentators ever since.

We can but think of the contrast between the sacred literatures of Moslems and of Christians. It is the contrast with Scriptures of a book which is, in largest part, the work of one man, a man of supreme genius, indeed, but without other elements of large cultivation such as even his own world would have counted that. Mohammed was a man of the people, a camel driver. He was moved to revolt from the religion of both Jews and Christians, as he saw them. He was overmastered by the feeling that those religions had nothing to say to his people. But one has only to mention Bagdad and Cordova to be convinced that the Moslem faith did produce, in time, a life of the mind and a civilization in the world which a man like Frederick II held superior to the mind and civilization of Christendom. The learning of the Moorish period in Spain, which was also the place and time of a great expression of the insight of the Jewish race, shone with a brighter light than did much of the Christian learning of the time. It was combated not by learning but, one might say, by the last and bitterest of the Crusades, under Ferdinand and Isabella, just before the discovery of America. Men then also, particularly the Jews among them, fostered the faith in immortality and used Aristotle in so doing. Meantime the scholastics, basing their teaching also largely upon Aristotle, taught that the rational soul was especially created of God and infused into the organism, either at the moment of conception or at a given point in the embryonic history. The implications of it are, of course, different. With the schoolmen, so nearly as we can understand, the soul neither grows nor decays with the body. It gradually unfolds its nature and capacities. Yet there is a sense in which to us, the coming into being of the rational soul, the self-conscious spirit, is the greatest mystery of the universe. In Paul's word, "There is a natural body and there is a spiritual body, a glory of the terrestrial and a glory of the celestial." But growth must be of man's own free decision, apparently, in the life of the man who deliberately chooses to put spiritual things before temporal things.

The growing rigor with which Protestants viewed the doctrine of the inspiration of Scripture hindered the advance, in those circles, of opinions which would have been—and for others were—the natural consequence of the revival of learning. Emphasis upon the word of Scripture had been originally intended to set men free from the authoritarianism of the Roman Church. It ended in setting up an authoritarianism as immovable and, perhaps we might say, even more immovable, than the claim of the authority of the Church. The Infallibility Decree of the Vatican Council in 1870 has never had the same effect upon the Roman Church which the teaching of the infallibility of the Scriptures had upon almost three centuries of Protestantism. And one result of the stiffening of the views of those who adhered to religion was inevitably the hardening of the views of those who dissented. The length to which deists and rationalists and, ultimately, atheists went in contradiction of what they took to be the faith, may be explained in good measure in this way. After Locke, free discussion, say, of our own problem of immortality, grew less among men committed to the Christian cause and ever greater among those who separated themselves from this, or from any religion at all. We came over the threshold of the nineteenth century with much this same antithesis. The rise of the sciences, with ultimately the doctrine of evolution, continued the same radical separation. In the single matter of which I am just now speaking, the view of the authority of the very words of Scripture certainly played for a time a decisive part. For some it plays that part even to the present day. The Scriptures were declared to say one thing and the doctrine of evolution another. Of course, many Christians now believe in evolution. The advance of man from the lower, and so far as we can see from the lowest, levels of animal life entails a view that mankind has come very slowly into the possession of a soul such as we now think of when we use that word. Soul, too, has been evolved with the higher life of man, and the higher life of man has been evolved with the ever greater ascendancy of the soul. This disposes of the view which has obtained in one way or another practically all the way from Plato to our own time, the view, namely, that the soul was conferred upon man by a special act of God. It would seem, on the other hand, to go further than any other thought to explain why man has evolved beyond the beasts which were without question his progenitors. By that same token, it presents to us the thought that the living soul may be that part of man by which, in its evolution as soul, men may pass beyond the conditions of life as we now know these. There may be a life of the spirit, which we have but scant means of representing to ourselves. And yet we do actually see that men who give free rein to the guidance of their souls, apart from the thoughts and endeavors of many of their fellows, are thus enabled to lay hold on things which are not alone higher than the objects of desire of primitive men. They are higher also than the objects of some men who walk the streets with us and live side by side with us and partake with us, and we with them, in many of the endeavors of life. It leaves us also with the question whether those whom we sometimes think of as neglecting, despising, forsaking their souls, have outlook for a life in the spirit.

The rise of the sciences, with the giving to man also his place in the long evolution of living beings, poses for us a question quite different from any of those which earlier solutions fit. It implies something of which Aristotle seems never to have dreamed. We do gather out of the process of human evolution, unimaginably long as our fathers would have thought, something about the progress of the race. That progress has been tragic, pathetic, glorious. We do gather faith and hope—if we are of those who can look at it with hope. It drives to despair those who can despair. But all such reflections seem better to fit the problem of the race, and we are thinking of the problem of the individual. The progress of mankind seems to make the world a better place for the good and a worse place for the bad. Even that sentence calls for instant qualification. Whom do we mean by the good? Do we not mean those who dedicate themselves to ideal ends and with these, of course, to the good of others? Yet no inconsiderable portion of our own fellows would call that the bad or, at least, whatever their assertions, their lives would seem to show that they considered it bad for themselves. They are willing that others should dedicate themselves to ideal goods and altruistic ends—and pay the price, as, of course, they must. In different words, those who largely get—and also fail to get—the good they seek out of this life and world—being such as these are—are such as care little, and grow to care less, for that which some other men mean by the good, the good, namely, of man's soul, of morals and spirit, and of the world of other men. These latter live for ideals of character for themselves and of the welfare and character of others. They feel that these ideals can be best fulfilled in a life of fidelity to truth and goodness, even at all costs. The goods of this world are best, or perhaps they can then only be called really good, when they contribute to, can be utilized for, things which are better still. Such men are in the world, perhaps in the very best sense, but, as was said, they are not exactly of it. They make their own world. The world does not make them. They are not subordinated to life. They subordinate life to themselves. The moral issues of life, the spiritual interpretations of life, these are really the life of those of whom we speak. We have all known men and women of whom something like that was true. This was their most real life. To some it was their whole life. If they have possessions, they use them for such ends. If they have not possessions, they use that fact to further their ideal of life and to convince their fellows that they still have an inestimable benefit to confer, namely, the highest sense of what this life is for. They are sons of God while they are still truly men, indeed, we might say that they are the truest among the sons of men. The riches that they are beggar any riches which they may have or, conversely, may not have. No poverty of outward life stands in the way of fulfillment of their purpose. It is the richness of their inner life which gives them direction and achievement. Their aspiration is for more life of this sort for themselves and more men who live it. These people go out of life shining souls. Some others seem to go out of life after finding that there was not much in life after all. And, strange as it may seem, that is ordinarily the verdict, upon these particular lives, of their fellow men as well. The type of which we are speaking is at bottom the type which monasticism in its great exemplars, both men and women, once set before the world. Only, they thought that it was necessary to go out of the world in order to live such lives. Perhaps sometimes it was so, then. But certainly among us a more potent example still is to set those same high purposes before ourselves and others while we remain in the world of men and things. That is an absolutely characteristic word of Paul concerning Jesus, "as poor, yet making many rich"—so rich that he could afford to be poor.

Men and women of the type of which I speak prompt us to believe that there is something beyond this life. Or, to put it better still, they prompt us to believe that there is more in this life than we had believed. Some of the humblest people in the world are those who most convince us of this truth. But is that argument? No. It is intuition, pure and simple. It is perhaps an intuition active in moral natures, and carrying along with it those who have been awakened to nobler issues. It is, for substance, that we find it impossible to believe that the most selfless life, the life set on highest things, comes to the same end with the most self-centered life, set on its own self-indulgence and its devotion to merely passing things. But why should the best things, even in this world—and also some things about which it may well be doubted whether they are the best things—come only to those who fulfill the conditions inherent in those things? This is especially true, if all the condition which is asked be just a state of mind, a life regulated by an impulse of which we are unable to think except as, in itself, a blessing both to the man himself and to other men, as well. All of which, in its beginning, at all events, I say again, is pure intuition. It gathers its evidence afterward. They have it who have it. They lack it who lack it. And perhaps no argument except the argument of radiant example brings it home to those to whom it once seemed foreign. In that respect it is like a great many other intuitions. That which seems in principle an abandonment of one world, which is close at hand and very attractive, comes to seem to those who take the step, to be the entrance upon another world of life, a life by which, as the saints have always said, heaven overlaps the earth.

On the margin of this central contention are many other questions about which, to my feeling, one who knows the limits of knowledge can enter only cautiously, if at all. But, at all events, it will hardly be denied that this is the heart of the question about immortality. I shall not be misunderstood as saying but that a life lived in this spirit, devoted to the highest things and the service of others in the interest of those things, has not its reward in this world too. I think it does. But it is a reward to those who care for this reward. I think even that I have known men who worked for their world in this spirit who felt themselves already rewarded beyond their desert, even if they contemplated no further reward. I think I feel that if any souls are worthy—I will not say of reward, I am rather sorry that I used that word—but, let us say, worthy of continuance of their devoted life, it will be the souls of those who have shown how desirable it would be that such lives should be continued. And some have worked for their world in this spirit even while they showed that their minds were not dwelling very much, and perhaps not at all, upon the problem of immortality. I will not say how much of the content and consummation of such a life imagination may have been able to point out for us. In that, I fear, much depends upon the quality of men's imagination. The forms of imagination change from age to age. Witness Homer in the eleventh book of the "Odyssey," or Vergil in the sixth book of the "Aeneid," Jesus in rhapsodic passages of our Gospels, Dante in his "Paradiso," or Milton in his "Paradise Regained." Forms of imagination change, as I have said. That may be, while conviction of the underlying truth does not change. That which happens to sinners is generally more picturesque than what happens to saints. Perhaps that says something about ourselves. The forms which the expression of it take have generally been poetical, artistic, which is often the appropriate, and perhaps even the necessary, form which intuitions do take. It may be philosophical for those who have talent for such expression. It may be just the serene conviction of people who are neither poets nor philosophers, but who are confident that the view by which they seem to have got the best out of this life, even as it is, and despite all its contrarieties and their sufferings, will not put them to shame.

It is not unworthy of note that the five great poetical visions of the future to which I have referred, have all of them this common trait, that the world of the lost is so much more interesting to us than the world of the saved. That is an observation which might lead to a cynical view. It is, I suppose, that life, as we live it and see it lived, lends more material to the imagination of the state of the lost. That might be only another way of saying that it is so because we are what we are. The race has not got any further than it has. But in point of character, we are fairly sure of the type of character to which we may attribute the fact that the world has got even so far as it has. Even those who might dispute this generalization would at least admit that Dante's description of hell is minatory, that his description of purgatory is rather insipid, and that his description of paradise took color from the notions of his time, although he was so overwhelmingly the greatest man of his time and one of the greatest of all time. Certainly there is the same contrast between Milton's "Paradise Lost" and his "Paradise Regained." One would do well to remember the text, "Eye hath not seen nor ear heard, neither hath it entered into the heart of man to conceive those things which God hath prepared for them that love him." Those are words of Paul. And if we are thinking of the other side of it, the same Paul said that "they who live after the flesh shall of the flesh reap corruption." Perhaps for our own anticipation we might take a leaf out of our own normal experience. The reward of faithfulness, as we see it, is to have more things to which to be faithful. Until, at least, our present powers have begun to wane, the great reward of having done something is to have more to do, more responsibility to bear. We count that our best reward in anything that we have done. And perhaps it is inevitable that when we try to picture the future, either bad or good, we can do it in no terms except terms of which we know. But when we rest in the sense that there must be a future for those who live nobly, or when perhaps we forego the pleasure, which is sometimes also a pain, of picturing what it may well be like, then we more simply rest in the confidence that unless life is a hopeless enigma—which we cannot believe—something worthier will be—perhaps that is the best form in which we can picture our faith in immortality. It is certainly the form in which some of the best men and women whom we know devote their lives here and now, in faithfulness, in any case, in a trust which their lives continually justify, and in a hope which may be better than any picture which we can make of it. Even meantime they seem to have got the best out of life.

3. OF GOD

We have spoken of Jesus as, we hold, the supreme manifestation of God as spirit in the life of man. That life of the spirit in the Man of Galilee we approached, in so far as seemed possible, from the side of history. The sources of our information in this sense are, of course, the documents known as the Gospels. Jesus' life, even more than his words, bears witness to that indwelling spirit. His influence upon the world from his day to ours bears the same witness. That, too, is history. We have spoken also of the hope of immortality as intuition. Such was the faith and hope of Jesus. It was the trust of many of his contemporaries. Indeed, it had become the trust of prophets. It has remained the trust of Christians. Yet it was a trust not undisputed by some thinkers of Jesus' own generation. These put a different interpretation upon the prophets. It was a point upon which philosophers who were not of his nation also reasoned. These reasonings, as well, have become a part of the inheritance of the world of thought. Indeed, back of all this, so far as we can trace religious apprehensions at all, this of a future life, in some sense, had apparently been one. But with all the evidence that we can gather for this belief, we have no witness which convinces us, and others, beyond this widespread, and perhaps we might say almost universal, intuition.

Concerning God, even as magnitude for our thought only, the case is different. From time immemorial, men have ascribed the origin and the governance of the world, and this far outside the world of human magnitudes and destinies, to gods or God. But we of the century just past are, of all men, least able to deny that our ideas of the manner of God's making of the world, and of his government of it, are different from the ideas upon these subjects which mankind has ever in all its long history accepted. And not merely is this true of our own planet and solar system. Our solar system itself now seems but a small affair compared with other systems and with the starry heavens as a whole. Moreover, not merely astronomy but geology also leads us to look upon the history of our earth in a manner very different from that of which even our own fathers thought. The evolution of the life of animals and of man shows greater marvels still. Within the memory of men still living, this state of things brought students of science, some of them, to feel that they could have no faith—not such, at least, as believers would require. Conversely, men of faith abjured science as almost equivalent to atheism. I marvel as I think how quickly that state of things has passed, for "erected spirits," upon either side of this great contention. If we are going to think of God in terms of creation and providence, of God as "our Creator, Preserver and Bountiful Benefactor," as the Prayer Book beautifully says, we have, at all events, to accustom ourselves to a meaning of all those words very different from that which the writers, beyond question, intended and our fathers in faith and love accepted.

In light of these things, we cannot say that the faith of God is altogether an intuition in the sense in which it may be reasonable to say that the hope of immortality is an intuition. God is much more than that. Nature and man give to our reason evidence of him. All of our ever-changing knowledge must find place in our conception of

God unless we are to leave either the intellectual life, or else belief in God behind us. Science, which represents our constantly enlarging knowledge of the world—and of ourselves as part of it—has, we claim, its place in our idea of God. This, therefore, cannot be the same idea of God which our fathers and mothers held and taught to us. No less, our knowledge of the whole history of mankind, on the side of its successive representations of God and of his working, must make its contribution also to our thought of God. Science, history, philosophy, as the reckoning with the reflection of mankind upon the highest human problems, all have place in the faith of cultivated men, or else, some must have no faith and some may have no enlarging cultivation. This modifies the forms in which we are able to hold even the intuition of God if, at the same time, we are to feel that the intuition is indefeasible. That intuition holds one side of man's nature unless, indeed, it is destroyed by his sense for intellectual integrity. Intuition holds us up to the connection with God of one side of the nature of our being. This not all our knowledge gives us. But this, again, not all our knowledge takes away from us, unless indeed we confound more naïve views of our unformed years, or the views of former generations in the history of mankind, with this intuition. Also, as we have often said in these pages, the intuition is not the same thing with its formulation. It is primarily of the intuition of God that I feel bound here to speak. It must be, however, quite evident that I claim neither that intuition voids our knowledge, nor does it excuse us for not seeking knowledge. On the other hand, the largest knowledge, and an ever-changing knowledge, is not incompatible with the life of the soul of which religion is the primary and indefeasible expression. Rather, I count that the life of the soul needs the knowledge and, conversely, advancing knowledge needs the life of the ever enlarging spirit which religion really is. This is true if men are to fulfill, on the one hand, their true and largest selves, and, on the other hand, to mold by their influence their age and the future of their fellow men. For the very reason that, upon us all, the age confers so much, we are under sacred obligation to achieve ever higher ends. I hope, however, that I have abundantly made plain that which we have often had occasion to remark, that it is useless to appeal to intuition except as equivalent to the larger reason.

One ponders the opening sentences of the ancient creeds, particularly of the Nicene and of the so-called Athanasian Creeds. One has the feeling how brief their introductory sentences are. "I believe in God, the Father Almighty, Maker of heaven and earth." One version of the Nicene Creed adds, "and of all things visible and invisible." That seems very little to say of God. Nothing is added except that he is the Father of our Lord Jesus Christ, of whom the Creed then proceeds to speak. The Athanasian Creed says at once:— "We worship one God in Trinity, and Trinity in Unity. For there is one Person of the Father. But the Godhead of the Father, of the Son and of the Holy Ghost is all one. Such as the Father is, such is the Son. The Father increate, incomprehensible, eternal, and yet not three Eternals, etc." Origen, who died nearly three-quarters of a century before Nicaea, had been in a measure in the stream of Greek speculation about God. But Origen had had to seek refuge in another see, and long after his death, was anathematized. The ancient Greeks had speculated much about God. Philo, an Alexandrine Jew, in Rome about the year 40 on some errand for his people, and who wrote in Greek, had also ventured into this area. He had even used the word *logos* to describe the revealer of the unknowable God. Epictetus and Plotinus speculated about God, Marcus Aurelius more sparingly. Yet in increasing measure all of them had viewed Christianity with hostility—or scarcely viewed it at all. It is true that the origins of Christianity were in Judaism, but by the time of Nicaea its constituency was widely cosmopolitan. Was the reticence of the creeds on the subject of God intended to avoid disputed topics? Christian Gnostics had shown to a demonstration that there were many disputed topics, and the more they were discussed, the more discussion there would be. Was it perhaps that the creeds were intended as well for the unlearned as for the learned? At all events, such are the facts. Later there came the period of the long decline of learning. This was the period of the spread of Christianity among the untutored races of the north and west of Europe which were to become the strength of Christendom. It is perhaps not surprising that speculation in the grand manner concerning God came again to take a foremost place only in the period of the Scholastics. It was in flower again in the time of Anselm's "Cur Deus Homo." It is in full fruit and potent seed in Aquinas. The Holy See in our lifetime, 1880, through Leo XIII, elevated Aquinas to be the pattern of reasoning concerning God —in a sense, the authorized Christian philosopher.

The Decrees of Trent had touched mainly upon topics of too immediate interest to enter upon this high course. The Renaissance had, indeed, stimulated both Catholics and Protestants, the latter especially, in their varied statements concerning God, his nature and works, with also providence and redemption. Yet the Protestant creeds, as official statements, were naturally largely confined to pregnant antitheses with Catholicism. Then, between the Reformation and ourselves, there passed over

Europe successive waves of philosophical endeavor, Deism, Rationalism and Positivism. Within our own century, there have been various efforts to find adjustment to the sciences of nature, of which the reformers knew little and the scholastics less. The inference to be drawn from all of this is not that God is not a problem for philosophy. But the fact is that Christianity has lived with many philosophies. That fact alone would seem to show that it is not identifiable with any philosophy. This is, however, only the same inference which we drew when we said that religion is not identifiable with any theology. Philosophy and theology are interpretations. Religion is the thing which is interpreted. Theology is, of course, more conscious that it is interpretation of an intuition, but it does tend toward rationalism. In fact, this may be said to be the *raison d'être* of theology. In so doing, it commits that which is ever living and mobile, religion, to that which is supposed to be permanent,—but which, for reasons of its own, proves not to be so. Philosophy, on the other hand, is fully conscious of itself as rationalization, and rationalization of many things besides religion. It also tends to obscure, or perhaps begins by obscuring, the intuitional element. Some philosophies, like the more self-conscious rationalism of the eighteenth century, had scant place for religion. Deism, although it called itself after God, left God largely unrecognizable. And Positivism, building only an annex for the service of man, proclaimed that to be religion. For psychology, it will be remembered also, that Comte had no place at all. In light of this, is it to be wondered at that the great theologies of the Reformation period seem now to some of us remote? In our day, studies of religion, and of many religions, have taken at least two new directions. They have addressed themselves to the critical and historical investigation of our own sacred literatures. They have engaged themselves also with comparison of other religions, theoretically, of all religions, with our own. With these have gone also studies of the applications of religion to life. Some of these are naturally applications to a life with which the reformers were not conversant, studies of the social implications and applications of religion in our own day. All this has had profound influence even upon the matter with which we are here immediately concerned, namely, the idea of God.

Moreover, the parallel of that which I here seek to describe has happened under our own eyes in another area. I mean that of the studies of the world of nature. These also have opened to us in amazing fashion in the last two generations. Men used to approach the study of nature also from the side of antecedent speculation. With some these speculations were philosophical. With others they were theological. Giordano Bruno had, indeed, anticipations of what we call the scientific movement, but parted company with tradition mainly upon philosophical grounds. Moreover, Bruno was burned at the stake. Galileo had much more perception of the new movement in the studies of nature but he, too, was silenced by the Church. He seems, nevertheless, to have declared that the earth does move. Successive generations found themselves in an inevitable conflict. The advancing knowledge of the sciences, almost from day to day, was giving us new notions as to nature and the processes of the universe. Time was, no longer ago than my own youth, when many conspicuous figures in the advance of science were openly opposed to religion. A still larger proportion were, at all events, indifferent. They found the theological explanations of nature no longer valid. That also has happily passed. This is, however, mainly because the theological interpretations of nature have passed. We approach the thought of God from the side of a real interpretation of nature itself, so far as we are even yet competent to that. Many men whose life has been given to investigation of nature find now no difficulty in believing in God. It is, however, a belief in God which can be correlated with knowledge of nature. Paley's "Natural Theology," or again, his "Evidences,"—with most of the books on the "Evidences of Christianity" which were read when we were in college—seem to us now among the most pathetically unnatural books which one could be called upon to read. I have a beautifully bound copy of Paley given out as a prize to an English Grammar School boy in 1837—one must suppose to guard his mind against the errors of science.

Contrast that with the open mind toward the results of scientific inquiry which characterizes the education of youth in our day. Contrast that with the frank and full expression of their own views of religion on the part of some of the most distinguished men of science in our day. In sum, what we find is that religion is, indeed, not identical with any theology, and perhaps still less with any philosophy. These latter are interpretations, each in its own way, yet even theology preponderantly in the intellectual area. That which they interpret is, however, an intuition which is at once more complex and also more simple than either. Both are justifiable in the effort to describe life as a whole. Neither is satisfactory when it forgets the specific quality of the thing which is being described. Both seek abstraction for that of which the glory is that it is concrete. They set limits to that which is universal. Religion is life itself—to those to whom it is a life. The religious feel that God is the source, the sustainer, and the end of that life. Christians feel that

Jesus is the supreme illustration of that life, as it was once lived by a man among men. This is the reasoning so often met with in the literature of the last generation. It was to the effect that we must learn more about God from the character of Jesus, and less about Jesus from speculations concerning God. It is the overwhelming impression which we sometimes get from lives of devoted people whom we know, that we learn more about God from those lives than from either philosophies or theologies. And yet some of these same devoted people still offer statements of religion, as if their statements were the substance of their religion. We may well know and be glad that they are not. Their religion is much better than their statement.

Perhaps it is one of the purposes of creeds to be brief. The meaning of Christ as revelation of God, the meaning of God as inspiration to men, was, and is, of more importance, and, particularly it is of more importance to masses of men, including the lowly, than reasoning about God. Creeds seem, however, to have been intended to be affirmed by all of those concerned with religion. One of their functions was to rally believers. The Athanasian Creed constantly repeats the phrase, "It is necessary to believe." The Decrees of Trent—to be sure in the midst of the struggle with Protestantism—have a kind of minatory cadence at the end of their paragraphs, "If any do not so believe, let him be anathema." Yet history shows that there had long been some free play of the imagination of the simpler peoples of the west and north of Europe over the Christian message. There were infiltrations of many pagan customs and ideas, like the use of eggs and the legend of the hare at Easter. There came a time, however, when Christianity had to give account of itself, and this to the mind of the world as well. Perhaps the rise of Scholasticism with its influence upon statements of faith might be described in those words. Anselm's effort to demonstrate the existence of God from the conception of a perfect being was an effort of abstraction of this sort. Despite its leaning upon Aristotle—or rather, upon so much of Aristotle as Anselm knew—it was of a different sort from classical Greek reasoning upon this subject. God on the side of his saving relation to men, God as represented in the incarnation, in the life and death of Jesus, had had all significance for religion. But God as he is in himself—the God who was incarnated in Jesus—what is God in himself? Upon that Anselm reasoned as a man of his time and training would—or could. Aquinas died more than one hundred and fifty years after Anselm. His "Summa contra Gentiles" has often been called the first great attempt at a complete theological system. Aquinas' point was, as had been that of Anselm before him, to deal with the idea of God in himself—beyond that of God as he is made known to us in the revelation through Christ. No one who has listened to de Wulf in recent years at Harvard could fail to be moved. But one cannot deny that religion is not philosophy. No more can one deny that scholastic philosophy has a history.

The Augsburg Confession, immortal when one considers its date, 1530, says:— "There is one divine essence which is called, and is, God, eternal, without body, indivisible, of infinite power, wisdom and goodness." The Thirty-nine Articles, 1562, say:— "There is but one living and true God, without body, parts or passions, of infinite power, wisdom and goodness." The Westminster Assembly in its Shorter Catechism, 1647, says:— "God is a spirit, infinite, eternal, unchangeable in his being, wisdom, power, holiness, justice, goodness and truth." There is, if we may venture to generalize, in these symbolical books in which the influence of Augustine was strong, a juridical view of the relation of God to man which was more or less decisive for the whole construction. The Scotch, with whom the influence of Knox was very strong, can hardly be blamed for that when we recall the years that Knox spent with Calvin in Geneva. The Hollanders also, against whom in the seventeenth century the Remonstrants contended, were not far behind in this regard. And whether from Scotland or from Holland, this view had for a long time great influence in America. It was a view of God primarily as Judge. There is another remark to make. In the long review of history, it is obvious that the Protestant confessions were particularly strong, and this with something like unanimity, upon the particular points which were then at issue. There were other points not then under discussion in respect of which the inherited faith was not—or not much—revised. There are also other points at which, under the freedom of the intellectual life which it is the genius of Protestantism to guarantee, and with the vast advance of knowledge in these four hundred years, it would be highly salutary if the Reformation statements could be subjected to revision. It helps somewhat that some men feel free to revise them for themselves. Everything is helpful except the feeling that they are statements once and for all. The world moves. We are in danger of impairing the appeal of a cause for which our ancestors died if we will not advance to issues of which they never heard. The liberty which that great struggle guaranteed ought not to be converted into a privilege to stand still. Movements, even slight and slow, in the direction of the unification of the Protestant cause might also be facilitated if this view could obtain.

It is agreed that the Deistical movement, as a movement in English theology, was launched by a brother of George Herbert, one of the saintliest of men. This was in the very decades of the settlement of the Massachusetts Bay Colony and of the founding of Harvard College. But from beginnings which promised good for both State and Church, Deism advanced to a condition of things in which men of practically no faith attacked not merely the Church and religion but even the State itself. The claim of the rights of reason having been denied, those who asserted them advanced to claim the sole validity of reason in every relation of life. Whatever came to be thought irrational was impossible. The rise of the sciences in its modern phase—most significantly, of course, since the beginning of the second quarter of the nineteenth century—presents to us again in our own lifetime the same dilemma. The first two of these movements urged in the abstract the right of reason as against authority. Even this latter, however, now forces modification of time-honored views of creation and providence. It gives to man place in the context of nature which at first seemed impossible of combination with inherited views. It is perhaps only to be wondered at that the consequences for faith have not been more destructive than they have. The truth seems to be that the rejection of faith, even in the face of such a state of things, is less than might have been expected. Moreover, this appears to show itself rather in hostility to the Church as institution than to the faith itself. This is, however, a state of things upon which only one interpretation can be put. The doctrine of God, with the thoughts of creation and providence as the reformers were able to phrase these, now lags far behind that which our view of the world compels us to believe. Concerning creation, with also the sustaining and progress of the universe, our thoughts are all oriented from the point of view of evolution. Relation of man to a gradual evolution of the universe of which our fathers never thought, is now for most of us a fixed belief. It is idle to say that these things do not demand changed ideas of God and make of the interpretation of faith in God and the divine order a changing thing. It imposes upon us a dilemma. Either we learn more of God in the process of learning of ourselves and of the world in which we live, or else, we learn of the world and ourselves, discarding the idea of the unity and control which the faith of God has always furnished. It would seem also to be clear that we have need to think of God pre-eminently as immanent in the world and ourselves—the true idea of God as spirit. It is this which we need in place of the urgency for the kind of transcendence of God which seemed so natural to our forbears.

The great issue for our time, incomparably the greatest, has come upon us with the rise of the sciences. I need not say again that I mean all the sciences, those of man and those of what we used to call nature. Rather, we need to recognize that man is the crown of nature and God is the source and the issue of both. For a time within my memory some thought that they could not be scientifically minded and remain religious. Some Christians, at times, a little disconcerted and regretful, agreed with them. That episode seems mainly past. But the issues are particularly bad for that part of the Christian world which inherits the priceless treasure bought for us by the Reformation. It is of the genius of Protestantism that it has no papal authority. It is not of much use to point back to the reign of Elizabeth and the Long Parliament as if they settled everything. Nothing ever settled everything. In these last three centuries there have arisen many of the greatest questions which have ever beset the world of thought. These questions have their repercussions in the whole area of life. Fortunately, perhaps, the world does not live—nor, for that matter, does even the Church live—altogether by the grace of those who themselves live in a perilously courageous pursuit of the intellectual life. It has never yet been so. And despite all our emphasis upon education of every sort, it is not likely that the Church will ever be composed entirely, or even mainly, of educated men and women. It would lose some of its grandest traits if it were ever to come to that issue. Yet even so, it is not good for the Church to drive from it, or to induce to leave it, those who do lead the intellectual life and whose wide horizon makes them feel, not always unjustly, that they do know whither they are going and why and how.

The period of which we have just spoken, the era of Deism and Rationalism, with also that of the rise of the sciences, is treated in one of his latest books, "The Idea of God," by Pringle Pattison. The substance was delivered as Gifford Lectures in the University of Aberdeen in 1912–13. The book was published only in 1917, in the course of the War, and dedicated to the memory of a son who had fallen in the War. The body of the book describes the struggle of the nineteenth century, "the duel between Idealism and Naturalism," as he calls it. The limits which I set for myself would in no case permit me to devote more than a brief paragraph to these questions. Moreover, the work is there done in incomparable fashion. The thing, however, to which I beg especially to call attention is the title, "The Idea of God." Pringle Pattison is a philosopher. Furthermore, under the conditions of Lord Gifford's foundation, the lecturer is bound not to offer any direct advocacy of religion. All the more, it is, therefore, of the intuition of God rather than of the idea of God that I propose to speak, the rational inquiry being, even down to the most recent years, thus nobly provided for. I consider that this other area of our discussion, namely, that of the intuition of God has a significance all its own in the completion of the study upon which we are engaged.

To Jesus Christ, as authentic figure in human history, as revelation of the quality of God as spirit, with the influence of God upon the spirit of man, we devoted the first part of this essay. Our further endeavor is, moreover, in line with what we have just been saying of the intuition of immortality for which there is no demonstration. It is of God as intuitively known in the souls of men that we would now speak. It is of God as source of emotion and enthusiasm, as guide of man's spirit, as light of an intelligence which sometimes seems almost to supervene upon our own, that I would write. It is of God as secret of power and peace that I speak. Our intuition of God changes with every change in the individual and his circumstance, as rational knowledge does not, or, does so only upon our will and effort to have it change. Intuition attended man in paganism. It went before and beyond the crude reasonings which practical contacts in life brought to men. "The pre-rational," Durckheim and Levy-Bruhl have called it. It is my point to show that intuition is the reasoning which also follows after and goes beyond the rational. We have seen how with the Greeks, reason, as also aesthetic quality, led some like Plato, and also Aristotle in his earlier writings, to types of speculation upon the problems of religion which, as such, have never been surpassed. Yet Socrates, with his daimon, remained an intuitionalist to the last. Bergson has said in his latest book, 1935, "We know that all around intelligence there lingers still a fringe of intuition, vague and evanescent. Can we not fasten upon it, intensify it, and above all, consummate it in action, for it has become pure contemplation only through a weakening in its principle." *

Plato drew some part of his philosophy, by which he was closest kin to Socrates, from his *eidola*—a word of which idols is hardly an adequate translation, and our modern word ideals, in its common usage suggests quite a different thing. Moreover, as everybody knows, the baffling thing about several of Plato's Dialogues in which Socrates speaks, is to judge how much of it is Socrates and how much is Plato. But the descent—ascent as, of course, they thought it—in the sophists marks the general decline of any reckoning with intuition. To some of the sophists, this appeared mere superstition, when not just priestcraft. On the other hand, we have in the Old Testament the age-long record of experience and reflection of a race which had little or no talent for speculation. They substituted for it, through the teaching of the prophets, a growing moral consciousness which in time purified their religion, as also, in turn, religion purified their morals. In the later prophets this becomes the great contribution of the race to the progress of mankind. To be sure, here also, a certain phase of religiosity sank into ceremonialism, or again, with Pharisees, into legalism. It is, however, by his profoundly religious intuition that the mind of Jesus was characterized. One might say that it served him in place of all education. For we do not certainly know that he had any education, except in the reading of the sacred book of his people, the being bred, most probably, in a synagogue school, and in listening to words of those who spoke in the synagogue. We are told of but one occasion when he wrote, and then it was in sand. Yet

* "Morality and Religion." Henry Holt and Company.

"the mind which was in Christ Jesus" became the phrase which summed the apostolic approval. When, however, we ask ourselves about the "mind which was in Christ Jesus," can we think of it otherwise than as almost, if not purely, intuition concerning God and man and their relation—an intuition which is otherwise unparalleled? With this went also clearly an intuition concerning morals, borne in upon him from the history of his people and, as well, from examples in the motley world about him. It was his conviction that morals based upon the sense of God, outgoing in the reverence for and care of men—it was this which constituted the natural pathway to the fulfillment of the life of a man's own soul and, as well, to that of the destiny of humanity.

For a while the purity of this apprehension placed adherence to Christianity within the reach of humblest people. Did not Paul say to his Corinthians, "Ye see your calling, brethren, how that not many wise men after the flesh, not many mighty are called." That was a good word to speak to Greeks. For the time came when the Greek spirit with its speculative tendency took the place of the simplicity which was in Christ. The Athanasian Creed markedly shows that drift. It was perhaps already the sense of this growing confusion of the spirit of Christ with the learning of the world which led some Christians of his time and afterward to censure Origen. It is equally true, however, that Christianity did not remain the religion of the humble only. Yet its conquest of the world of mind was bought at a price. Just so also, its conquest of the secular power was, presently, paid for in the coin of the world. The history of Christianity has illuminated these reciprocal relations ever since. As religion, Christianity has shown itself capable of composition with philosophies in their succession. But it has sometimes also almost been displaced by the intellect which it thought to make only its ally. At first, this was with the later phases of the formal reflection of the Greeks. With the scholastics it was still a part of the Greek inheritance, but much modified by the thinking of the millennium which had intervened. And, for a vivid contrast, showing how the same thing happened with the faith of the Great Arabian, one has only to turn to the verses of Omar Khayyám. The Reformation formulae revealed some effect of the revival of learning, but hardly so much as one might have expected. And perhaps we should say here again that, just as in its beginnings, so also in the actual time of the Reformation, the movement did not arise exactly from the side of the learned. Is it any wonder that, as we have said, the Reformation symbols all now show need of revision in light of newer movements in philosophy, and especially of the advance of science? But what is it which has brought to the consciousness of Christian men the sense of this need of readjustment and re-statement? Surely it is, again, intuition—new intuitions about God. These are in light of new knowledge about men and the world, and in the light also of our feeling that our old imagery, taken from the life of man, does not cover all of our new conceptions of God. It is the sense—which is also, if you choose, a phase of intuition—that individual men need not be divided within themselves, knowing no science in order to keep their faith, or else, having no faith in order to keep their science. The age, the world, must not be thus divided. It cannot be thus divided. For individuals, religion would only perish in such division. The man of knowledge of their history knows why statements of faith made in past ages could not possibly have taken cognizance of the advance of knowledge which we witness. The man of intuition may not know why, but he is vividly aware of the fact. It may be a very human obligation for a man of some measure of the newer learning to make plain to the man of intuitive faith why he feels the dissonance of which we speak and how this might be remedied. Such a little service rendered might diminish the danger that a man lose faith altogether, meanwhile quoting men whose life in the mind he respects, as justifying that loss. It is this dissonance between what a man feels and what he is told he ought to think, which did not exist for those who, ten generations ago, gave form to our Protestant creeds. But the dissonance now exists, and will increase.

Let me illustrate. To many writers of Protestant systems of theology, especially the older ones, it seemed the only logic to begin with the topic of God. For obvious reasons we have followed in this book the inverse order. We have done this with the hope of gathering material for our inferences concerning God from nature and from the history of man. The difference might for the moment seem more apparent than real. Because some, even of the classical systems have, under the topic of God grouped their material under headings bearing the titles, Creation, Providence and Redemption. The difference, however, becomes decisive when we say that we, of course, cannot speak of creation without reference to the sciences, particularly astronomy, geology and biology. We cannot speak of providence without reckoning, at least, with psychology and history in all its aspects. We cannot speak of redemption as something simply done for man, conferred upon man. We have to speak of it as something in which, even in the individual sense of it, every individual man has been and is and must be co-worker with God. And in any corporate sense of it, in the sense, that is, of the hope of the world's becoming a better world, it is even more evident that man must work together with God, as also, of course, that God must work together with men. It is, we might say, only with these modifications, enlargements of meaning, that those words creation, providence and redemption may still represent to us the matter with which we are here concerned. It is thus only that they may furnish us the basis for inference concerning God himself, and this exactly from the point of view of religion. Even down to our own day, formal teaching in some theological schools has not widely departed from the inherited scheme. But it is in respect of what is taught under these headings that the vital difference reveals itself.

It is in religion, primarily with God, as person that we have to do. It is also with man as person that we have to do, and this in the most intimate and decisive aspect of his personality. The participation, the necessary cooperation of man himself in his own salvation belongs to the highest ideal of it. We correctly feel that no discussion which neglects or minimizes this aspect of the matter will suffice. The picturing of God in terms of a magnified man, as he appears in the first chapters of Genesis, is to us inadequate. The larger knowledge of the nature and development of the universe, of the evolution of forms of life and of the origins of man, suggest something quite different. That other was, indeed, the imaginative, poetical form in which earlier mankind might apprehend creation. It certainly presents the matter in a far nobler form than some other narratives of human origins with which it might be compared. But astronomy, geology, biology—to name no others of the sciences—have caused us now to infer that the world in all its multiformity was not created by fiat in that way. Concerning the origins of life we still speculate. But man, even such as he is, would seem to be in the continuity of forms of life of whose age and variations, and of the causes of whose variations, we can as yet make no adequate presentation to ourselves. A Bible lies on my desk as I write which was printed in London in 1865 by the most famous of all the societies for the publication of the Scriptures. It bears at the top of the margin of the first chapter of Genesis the date 4004 B.C. These are the figures of Usher, Archbishop of Armagh and Primate of all Ireland, after 1625. One of his books, "Annales," published in 1654, had contained his studies in biblical chronology. His dates were inserted by some to us unknown editor on the margin of reference editions of the Authorized Version. I do not know how recently they ceased to be thus printed.

No one knows the date of the creation. Or rather, in the sense in which those truly learned and devout men assumed it, there was no such creation. Astronomers and, again, geologists, and also biologists, just now append a varying number of ciphers, to any figures they may give us as to the age of the earth or of our solar system, and admit that there is much more that is unknown about the universe to which the figures are supposed to apply. Life on our earth, we must suppose, was made possible by changes of temperature. But it is difficult to say how rudimentary such forms of life were. Almost the only thing we think we know is that the series was very long and that man is at the end of the series. But the point for us now is not how much less creation, in the sense of finished achievement, then meant. It is, rather, how much more creation, especially of man, now implies. Or, to put it differently, the point is how much more of his destiny man, as the highest object in creation, has still to work out for himself, with the aid of God. Because it is quite clear that in his evolution he has long since passed the point where by one decisive factor he has become a conscious, free and responsible self. The aid of God is, now and long since, conditioned in man's own willingness to seek the higher and the highest things, and to avail himself of God's help in the achievement of those things. He must make these things to become part, and the highest part, of his own life. He rises by them, and they, in turn, rise by him. In the noblest sense, man has become co-worker with God in the achievement of his own destiny, and in his contribution to the high destiny of other men. Therewith he has become something different from any other object in creation. He has ceased to be altogether an object. He has become a subject in creation—and re-creation. All that for which untold ages waited has come at last to be shared by one whose intelligence and freedom and responsibility is the issue of that waiting. The old word "likeness of God," and Paul's word about being workers together with God, get new and vaster meaning for us in the light of all that has gone to make us men. And as men, we can never again lay upon God alone all the responsibility either for our own salvation or for the saving of the world. We have to take a man's share in that work ourselves. Not even our damnation can we lay to the charge of God alone.

And just as in the case of creation, so now as to providence. We have to make new interpretations into which the total of a knowledge of the nature of the world and of ourselves, at which we have only recently arrived, can be fitted. The age-long teaching as to a finished creation on the part of God, "by the word of his power," has been transformed for us. Evolution of the universe and an age-long process—aeons long—of the development of life, including man, takes its place. The poetical form in which all this was described many centuries ago does, indeed, in its beauty, and particularly in its moral meaning, transcend many other accounts of the beginning of things which we have come to know in other literatures and religions. That fact in itself may be witness to a relative maturity of the description as we receive it. But it is imagery, poetry. The exalted form in which the moral dilemma of man's life is portrayed, with also perhaps the form in which the faith of Scripture was held by even our own parents, caused it to be believed in all literalness by some of them, not to say that the simplicity of it commended it to children. But also it needs no saying that much of this has been replaced by new thoughts of the development of the world, particularly of the world of living things, the emergence of man as we now apprehend this, with also the long progress of mankind of which only a few generations ago we had no idea.

So is it also in relation to our thought of providence. Here, too, the traditional imagery has been—imagery. Exactly in such a matter as is the care of God for man and the faith of man in that care, what could be more natural, inevitable, than that the solicitude and trust of man and the care and guidance of God should have been expressed in language of the most fundamental, as also of the most exalted and exalting of human relations, the language, that is, of the family. "My Father," and "your Father," said Jesus. "Like as a father pitieth his children, so the Lord pitieth them that fear him," says the Psalm. In fact, this is one of the almost universal images in all religions. Again we say, how could it have been otherwise? Why should it have been otherwise? But as to providence, we hardly need to be reminded of the larger meaning of a word which conventional usage has often narrowed. It is the grand idea of God's wisdom and care, his foresight and love, his aid in the best sense of that word, his control of all things in the best interest of mankind. But in the usage of some this sense has tended to be limited to intervention in the course of nature or in the progress of affairs which were esteemed to be beyond the control of men. It has been thought of as escape from things not reckoned with, or as the turning to our advantage a situation which it may be had passed beyond our control. I should not like to speak irreverently even of such a view. I should not like to speak slightingly of that great text concerning God "who will with the temptation [trial] also make a way of escape, that ye may be able to bear it." These also are spoken of as God's providences. And those upon whom unsupportable burdens in life have fallen may view these also, as their great providences. We may be grateful, if life does present these aspects of providence, sooner or later, perhaps in the life of everyone of us. Yet there is also a much more heroic aspect of the matter. Comfort in our tribulation is not all. Stimulation to accept with joy great opportunities may be another aspect of the providence of God, and one for which we might well be as grateful, if not even far more grateful, than for any deliverance. Responsibility to bear, power and joy in bearing, may well be as noble an aspect of the providence of God as any deliverances of which we ever thought. Brave souls have often regarded these as their greater providences.

But again—it is imagery. And as the noblest aspiration of a man for his son is that he shall become a man, so the noblest of the purposes of God must be that his son shall be a man. That fact lies upon the very face of Scripture. That fact is fundamental to the teaching of Jesus, although also one sometimes feels—or thinks he feels—Jesus' consciousness of the distance between himself, with all the splendor of his insight and goodness and, on the other hand, the best even of the men whom he had chosen. But the sense that his followers must be men deepens as he himself becomes more and more aware that he must go away from them. In Paul the feeling mounts to a passion for raising up men who, in the responsibility of a great cause, are to be men in Christ Jesus. We fall back upon the other view in the moments of our depression, of bewilderment, of our sense of inadequacy, of defeat, perhaps especially when we feel that we have deserved defeat. Yet here, too, the best sense that we have is perhaps the sense that we are not exactly children. We contemplate the course of history, so far as we can understand it, or ponder even only the lives of men about us. And the thing at which we perhaps most of all wonder is the fact that man has long since arrived at the stage when he takes—and, whether he will or no, must take—a large part of his own responsibility for what he does or does not do—for what issues are, or are not, to be. Man is his own fate in a sense for which the animals, so far as we can see, present no parallel. This is the price, you might say, which man pays for the fact that he is a man. He makes society and society makes him—or unmakes him. He builds up institutions, and these build him up—or pull him down. No belief in evolution can wipe out this high distinction of man from the other animals. His destiny and the destiny of the world is so largely in his own hands that we say sometimes in a kind of desperation, "And God can do nothing about it."

The religious man finds two solutions here—or rather, two aspects of one solution. He throws himself upon the greatness and goodness of God in the sense of his own inadequacy. In order of time, and with most men, he is likely to have proved his own inadequacy first. But in either case the normal course is to recur to effort of his own. The issue of a true faith in God is thus in the normal case the enlarged sense of our own responsibility, with also perhaps the discovery of powers which are our own and yet are not our own. In other words, the issue is effort, not passivity. It is courage, not discouragement. It is the sense that one owes all that is possible in that direction to his fellows. We owe it to ourselves. We owe it to God. This is the way in which perhaps is it best borne in upon us that God is spirit, that he exerts his power first in us, and only then through us. We are baffled by the sense of the guidance—providence, if you wish to call it that—of life upon the earth up to the point of the appearance of man. But with the appearance of man, we seem to have entered upon a new stage, in which the activity and freedom and responsibility of man himself is a necessary condition of the further development of man and of all mankind. We can hardly do otherwise than view the whole history of mankind in this light. That is an extraordinary word which one of the discourses in the Fourth Gospel puts upon the lips of Jesus himself, quoting the Psalm, "I said, Ye are gods" and Jesus proceeds, "And if he called them gods unto whom the word of God came—say ye of him whom the Father hath sanctified 'Thou blasphemest' because I said, I am the son of God?" Exactly in the areas of which we speak, that of the achievement of the better things in life, with the reflex of these in ourselves, it is clear that there is that which God cannot do for us, or rather, can do only in and with and through us. The whole point that I would make is that in all the higher things of man's life, in the area of the moral and spiritual, we can but co-operate with that which we may still most wisely and truly call God's providence. But we cannot escape our own responsibility. And this is true not merely for our own destiny but for our share in the destiny of our fellow men. When people talk of the providence of God, they think often of it as something which comes to them. Our soberer thought must lead us often to the sense that it is something with which we ourselves have much to do. The providence of God in the inner life of man is often the greater providence. And this is true not alone in men's own lives but in the lives of those about them and of those after them. This is the point of our constant emphasis that God is spirit. The language which speaks of the hand of God was natural perhaps to our infancy. It has been natural in the long tutelage of humanity. It is natural now in the times when our feeling is in the ascendant. But the profounder truth is that we are workers together with God even in the things in which we derive all our comfort from the fact that it is he, God, who works within us "both to will and to do of his good pleasure."

It may be that we shall have less to say here in this place under the heading of redemption. Twice already in these chapters we have spoken of specific views of the atonement which have held such large place, particularly in classic Protestantism. The etymological sense of the word redemption is, indeed, that of buying back, of buying off, of ransom, release, through a supreme price paid, a substitution offered. Christ's sacrifice, freely made, was accepted of God as in our stead. Theologically, if we could find an adequate sentence in summary of the age-long teaching, it would be something like this. Redemption is deliverance of man from consequences of sin through the obedience and sacrifice of Christ, our Redeemer. The word premised, only too truly, that man was in bondage to the power of evil, sometimes a spiritual power external to himself, or again, to evil passions and propensities within himself—or both. He could be delivered from this only by the suffering and death of Christ on his behalf. In usage, redemption thus covered the ideas of atonement, justification, regeneration and sanctification. We have no need to repeat what has been said in other connections in these chapters. We are not in bondage to the devil—whatever meaning we may find summed, in one aspect of it, in the apostolic phrase, "sold under sin." We are not debtors to God in the sense that someone else could pay our debt. The thing goes deeper than that. Paul's own image of our becoming "new men in Christ Jesus," his phrase about our "putting on the new man," with also Jesus' own loved and oft used image about "new birth" goes deeper than that. Some theological representations, fortunately now passing, were enforced by still cruder interpretations. It was not thought to be within the power, or even within the will of God, that men's sins should be passed over in pardon and thus all made good again. Someone must suffer. And the sense of this loving suffering on man's behalf was the occasion of the awakening of men to the sense of the magnitude and fatality of evil. Men would be moved by that, not alone to a sense of the purity and majesty of God, but also, to a sense of the love and sacrifice of the mediator. Man must be awakened to resolve upon a purer life for himself and, as well, a life given to the service of God and to the help of others. All of this is, in one way, true of life as it is lived. But this imagery lends itself only too easily to the thought of our guilt as imputed to the Redeemer and of his righteousness as imputed to us. It needs no saying that there is something transactional, unreal, about the very supposition that man's real guilt could be ascribed by the All-Holy to another and the righteousness of the other avail for man himself. That is just a schematization, a rationalization, on the part of some who would be offended at the very word if it were used of something which actually happens all about us, and happens all the time in the verity of life. The greatest power for good in the world may well be the suffering which those who do evil bring upon those who love them. They bring this suffering upon those whose lives are not thus stained—or not in the same measure—but who are more than willing to bear all the consequences of other men's folly and sin. These do this with joy if only the other can be led to see and abjure the evil and give himself to the good. It is somehow thus that we can rid the thought of redemption of any survivals of conceptions external to the history of souls. Such souls are in their own smaller way our saviours. But this saving is something which only the man himself can do. It is thus only that we can rid the thought of redemption of anything external to the soul itself. We feel that we must free the transaction from being just a part of a scheme of things, a plan for making good something which has gone wrong in the world. That is not the problem. The problem is to make good the man through whom it has gone wrong. It is only so that one makes this vicarious suffering a part of the necessary, the sublime order of nature of the moral world. It is somehow thus that we open, even to such men as we ourselves are, the privilege of taking part in Christ's own work, "filling up that which is behind" in Christ's work —in Paul's great phrase—the work of God who is spirit in the world of men, who are spirit, too.

It is no great wonder if the typical point of view for the reformers was, by and large, salvation by faith, and some said, for emphasis, by faith alone. It was easy to accuse Catholicism, particularly in the time of the

Reformation, of putting too great emphasis upon good works, especially when, in the long sequence of the power of the Church the very definition of what works were good had led to gravest abuses. It was easy thus to exaggerate in the single matter of the indulgences. The long ascendancy of the clergy had led to specific, perhaps one might say, to very ecclesiastical, views of what was good and meritorious. But one cannot know half well the history of the Middle Age and of earlier times also, without knowing with how many souls the emphasis was quite elsewhere. The emphasis was upon an inner life of which good works were the natural fruit. Augustine, to mention only one name, was a passionate teacher of the gospel of grace and of good works as the fruit of the divine grace. His view, as we can hardly help feeling, was the sequel of the tragic contrast of his own saving experience with his earlier mode of life. In that fact we may find some explanation of the influence of Augustine with many of the reformers. This thread, in many men and women in the Orders, as also in the secular life, had never been lost, although Protestants do also owe much to the fact that it was among them so zealously taken up. But the Protestant emphasis, tending to become an exclusive emphasis upon faith as over against works, had also its own evil consequence. Witness the affair at Münster, and listen to the constant effort of loftier spirits to bring home the lesson that true faith could not be without its own fruit in a good life. After all, while it is quite true that life must go before work, it is equally true that work must follow life. Works are the evidence of this life as truly as of any other phase of life. We were all too young to know it when we were born. But being born has natural consequences. This is as true in the life of the mind as it is in the life of the body. And it is, I had almost said, even more true of the life of the spirit. Great is the mystery of life, and greatest, perhaps, is the mystery of spiritual life. But the signs of it are not mysterious. In fact, it is the signs which usually reveal with some definiteness of what sort the life is. "Now the fruits of the spirit are these," said Paul. The fruits of the redeemed spirit make their contribution to the redemption of the world. We are "workers together with God." Few greater words than these have ever been spoken. Perhaps greater is only this word: "For it is God who worketh in you, both to will and to do of his good pleasure." The fruit of a redeemed life is its contribution to redemption, of the man himself, and of his fellows. The question as to what happens to us after that, we sometimes think we might almost leave in abeyance. To be taken up in the allegiance of our own free spirit into the work of God, the God who is spirit, to share in his influence upon the spirits of men, and in the transformation of the world into a world of the things of the spirit—this would seem to be almost reward enough, even if that should be all.

We seem, in what we have here written, to be trying to describe God in terms of what he has done and is doing for men, in terms of that which he is to men, in terms of what he is to the innermost self of ourselves. But what else should we do? The first chapter of Genesis describes God's work of creation in terms natural to the man who wrote it and to the men for whom he wrote. We in these paragraphs have sought to limit what we have to say of God to his relation to the souls of men. As to God's relation to the world of nature, we realize that we do not understand that at all as the author in Genesis did. We have to understand God's work in creation, in so far as we understand it at all, in light of the amazing truth which the sciences have brought to us, most of it, almost in our own day. It is this knowledge which makes the older poetry of representation seem to us no longer to represent the standpoint which in the prose of science we are compelled to occupy. So also, when we try to say something real to ourselves about providence. We have to try to think what providence means in its largest sense to men such as we are, in light of experience which we ourselves have had and which the long history of man reveals. We have to think of God's activity in the world of men as we are able to present it to ourselves in the veritable world in which we now live. What does the care of God mean to men like ourselves, in experience similar to our own? And even when we speak of redemption, it is indeed highly instructive to recall what other men and ages have thought about redemption. But the best part of what we say is that which really describes what God means to us and to men like ourselves in this world and in this day. It is the only world we have. And it is obviously a world in which we are to do our part to make it a better world, and so also to make ourselves better men. Or, to put it more profoundly still, we are made better men by the life and work which our time and place present to us, and in which we draw ever upon wisdom and power greater than our own. Surely it is so also with redemption. We infer God from our own needs and wants, indeed, from our own defeats and victories in the inner life, in the outer life, and in the life of the world of men about us.

We might make abstractions, in the area of pure thought as to what kind of being God must be. But that is the task of philosophy. It is not directly the task of religion, as is evidenced by the fact that many men and women live outstanding religious lives who are not philosophers. In religion what we seek is that which God actually is in the moral and spiritual experience of men, and best of all, if that can be, in our own experience. In that sense every view of God takes something of its form, yes, even of its substance, from ourselves, from our time, from the problems of our race, and of the world in which men live and work about us. It is that which we really draw from the sense of God in our personal experience. It is that which we believe to be the secret of the shining experience of men and women, great and simple, whose lives we have observed. It is that which we need to think of in such a study as this. And perhaps we think of it best when we do not go outside of our own problem, although we perfectly well know that the God of the universe, as it is, must be the God of many phases of life besides the one with which we have immediately concerned ourselves. God is what he is for all men and all the interests of men. But this is the thing which we have thought ourselves most bound to say, in this connection.

And do I need, beyond what I have just said, to summarize? God is, for this specific discussion, the counterpart of our souls, or rather, if we may make bold to say it, we are in soul the counterparts of God. We are sure that it is soul which makes us men. It is from this point of view that we bear the likeness of God. About all else we can have our theories and grow in knowledge by finding out whether our theories agree with the facts. A large part of the history of mind could be summed in that one sentence. Indeed, in the life of the soul, we advance in knowledge, both of our own souls, and of the souls of our fellows, and so in knowledge of what God must be like. But the soul of man is something which we think has no parallel in the universe, unless it be God.

And if there be no God in the sense of which we speak, then whence and why these aspirations? Or, to put it differently, how could we be what, in our best moments we think we are—how else can we understand those achievements which men make in the spiritual life and, in making these, make a spiritual life more possible and actual for their fellow men? For religion what we need to know is how we are to be conformed to the mind and will of God. The mystery of creation and providence is great, and, like all things which pertain to God, I might say even of those which relate to this world, the mystery grows only the greater the more we know. But the mystery of the life of man in mind and spirit is greater than any other mystery. If there is nothing in the universe corresponding to this, then what is the meaning of our being what we are? Why are we not fulfilled in the life of the animals? For, on one side of our being we are the kin of all the animals and they are our kin. And—what gives us even more food for thought—some men are, or at least they sometimes seem to us to be, close kin to the animals, closer kin, we sometimes think, to the animals than to God or even to the best of men. That is, again, one of the mysteries of the universe. Are we men, in the best sense, only in so far as, having souls, moral capacity, spiritual destiny, we find our fulfillment always and only in something beyond ourselves? Of the animals, so far as we understand, we cannot say that. It is obviously in man as soul that we are to find the image of God and, again let me say, in so far as religion prompts our quest. The idea of God suggests a thousand things beyond this one, but much of that we can well leave to philosophers and scientific men, to those, that is, who deal with the problem of the universe as such. For religion, what we need to know may be gathered from the needs and wants of men's souls and from the achievement of great souls which have not lacked in the long history of mankind. It is what we find written in experience of souls and, pre-eminently, it is the quality and passing greatness of the soul of a Man of Nazareth that suggests to us what the God of our souls must be like.

PART IV

REALITY AND REALIZATION

Part IV

REALITY AND REALIZATION

REALITY

A popular assumption, formerly rather widespread, held that science has to do with the material universe. After the middle of the last century, the sciences of physical nature did indeed celebrate spectacular triumphs. The succession of achievements has continued. That presumption may have had to do also with the temporary discrediting of philosophy, or, at least, of the old idealism. The case was made worse for religious knowledge by a somewhat panic-stricken retreat of some advocates to extravagant claims concerning the supernatural. Literary and historical investigation of the documents of revelation, as also of authoritative dogma, with comparison of religions, recognition of stages of development of all religions, have modified this. Votaries of science recall days when discoveries were banned and, indeed, an occasional discoverer burned, in the name of religion. They have found happiness in availing themselves of liberty achieved. Some heartily accepted the "cleaving of the universe in twain with an axe," which rather logically followed the view upon which irreconcilables among their opponents insisted. Sciences of the material universe have indeed conferred untold benefits upon the outward life of man. They have had some share in breeding up a generation gratefully intent upon such benefits. Benefits which religion, and even morals, confer had, for many, somewhat paled in comparison. Again, there was current a rather unhappy limitation of the sense of what it is to know. All that seemed to fall outside this limitation was consigned to the limbo of the unknowable. That presumption, too, has passed. The sciences of physical nature did, indeed, begin anew their triumphant march with the most obvious. Not even in physics and astronomy, however, has mechanism survived as an adequate interpretation. As difficulties in the sciences of life emerged, what was called vitalism was summoned to the aid of mechanism. Vitalism, at least as once apprehended, appears now to be a somewhat mythical explanation. The sciences of living things had logically to seek to begin with the lowest orders. Lowest forms of life, it appeared, could still be thought of in terms of action upon them of environment. Higher forms obviously contributed to the change in themselves by reaction against their environment. They ultimately changed environment. Feeling, will, entered into these reactions. A measure of independence within environment became quite as obvious as was dependence upon environment. In latter years a whole group of new sciences have been developed, sciences of the higher aspects of life. In no case has there been thought of abandoning the basis of observation and induction characteristic of the sciences. Conversely, impatience of philosophy might be regarded as mainly one of the aberrations of the youth of modern science. This also is already passing. Among the sciences of the higher life of man, study of religion in its inner nature, and of many religions as issues of similar impulses, has vastly altered the view with which historians approach the problem of religion. This has made possible application of the principles both of science and of philosophy to problems of religion. Authority of religion is one of the very things into which history and philosophy and, in a measure, even science, have to inquire.

We are accustomed to consider environment as we approach any problem of development. It is against the world of its surroundings that every living thing reacts. No words were more familiar, even in the early discussions of evolution, than the words *reflexes, reflex activities*. We do not know how far something which we may call vital goes down into the world which we used to assume to be inorganic. We do not know where incipient, responsible self-direction begins in a world which we assume to be barely organic. With our present knowledge, it is easier to assume infinitesimal gradations than to suppose that the universe is really divided into three conventionally separate compartments, of brute matter, life, and the consciousness guided by intelligence which reaches its consummation in man. Men spoke of emergent evolution. We may be sure of the point where new phases emerge for our recognition. It is harder to say that this is the point where new elements actually entered into the long sequence of changes. For that matter, it is not certain that they were not there from the beginning. Perhaps it is an assumption that there was a beginning at the point where changes of temperature would seem to us to have made possible the organic world. At all events, well below the lowest levels at which we think we detect consciousness we note an impulse of a living thing to find or to create for itself a more favorable environment. At the level of man such an impulse is not merely beyond question. It might be said to constitute, in one aspect of it, a clue to the higher life of man. At this level not merely does the living thing work to change its environment. The changing environment works also to alter the being which lives in it.

Things toward which human hope and age-long endeavor have gone out must in some sense exist. Truth, beauty, goodness must have real existence in our environment, related to aspiration and effort from within ourselves. They must be real values, entities, in the universe which could have produced man, even such as he was—and is. They correspond to that which at his best he seeks to be and, as well, by transformation of society, to help others to be. Nothing is more certain than that the man of science believes that there is in the universe a truth which it is the aim of the life of men of his sort to explore. It is this constant effort—with, at times, at least, happy achievement—to transfer some portion of this reality, thus far unknown, to the realm of reality known and fitted to be worked with—it is this which constitutes the life of scientific men. Men give themselves with confidence to this quest. They are participant in a movement which in our time has achieved most notable results. It is not that their research deals always with the world of things material which the uninitiated might esteem to be the more solid part of reality. It is that they seek the principles of things which material aspects of the universe merely exemplify. It is because of the nature of a problem to which the empirical is the right and only method of approach, that men of science have this kind of confidence. They belong to a movement which has won great triumphs in our time by this method of approach. They have this confidence. It is here that they are at home. Defeat never makes them doubt that beyond present knowledge is a larger knowledge which is the object of their quest. Reality must reveal itself in ever greater clarity. It must at last do away with mistaken hypotheses which men have, as in so many other things, made and used along the line of their approach.

There is hardly more uncertainty among such men about the reality and power of the world of moral facts and values. Possibly they never gave so much thought to facts and forces of this order. Everybody knows, however, that in some sense facts of this order do impinge upon every man's life. In very truth, these are the facts which are in a way every man's business. They are much more clearly every man's business than the inquiry into, let us say, astronomy or physics or chemistry. We may cheerfully borrow our notions about these. We borrow at our peril our notions about morals from some tradition of the past or some impressions, crude or even false, of men about us. If we are not right—and we never can be more than partially right—the things in which we are wrong take toll upon our life. They take toll upon the lives of those about us and upon the lives of those after us. Truth of this sort needs to be the object of every man's quest. The fact that truth about the right and good so often is and so long has been unknown or, at most, inadequately known, has been the secret of many of the major evils of the life of mankind. It has been the secret of far greater evils than is ignorance of the laws of physics or of chemistry. We are fain to think of errors in science as corrected by facts which it is the business of science to find out for us. We are apt to think of errors in morals as avenged by government or, in the last analysis, by God. What is more significant still, ignorance is here not the only evil. Here the will to do the good which is known, or at least partly known, is often also lacking. This willingness to do the wrong in face of a known right has been the source of more evils than all our ignorances combined. This problem demands something very different from mere increase of information. Part of the world daily goes against the information which it has, or could have, if it would only observe and reflect. Because it is certain that in any larger view of man's life and destiny the right has such a way of avenging itself when the wrong has been done, that few, whether scientific men or not, have doubts that there is such a thing as the right, the good, and that it is an aspect of a most imperious reality in the universe. It has a truth of its own sort and one fully as awe-inspiring in its might as is anything among the realities of our material relations. The truth is itself more awe-inspiring, because the consequences being in the man himself, there is no chance of escape.

The world of the beautiful has less power to impress itself upon those who do not seek it than has the world of the good, or again, the world of the true, in the sense of the truth which is sought by science. Of course, in a large sense, all these things can be described with the word truth. But in the area of that which makes appeal to the sense of beauty, whether beauty of form, of color, of sound, or in any other relation, it is perhaps more true than in either of the areas just mentioned, that it is only those who seek who find. Or to put it more drastically, this magnitude never finds those who do not seek. The world of the beautiful does not seem to be armed with the terrific power of self-assertion which belongs to the world of the good, or, again, even to the world of the true, as, for example, in the fact that water will not flow up hill. The wrong finds us. We find beauty or go without it. Given time and scope enough, nothing prevents moral evil from bringing men and the race to book. Empires and civilizations rise and fall by it. All the enhancements of power which science has conferred upon us are quite helpless to reverse the moral judgment of the universe when men or nations make unscrupulous use of the powers of nature or of their own powers. Men may decide to have nothing to do with morals. The only issue is that morals have to do with them. But music and art and poetry are shy. They are for those who seek for them. The world of the beautiful has apparently less, and perhaps I might say, no power to impress itself upon those who are not impressed by it. Nevertheless, those who seek mock at those who think that there is nothing here to find. In the large, people who do not seek it do not find it. But nothing could convince those to whom it is something, or rather, to whom it is the supreme thing, that here is not also a fact, reality. For them it may be the grand reality.

There have been, however, and still are, some, perhaps many, who, advancing from the side of physical nature, or again, from reflections upon man, feel that, at all events, the conviction of religious men that their world is also a real world, must be an illusion. There is nothing, as they think, at the end of that road, the end of religious thought or endeavor. The outgoing of these aspirations, at all events, is vain. That feeling, at least, is a mere self-deception. At all events, it is worthy of note that science, even if we go back to the Chaldeans and the Egyptians, from whom the Greeks learned much, is a comparatively recent interest of man. Its progress has, moreover, been for long periods disastrously interrupted. Its signal triumphs are quite recent. Its ascendancy is one of the newest things in the world. The extension of a scientific effort to find out the truth about man and religion is the very newest of all. Effort of man to find out some other truths about himself, secrets of his own spirit, implications of that spirit in the universe, are far older. They are more continuous. They have been far more nearly universal. Efforts, in Paul's touching phrase, "to seek after God if haply they might find him," go back to primitive times, more primitive than any of which we have any other knowledge. The study of these early efforts has come to constitute one of the great aids, and in a certain sense also, one of the great problems of those who would really study religions. For, interesting as is primitive man and his religion, no competent person really believes that we can form an adequate idea of religion from its earliest known stages. Cordially as we admit the evolution of religion, we do not admit that religion is best understood by the study of its origins. Rather, it is to be interpreted by its highest exemplifications, as also by the whole of its long and varied history. The highest things in it, which are really the most characteristic, come to their manifestation only in connection with the highest life of man, intellectual, moral, social. It is conceded that early man was a creature largely of his emotions and, indeed, of very rudimentary emotions. He was more profoundly moved by the emotions and imaginings of those about him, than disposed or even able to take a stand for himself. Religion is now and will always remain in its own way a matter of feeling. It is a matter of intuition like the arts. But no one conversant with the history of religions would hold that religion is not capable of combination with the highest intellectual life of successive ages, ever since there began to be any intellectual life worthy of the name. It is by that interaction that religions have become worthier. It has in its institutionalized forms only too often been hostile to the advance of knowledge. But that was in large part because it was institutionalized, and institutionalized either upon the basis of myth or dogmas, or even of the interests of those who had interest in it. Despite what many men feel as to its remoteness, it is, of all the four elements of life of which we here speak, the one of by far the most universal appeal. The most ignorant man may feel the appeal of religion. When he tries to formulate it, his formulation must, of course, be judged by his competence for any formulation. For that matter, the formulations achieved by the wisest of any age have a right to be judged by the level of knowledge of their age.

In light of these considerations, it requires some hardihood to declare that, of course, the magnitudes with which science deals are reality, that morality also deals with reality. We might even concede that the arts are real, for those for whom they are real—but religion is pure illusion. Despite every error in apprehension, in defiance of having been victimized by taking wrong roads, despite every perversion which has been thrust upon them by authorities and every disillusionment which a man may have brought upon himself, men have never given up the search for this reality. At the present moment, in the very emphasis upon the outward life, there is no evidence that the struggle for the validation of the inner life is being given up. The certainty enforced by all of human history is that in the measure in which the inner life is given up, the outer life will take its vengeance on mankind. There is no other remedy for the evils in which the freedom of the moral world so often issues. There is no recourse save in the free allegiance of a man's own soul to that for which religion at its best has always stood. It has a long series of errors in its past. It is, however, to be remembered that it has a longer past than any other phase of human life. It has, moreover, been involved, first and last, with almost all the other errors, even the atrocities, of men and States. It may even be sardonically remembered that States, almost uniformly, and until modern times, have sought the sanction of religion even for being such pretenses at government as some of them were. They sought to buttress their authority by claiming that sanction. On the other hand, organized religion has gravely erred in claiming to be superior to the State within the State's own province. There was a time when it claimed to be superior to science. Religious law was long thought superior to law. There was a time when almost all art was ecclesiastical and most learning was confined to clerics. What institution or what cause could have failed to be demoralized by those mere facts? But not only has that state of things measurably passed away—and no men are happier that it has passed away than some among us who most sincerely have the interest of religion at heart. It may be that some men still feel reactions from that old unwarrantable state of things. In our world and at the present moment, we see in some nations just the converse situation, the State attempting to dominate or minimize or eliminate altogether the religious interest. We still meet representations concerning religion which are quite opposite to the attitude of mind of enlightened and unselfish and responsible people among the religious. We are not, however, greatly impressed, in the light of a long human history, with the effectiveness of the effort of governments to cancel the religious interest. Not all people who think themselves irreligious are ready to believe how grateful some of the most truly religious are for the fact that other departments of life have shaken themselves free from immemorial complications, and are ready to take their share of responsibility for the destinies of mankind. That leaves the religious free to take their real responsibility, and to try to illustrate their conviction that true religion is a supreme aid to any true man in bearing his part in the life and destiny of the world.

REALIZATION

We play with the word *realize*. We say that a hope has been realized when we see it at last achieved in fact before our eyes. We may say also that a man has realized something as an aim, an exacting purpose, which will carry him through every contrariety until at last it is achieved. Or, perhaps, in the scope of mortal life, it has not been achieved. Does even that make him doubt? It is this last which is the primary realization. It is the event in the ardent mind which draws the other, the realization in outward fact, after it. Was the man necessarily the victim of illusion even if he never lived to see the outward realization? What is more august in life than to hand on the torch of one's endeavor? The most heroic chapters in the history of humanity are of that sort. Realization is, first, in mind and heart. Indeed, it is precisely those who have given themselves with ardor to such realizations of truth as the race has yet achieved, to whom these realizations themselves seem at the best inadequate. It is such men who count what has been achieved as but a forecast of what is yet to be achieved. They now give their whole selves to stir others to continue the pursuit, not counting cost. The most vivid thing about them now is their realization of that which has not yet been realized. It is exactly from the realm of the physical sciences that this view is enthusiastically proclaimed. It is followed with all the energy and confidence that men possess. It is transmitted to students with the feeling that to have re-created a mind, in this sense, may well be something far more significant than to have made a discovery oneself. Truths unknown and applications of them until our own day never made are now veritable commonplace. There must be more reality in the universe which is not yet discovered but which answers to our quest. A lifetime in a university has convinced me that there is no spirit higher than this in academic life. It is the faith of scientific men that there is this unlimited truth which we sometimes describe as if it were literally "waiting to be discovered" and utilized of men. It is not too much to say that many a man's religion, that, namely, which really inspires and controls his conduct, is a faith of this sort. It is this allegiance which, in its own way, takes the place of other devotions. The primary conviction of his whole life is that there is truth which as yet no man knows. It is, however, of the sort which he knows how to pursue. He hopes to attain it. If not, it must be the reward of the effort of those who are about him or of those who are to come after him. It is this belief which creates and re-creates the worker himself. It helps him to do his part in re-creating the life of others. It changes our world as we respond to the unknown truth in the world. No one who companies with men of every branch of learning as in a great faculty fails to feel the kinship of this enthusiasm.

It may be true that some part of this enthusiasm is due to novelty. Freedom has been won in whole branches of an inquiry which for ages was suppressed. Even if not that, they lay remote from the area of men's organized intellectual activities. Some part of the popular acclaim of the sciences may be due also to the fact that discoveries have found application in increase of comforts, in enhancements of power which every man appreciates. The air of simple reasonableness which the whole effort bears, the unhesitating abandonment of false solutions—all this gives to efforts in this general area a prestige, has drawn to it a sympathy, which no other area of intellectual endeavor just now enjoys. In the revolution of which we are speaking—a new Reformation, one of the most distinguished leaders, Pupin, dead in this very year, has called it—science has been true to itself. New discoveries have rendered obsolete interpretations not long ago esteemed to be irrefragable. Men outside these areas of inquiry find it not always easy even to understand when experts explain. Political, as also social and religious revelations, have to gather masses of men before they can prevail. They sometimes have painfully to await a leading person. This also is a contrast which they seem to present to movements of successful leadership in science. Perhaps this is only a superficial contrast after all. Science also has its history of tentatives which have failed, it may be for generations, before success arrived. Movements profoundly concerned with feeling and will would seem to have to gain their force before they win their light. In scientific movements in general, the reverse is the case. They see their light and then gather their force. Issues in this scientific reformation in the midst of which we stand are, by frank confession of its votaries themselves, by no means always clear. But theories of matter and force which have done duty at all events since Newton are discarded. Results long esteemed beyond all question are now thought to be not results at all but only mistaken theories. In astronomy and physics the best knowledge seems for the moment to be leading mainly to further and more tremendous questions. Certainly the candor with which new issues are faced is, all of itself, our greatest ground of confidence. Herein lies a lesson for those of us who work in areas where mathematics are of no avail. The certainties we seek pertain to qualities rather than to quantities and measure. They depend upon our perception of those qualities. Our thoughts have to do primarily with human elements. These are always mobile and despite our best endeavors they remain mysterious. In a sense, the more we know of them, the more mysterious they grow. It is a comfort just now to feel that there are other inquiries which also lead off into mysteries unfathomed and perhaps unfathomable. But one thing which is certain to all men of science is that there is such a thing as truth to be discovered. Another is that truth is constantly demanding more adequate interpretation than it has yet received. Another certain thing is that truth is ever ready for new application to the lives of men, or, if you prefer to put it so, the lives of men are always subject to modification through the knowledge of new truth. And still another thing of which the successes, as also the failures, of ten generations make us certain, is that we have not been wholly mistaken as to where and how we have to find the truth we seek. Of nothing is science itself so devoutly convinced as of this, that truth is a quality, a magnitude, in our universe which exists for us to know and we exist to know it.

I feel at times a sense of the naïve in the unconscious assumption among some of my scientific friends that in their area is incontrovertible truth. I recall how often their truth, now acknowledged, has been controverted and, what is even worse, how long and widely it was utterly neglected. Ignorance reigned. Men were content to have it so. They sometimes conveyed the learned impression that there was no such truth, no truth, that is, beyond their own philosophical and religious speculation. Times change. Faith is still the being confident of things not seen. And statements of that truth which, much less than fifty years ago, were put forth as final have long since been abandoned. That in a chapter on reality in religion we take our departure from this reflection has its reason. It offers us the thin edge of the wedge. The procedure presents a contrast to that formerly prevalent in philosophy, and a still greater contrast to teaching still common in theology. Yet much less than a century ago, among theologians in general, the converse of these assertions was true. What we now ask, especially of theologians, is that they should take to heart the lesson which here in the sciences is plainly written for all who will to see. It is the lesson, namely, that much that we have taught as doctrine and even made permanent as dogma is, in any case, and of necessity, not the fact itself. It is interpretation of facts as we once saw and felt them. It is reflection upon facts. And two things happen to interpretations and reflections, and these two things have happened and are now happening with accelerated pace to much of the theological interpretation which has done honorable service in time past. The first of these is that changed modes of thought bring to our cognizance new facts in the inner life of man just as truly as the methods of inductive science have brought to light new facts in the world about us. The other change to be observed is this, that with advancing knowledge, in all areas—and just as truly in our own—principles of interpretation change. Interpretations esteemed valid a century or even half a century ago are no longer valid for religious men, if these are really in touch with the varied knowledge of our time. We become thus responsible in some measure at least for the alienation of men from religion, if we set forth as the substance of religion that which is really only an interpretation of it, and in some part an antiquated interpretation. We condemn ourselves to remain men of a divided intellectual allegiance. We insist on applying to that which we claim to be the most important of human knowledges modes or reflection which we ourselves no longer use in any other connection. This is the realization of which more than of any other we now stand in need.

1. THE TRUE

There are lines of Goethe of great beauty and significance which are practically repeated at an appreciable interval in the poet's life and in quite different connections. More perhaps than in any equal number of words, the largeness of the poet's spirit is expressed. The verse has the ring of self-dedication and a challenge to men to give themselves to the highest. It is taken from a poem entitled "Generalbeichte," which is thought to have been written in 1802. The stanza runs:—

Willst Du Absolution
Deinen Treuen geben—
Wollen wir nach Deinem Wink
Unablässlich streben
Uns vom Halben zu entwohnen
Und in Ganzen, Guten, Schönen,
Resolut zu leben.

Almost the very words of the next to the last line repeat something which the poet had written perhaps some years earlier in verses entitled, "Ein Epilogue zu Schiller's Glocke." The reference is to Schiller himself. It is to be noted, however, that Schiller died in 1804. I am therefore not quite sure of the order of precedence.

Indessen schritt sein Geist gewaltig fort
Ins Ewige des Wahren, Guten, Schönen,
Und hinter ihm in wesenlosem Scheine
Lag—was uns alle bändigt—das Gemeine.

It would be difficult to say what mood of the poet's reflection determined the order in which these several elements in the life of the spirit are named. We cannot tell whether there was particular significance in the slight change of the order in which the words fall. In a way, nothing could be more characteristic than is his beginning, in the one case, with the word for the Whole, the all-inclusiveness of the meaning of the universe, the world of things toward knowledge of which we are to strive and of the life, which in striving, we are to live. Yet, also, nothing could be more characteristic than is also the other setting. Here it is truth upon which the emphasis is thrown. To Goethe nothing could be good or beautiful which was not true. Then, in both cases it is the good to which wholeness and truth are to lead. And, in turn, in both cases it is the share of beauty in the good and true which is proclaimed. Over the one stanza—the Absolution—hangs the recognition of shortcoming. In both connections there is resolve. The first poem is literally a form of prayer. In the second, self-dedication takes its departure from a loved example. It touches, in closing, upon that which often makes high resolution vain—the ordinary, the accepted, which Goethe so often thought of as the enemy of both the good and the true.

If anything is being contended for in these chapters, it is that in seeking the truth about his universe and himself, in availing himself of that truth and living by it, man has all his hope of the fulfillment of himself. It is in this that he makes his contribution toward "that consummation and far off divine event toward which the whole creation moves." Mankind stands and has always stood over against his world, using the power of reasoning with which he alone of all creation is in such degree endowed, to find out what the universe is like and how it works for men who work with it. His world in all its might and mystery stands over against him. It answers his questions when he learns how to ask them. It lends its might to him when he discovers how to get and use it. It makes itself his ally in things in which his own forbears for uncounted generations found nature hostile. It is subjected, one might say, to one of its own creatures. Man is by no means one of the strongest even of creatures such as walk the earth in our own day. Still less is he to be compared in strength with creatures who in helplessness have perished, while yet from their bones man reconstructs in his own mind a past which was already old before men were at all. Other solar systems he makes his own for purposes at least of understanding movements and vicissitudes of his own little earth. He is not shut up quite, even as were men only a generation or two ago, to helplessness in face of diseases, plague, famine or devastation through the elements. Resources of nature have always been there waiting for him to avail himself of them. And again, in problems which are preponderantly those of human nature, questions of commerce, of government, questions which civilization creates and sometimes solves, and also, often fails to solve, the history of mankind is unrolled to help him. Even in all of this, the key must be in knowledge of what human nature is, what men have done, how they have tried, and perhaps why they have failed. Problems of the inner life are those in which each man seems to start from the line for his own self. Yet treasures of the literature of all humanity are there, embodying the experience of unnumbered generations. These set forth men's aims and efforts, failures or success. Poetry, drama, the literature whereby one knows the hearts of men, help us to know our own hearts and to realize what human life is like. Treasures are on every hand to know, and we are here to know them. Life is essentially an unending quest of truth. It is effort, always inadequate, to solve the mystery of it. It is love of it, joy in it, power through it. Man is changed in his own inner nature by his struggle for conformity, perhaps we should say glad allegiance, to what is true in his environment. Few men have ever shown greater fidelity in search for this truth than did Goethe in his long, privileged and arduous life. There is something in his placing of the word for the good next to the word for the true. For if ever a man sought truth in all its wideness, newness, oldness, endlessness, it was he.

The approach to the general subject of this book, the nature of religion, was chosen intentionally. It was the approach to the question of religion from the side of its truth. It was the relation of religion to valid knowledge and of valid knowledge to religion which first engaged us. Of the various pursuits of truth also, we—and again intentionally—chose first that which has been uppermost in our own generation, the study of external nature. It has indeed been obvious to us that religion has methods of awareness quite other than those in use in natural-scientific inquiry. Yet we have contended that knowledge is in a deep sense one. It is pre-eminently our contention that religion is natural to man. On its subjective side, religion is awareness of a need of man's nature, with also discovery of sources of fulfillment of that need. It is also plain fact that some arguments against religion —or the still more injurious state of mind which assumes that there is no longer any need of argument about it—have their source in a tacit assumption that the religious world is a world all by itself. Some of the religious have, we must own, in their argumentation, given ground for this assertion. Religion is believed in by those who believe in it. It controls those whom it controls. But its magnitudes have no place in the environment of every man's life. It is in this sense that we have sought to set forth that there is in man a need and also a desire to know the truth, in this relation as well, and to conform his life to that truth. Jesus said, "Ye shall know the truth, and the truth shall make you free." Yet much presentation of religion has spent itself in arguing that religion is a state of being bound to something. And, indeed, the very word *religio* describes a state of being bound to something. But is not the scientific man bound to what he knows to be true? Is he not set free from what he now knows to be not true? If this is so, there must be something in man's environment which corresponds to this desire, something which fulfills the need of men to find their truest freedom in being bound to something. It is precisely thus that religion takes its place in the development of men, a place which is taken in no other way. Or, perhaps I should correct myself and say, that we are all bound in our relations to those whom we love. But in those relations we find our most perfect freedom, or, if you choose, freedom to the longest approaches to perfection which human life affords.

Just now to many minds, and this partly through their own absorption, physical facts may seem to be about the only facts, the only hard unquestionable reality. And by a law which we have already noted, the aspect of reality to which we devote our whole selves makes of us selves who are likely to be absorbed in that aspect. Men who make of a limited thing their whole life must not be surprised if they find themselves limited men. They see and feel vaguely and perhaps, at last, not at all, any other than their own chosen aspect of reality. The fanaticisms of religion have always been cheerfully accounted for in this way by those who do not share them. But all about us are similar examples of an obsession by pure specialists in any of the directions of which we have been speaking. Beside the truth one knows, or gives oneself to knowing, it is of value to realize that there are other men and other truths. The sum of reality is made up of them all. We are quite familiar with the fact that there are some for whom the world of beauty, beauty of form, color, sound, is as good as non-existent. We are fain to say that this has a reason which is quite intelligible. They do not give themselves to it sufficiently. How should it give itself to them? No man in science ever made great achievement who did not give himself to science. How should he? The answer concerning religion is in exactly the same line. To say that men could have achieved a character such as all men of just judgment must concede to some religious men whom they have known, and then to say that it must be all hallucination, is absurd. That is clearly as short-sighted as it would be to say that there is no world of nature waiting to reveal itself to men who devote themselves to the study of the world of nature. How can you account for the outgoing of men's hearts and lives in this or that direction, if the experience of mankind has not shown, the record of achievement made quite clear, that there is that which waits for its interpretation upon those who wish to interpret it. It waits in its realization for men who long to have that particular aspect of reality realize itself in them. This paragraph specifically upon the true may well be brief because in a way it has been the effort of this whole book to search for the truth in religion. What is necessary is only to emphasize the necessity of devotion to it, of utilization of it, if one is to fulfill his life in the manner in which it is quite clear that all other aspects of life fulfill themselves, in those, namely, who give a hearty devotion to them—and not otherwise.

2. THE BEAUTIFUL

Again, take the area, not of what we somewhat arbitrarily call truth, but of beauty. Of course, one who loves beauty, whose life goes out to it, holds that beauty is also truth. Keats thought so. Not quite everybody follows him. One looks at a piano. It is an amazingly complicated mechanism. It is admirably responsive to a purpose which has wide acceptance. The mechanism is, however, not the thing which impresses us. A violin is a still more wonderful instrument, perhaps because it is a so much simpler mechanism. Both are created to respond to a skilled hand. And to what does the skilled hand respond? One moved by music, however, does not think at the time of any of these things. What happens is that a musician makes music—that is, this is what happens to those to whom music appeals. To others, perhaps, he merely makes noise. The musician produces, or reproduces, from and to a trained emotion, a quality in human life. This quality may cover almost the world for which the musician lives. He makes others also, according to their several degrees of receptivity, to live for moments in that world. To these it is real. It is something which through written music enables new generations to share the inspiration of all times. It lifts us, even in memory, above the harassing, the transient, the inane. It opens a way by which we can in moments of weariness and sorrow transcend ourselves. It enables us to help others to do the same. Music, and equally, other expressions of beauty, render this service to those who have in themselves that which opens them to its reception. But in a measure this is true of all our receptivities. Training for such production or reproduction, and even for more perfect receptivity, has been gained in long drudgery. Habit works transformation of man's nature to respond to that which music in its fullness has to say to him. All the world cannot say it to him who has no such receptivity. I am not sure that the distinction often made that the sciences deal with quantities while the arts, with ethics and religion, deal with qualities, is a true distinction. The tissues of life hardly admit of being divided by the shears quite in that way. At the same time, it is true that beauty, as also goodness, of which we shall speak later, belong to the world of quality.

Or take the case of singing. Here a trained voice is in itself the whole apparatus of expression. It has itself become, under discipline, an instrument quite as wonderful as the pianist's hand. It seems even more subtle, less obviously comparable to mechanism, more directly the simple means of transmission of emotion. It has a living quality of the personality of the singer. It is the means of creating emotion and transforming personality in the hearer. It is a natural outlet of power, of passion, or of pathos. It is a living description of beauty, or again, of terror. Like those others, and by the same token, it may descend to the level of the banal and the unworthy. Or, it may transform "things common until they rise to touch the spheres." This means of uttering the heights and depths of feeling in the singer and of creating like heights and depths in those who hear, is older than any instrument. It seems likely to outlast them all. No great singer doubts the existence of a quality which lies out beyond his best attainment. Yet it is this which gives itself to him, in some measure, as he gives himself to it. It even enables him to give it to others—to those who really hear.

For there are, of course, those whom music leaves untouched. Races, even, differ in this regard. Tradition, convention, are not without influence. But, in the last analysis, one may say that those whom music leaves untouched are probably of those who leave music untouched. Denial proves nothing to those whose experience proves the contrary. Even in inquiries concerning the material universe, aptitudes are gained by application. Discoveries seldom happen to those who have no fitness to have them happen. "Seek and ye shall find."

Things of the same sort might be said of painting and architecture. Most of all, if we may take still another example, one might argue from poetry. The common speech of men is necessary to our intercourse. Prosaic, utilitarian indeed, and often diverted to things base or of injurious intent, yet this, too, has been from time immemorial means of the preservation of the glory of the past, of uplifting of the hearts of men in present exigency and to vision of the future. It has been the means of penetration to the inmost secrets of men's souls and the method of depiction of the grand drama of life as it goes on about us. It is something never to be forgotten when the right word has been found by the man who had genius to find it. In this case, it is a man in the whole of his being who is the instrument. Men who have had this quality have never hesitated to speak of it as of something which had been given them to say. The whole man is fitted, perhaps by the travail of his soul, to transmit something of the meaning which life has taught him. It is not that they by sheer effort make what was not there before, although in all high things there must be effort, too. It is that something of reality in the universe meets their endeavor. It is conferred upon them and by them passed on to others. Men of this sort we speak of as men of genius. The greatest of them have had the sense that in a supreme moment they went beyond themselves. Archbishop Söderblom has said, "The emergence of genius is in its way a constant demonstration of the truth that the essence of reality is creative. But the most miraculous thing which men have done at all is, I suppose, the creation and continuous re-creation of language. The language which, beyond all else, distinguishes man from the animals from whom we assume that man is derived, is ordered speech. This is the instrument of his self-expression, and likewise of his guiding and re-creative influence upon others." If we take poetry to be the language of feeling, it is no wonder that poetry is older than prose. Man was apparently a being of feeling before he was a being of what we call reflection. Long before writing it would seem that there were songs—at least, the earliest written songs which have come down to us seem already to have had a long history behind them. Older than Homer is supposed to be the mythical tradition out of which our Homer is made. It was creative imagination, proud racial consciousness, joy in life, fortitude in calamity, which had made his people what it was, long before the Homer whom we read had spoken. Pindar's mistrust of his own age, his saddened turning to the past, his search in it for principles which could guide a better future, treads already a path which poets have trodden ever since his day. Plato, surely among the greatest of philosophers, never passed wholly beyond the poetic mind. The high civilization of the Greek States produced tragedy, comedy, lyric, immediately appealing to us both in the greatness and the meanness of our civilization. Genesis and Judges are of the sort of stuff of which we speak. Psalms and Proverbs, Job and the Wisdom literature, belong, in their surpassing expressions of love of nature, in their consuming interest in the problem of the life of man; prophets in their depiction of the evils of their present, in their clear vision and their glorious hope, all belong to the great poetry of the world. And this poetry itself, by dint of what might be called a mere historic sequence, is canonized in the Christian church. Few of us but will admit that, compared with these, the law-giving and long stretches of the history, leave us cold. In Coleridge's phrase, it is the poetry which "finds us." Add that the Protestant insistence upon it all, as even an external authority, has made it known in more than six hundred languages and dialects of practically all the peoples of the earth. Moreover, through the long night after the fall of the Roman Empire, this was almost the only widely known literature of the northern and western world. What by and by grew up beside it was, again, just as in the ancient world, a literature of songs, legends, the songs of Roland, the Niebelungenlied, the Tales of Arthur, a whole world, again, of imagination and emotion, of loyalties and courtesies and charm, upon which the heart of Europe fed itself for half a thousand years. From it in no small degree the dramatists, even of the times of great Elizabeth, drew their plots.

After the Renaissance, with the new birth of intellectual freedom, there came, in every greater nation in Europe, now more and more in the vernaculars, such a revival of poetry of every sort as had not been known since the decline of the classical civilization. Of this literary revival our own age is the heir. In our time, a mass of literature of every sort is daily and hourly poured forth upon the world. This is partly through the invention of printing, and again, through the development of means of communication, and doubtless also through the great increase in the proportion of those who can read. Every one of us has to choose for himself that part, out of these infinite riches or, as it sometimes seems, of means of infinite inpoverishment of man's spirit, what he decides to use. But it will hardly be denied that it is in the large sense the literature of feeling that helps us to find and to keep our souls. Much of the rest of it we must simply glance at if we would keep our fitness to meet the emergencies of the day. Some of it might even be omitted in the same interest. Not to have formed a taste for good reading or, again, to permit the pressure of the world to prevent our indulgence of this taste, is to have impoverished ourselves. Just as before, it is a case of wish and will. One cannot quite say that it is a case of acquired taste, this taste for great literature. For it is a taste, by and large, which uncultivated people often have. It was this which in our childhood we loved. It does not require cultivation to bring it alive. It does require choices to keep it alive and through it to advance in alertness toward nobler things. It is the door to a world from which we cannot afford to permit the dullness which life presents to us in plenty to shut us out. It is when we simply permit high things to come in and make their abode with us that they work their miracle upon us. Interest is necessary, but not necessarily the interest of an excited moment or of an exhausted hour. There must be in the universe outside ourselves this something which gives itself to us, this answer to all that which in the highest moments of their lives men seek.

This is the sort of thing which in common speech we mean by inspiration. It is obvious that, in the sense vital to our discussion, the thing we seek to describe is of far wider application than some current discussion as to inspiration of the Scriptures would lead us to suppose. The student of astronomy, of biology, of medicine, has his inspiration. It is the joy he finds in the effort to discover and to apply the particular truth which belongs to the area of his endeavor. It is the confidence which upholds him in his defeat. It is the elation which comes with his success. He has always believed that the truth was there for him to seek. The faith of it upheld him while he sought. It is still more a revelation when he finds. It makes further inquiries requisite. We are accustomed to use the words inspiration and revelation in speaking, possibly, of poetry or of music and of art. Many men have fallen into an unfortunate convention in the use of the same words in relation to religion. The qualification must come, of course, from the nature of our particular endeavor. But what is here involved is that we perceive that in all these relations of life there is an insight which can, with its own appropriateness, be called inspiration and revelation. It is a view of nature which is touched with the imagination, perhaps also moved by the sufferings and hopes of men. It is nature seen through the medium of human life. It is emotion seeking uplift and support, power and peace, through nature. It is finding escape from the trivialities of life and the distresses of mankind by claiming the rights of one's own soul and the rights of other souls. In a sense these few words about the transcendent world of truth and beauty may suffice. They are to us in our main endeavor only illustrations. With the good and the holy we are, in a discussion of religion, more directly concerned. To them we advance. But it is worth these words to have shown that the good and the holy are not isolated. They belong to a world of reality and realization to which the true and the beautiful also belong. The method of appropriation and achievement is the same. That method is occupation with them, surrender to them, domination by them, fulfillment of ourselves through them.

3. THE GOOD

We chose in this chapter on reality and realization to speak first of the true. That order does homage to a prevailing temper of our time. It was the advance of the sciences of nature which served us for point of departure. Here it is easier to prove that nothing is now true which does not accord with facts now known. Look out upon the Campagna and reflect that if the Romans had known that water enclosed in iron pipe—and if, incidentally, they had known how to make such pipe—would have tended to rise practically to the height in the hills from which it came, we should have no aqueducts to add to the poignancy of our reflection upon the "glory which was Rome." Of course, when we think of it in this way, it must surprise us that the widespread enthusiasm for the pursuit of truths of external nature which has marked, say, the last one hundred years, should have come so far down in the history of mind. Beginnings of such study were indeed made by Greeks half a millennium before Christ, both in Asia Minor and in southern Italy. Then, the thought of the Greeks turned in other directions, to philosophy, statecraft, to the moral and social world. Egyptians had known also how to place stones in their pyramids which would baffle a modern engineer. We read about hanging gardens of Babylon, but we do not know quite how much to believe. The physical sciences were condemned to a millennium of neglect. The Greeks turned to the kingdom of the beautiful, and presently also to the kingdom of moral and social reflection. Their thoughts have become a universal heritage. There was, indeed, an outburst of interest in the physical sciences among Moslems in the valley of the Euphrates while Europe was still hopelessly in the Dark Ages. Then came another arrest until, almost, our own time. Meantime, religion and morals held the field. It is, however, the question of the good, the realm of morals, of which we propose next to speak. That which was good to do seems in earliest times to have been determined largely by what others did. The tribal spirit, clan wisdom and impulse, had its way. The very word morals, as we have said, seems to be derived from *mores,* the customary, the practices of the peoples to which men belonged. Even forms of religion are held to have had origin in the sense of responsibilities within the group life. Governments, perhaps we should say leaderships, as they then arose, laid down what members of the clan must do. It was then but a short step to the use of force, often not in the interest of the people and of posterity, but in the interest of ruling classes, and ultimately, of the potentate himself. Leaders in religion also made themselves lawgivers. They availed themselves of awe and reverence. They drew upon superstition. They promulgated imaginations in the name of gods or God. The history of religions is at this point profoundly instructive for the history of morals as well.

But for us, for all deeper thought concerning morals, the actual touchstone is neither civil nor ecclesiastical. It is rather—in reference to a particular injunction or prohibition—is it really in its own nature and in the light of the nature of man, right or wrong? Does moral truth agree with it? This is the reason why there has come to be a science of morals as also of government. The purpose is to find out what is real in the realm of that which is set forth as right. We are no longer much impressed with sovereign assumptions. We are likely to be aroused by threats. We dispute the State. We reject the decisions of our own democracy, if we think they are mistaken. So often have religious leaders or ecclesiastical institutions proclaimed that that was wrong which proved to be right—or the converse—that even here we are not too humble. It may indeed be that we are making these disputes on the basis of selfishness, merely pitting self-assertion against authority. That is a very old story. If, however, we do this with a feeling of responsibility, and as we gain consent of right-minded men, we no longer hesitate. The last question is, Does this which is proclaimed as right rest upon the truth, so far as we yet know the truth, as to moral relations? Is the claim that this is the right, the good, sustained by experience? Are facts on its side, or, better still, is it on the side of the facts? We can alter the injunction. We cannot alter the facts. The facts themselves also change, with the evolution of man and with the success or failure of men's institutions. Perhaps only by mistakes in our efforts can we find out what the facts are. A good part of human history, especially of moral history, could be described in that single sentence. It is a statement like that which aligns our inquiry into the nature of the good with all the other rational and scientific inquiries to which we commit ourselves.

We come here upon the principle which we have already dwelt upon as to the truth in the area of the sciences. After all, the so-called laws of nature are merely such as men, wise as to nature, have been able to set forth. New facts require the formulation of new laws. Even new insight into old facts does the same. Reality judges the law, and not law reality. Human history is, however, in this particular of morals many times longer and more complex than is any history of science. We speak of the laws of nature. And only a generation ago rather uncomplimentary contrasts were occasionally drawn between the calm effectiveness of the laws of nature and the working of what were called the laws of men, and still more if these were alleged to be laws of God. Forces of nature do not pursue the course they do because there is a law that they shall. Quite the contrary. Forces of nature follow the course they do because of the nature of the forces and of the facts with which they have to do. The laws of nature are not laws at all. They are only our generalizations from observed facts. The law is deduced from the course which the facts pursue. When further facts become known, with also modes, to us new, of operation of forces in relation to those facts, it is the laws, and not either the forces or the facts which have to be revised. The very phrase, "law of nature," is nothing but an importation from another area of the knowledge and experience of men, namely that of government. It is a misnomer. Conduct of nature was naïvely carried back to a supposed ordinance of God. In reality, the law was inferred by men from the conduct of nature and often, also, from the disastrous conduct of men. Even within its own area, that of the ordering of the conduct of men, the conception of law has undergone and is continuously undergoing modification. We may owe something of our clearer feeling about the necessity of law meeting facts, to examples set us in the sciences of nature. Also, we may owe some of it to reflection upon vast changes of government, in the modern world, which people gladly impose upon themselves. For long ages in the lifetime of mankind, law was thought of primarily as the expression of the will of a ruler. If the ruler were wise and good, his laws sought the good of those subject to it. But even that was a good deal of a presumption. Did he know? Or, if the very power of the ruler tempted him to abuse it in control of the conduct of men in his own interest, as often happened, then the issue was evil. The recourse was to overthrow the ruler. The process often resulted in the mere substitution of another ruler of the same sort. The impulse to democracy in our modern world can perhaps be traced to the Renaissance, with its reflection upon the ancient world. It obtained its full development as principle only at the end of the eighteenth century. It was a brave effort or, at least, it was a courageous ideal, for the remedying of some old evils. Once the first idealization of it was past—and in the period following the French Revolution, its idealization passed quite rapidly—we have become aware that democracy also may be the source of selfish and stupid, of violent and possibly fatal legislation. But it is at least the hope of democracy that laws can, by process of trial and error, be brought into ever-clearer conformity to the nature of man and of society.

It is not surprising that, in the long ages in which the source of law was thought to be the personal will of a ruler, the divine order should have been thought of after the same manner. Think of the long history of the language about God as king, of the attribution to him of supreme wisdom indeed, but also of unlimited power. The ascription also to God of all wisdom and power in control of nature, with also belief in interventions, at his pleasure, in the course of nature for the good of man—all this seemed to follow of itself. But the long history of the evolution of morals shows that men have had no such clear vision, certainly no miraculous intimation, as to what God intended. Humanity has had to learn that by disappointing and distressing experience. We seem at times to be indefinitely far from having learned it even yet. Whatever the will of God may be from and to all eternity, we do not know. We learn a little of it in the progression of ideals and devotion of men to the good with, indeed, also, progression of ideas as to what is good. We have to find the nature of man, and learn no small part of the right, in the long experience of humanity. Any revelation from God which we can understand comes to men in and through this experience. Take, for example, so illustrious a mind and so lofty a moral nature as was that of Jonathan Edwards, the great teacher both of theology and philosophy in this country in the eighteenth century. It seems almost incredible that a mind so great could have esteemed the problem so simple. Or, again, that he could have been so sure in his pronouncement of the eternal bliss of some men and of the eternal damnation of others. It was perhaps one of the last high exhibitions of the result of abstract speculation upon the whole vast problem of morals with which we are concerned.

Tribal customs, laws of Solon, laws of Moses, laws of any State or Church, can be nothing, from the human side, but just interpretation in the light of facts then known, and in the light, quite as truly, of ideals, which perpetually change. Ideals are better if men are better, tragically worse if men are worse. It is only on this basis that we can develop a science, and then also a philosophy, and finally, a theology which comports with the facts of a moral world. And it does not, even then, continue so to comport, because both knowledge and experience change. Among these all, and most of all among the theologians, reigned a view that the nature of man was evil and only evil. The case is bad enough, but not so bad as that. These ideas dominated centuries of religious teaching. Salvation of the individual man came to seem to be purely a matter of divine intervention on his particular behalf. When one reads the literature of Deism in the latter part of the eighteenth century, can one wonder at the revolt that these ideas provoked? Men brooding over the life of mankind were unable, some of them, to believe that the divine in life could be represented in such terms as those. Philosophies of the first half of the nineteenth century revolted almost as vigorously as did the rationalism of the last half of the eighteenth century. It is perhaps one of the "uncovenanted" mercies of the scientific movement that we have been caused to ask ourselves questions even more fundamental about the nature of man. Also we realize that we have no such exhaustive knowledge of the moral nature of the universe as would be implied in theories like those of which we speak. Furthermore, what knowledge as to human nature we can expect to gain from the course of life and the destinies of mankind we shall gain only by the study of man's nature on its best side as well as on its worst. Man's age-long wrestling with the problem of evil, his achievement in the direction of the good, also his incredible achievements in the direction of the evil, do not, any or all of them, lead to quite such a theory as to either God or man, as that of which we spoke above.

It is upon this basis alone that we can have a science of morals and, incidentally, of government. The purpose is to get at the facts, to find out what is real in the realm of the good. As we just said, we dispute the State, our own State, when we think it is wrong. We think that is our sacred duty if the State is ever to be better. This is no small part of the substance of political living at the present. Often as it leads us to the wrong, we are at least sure that this is the only path upon which we can hope to be led to the right. Of course, we too, may make, must make, these decisions on the basis of our own individual judgment. We do often make them on the basis of selfishness. That is an old story, too—one of the oldest. Bad or mistaken laws have to be changed. The moral life of men with which they deal moves. Knowledge moves. Ideals change. Purposes change with them. This, I think, is the fundamental fact. We lay down laws and set up governments to change characters. If we succeed in changing characters, we have to change the rules. And if we do not succeed in changing characters, then also we have to change the rules. Too much rule is bad. Too little may be worse. But, in the last analysis, right is not made by rules. The rules must rest upon the right. For all that we permit ourselves to say about that grand abstraction, the unchanging right, the concrete right here in this world, is always changing. The word *absolute* was not made to conjure with, not even the absoluteness of God. We can make God the Absolute only by making him cease to be God. Our faith is that there is always a right on beyond the right as we know it, to which our right, if it is right, is at least a stepping stone. It is a stage which must be passed through. This trust sustains us in the struggle.

There is no more perfect illustration of the contention of these chapters. In our universe is a reality which we call the right, the good, seen at least partially, now and then embodied partially, acted out imperfectly, here and there. Men have pursued it as best they could, some times out of the love of the ideal, sometimes also out of the terror which the flaunting of the opposite ideal brings upon us. They have never embodied it more than partially. They have often pursued it under illusion. They have sometimes fled from it in anger. They have failed and tried some new form of self-assertion. Here lies, however, more than anywhere else the secret of destiny for individual men and for the race. Depraved by bad morals, all the results of science may be wasted on us if we let them enervate us or lead us only to more selfish living. The very power over nature which is thus given us may be abused to degrade ourselves and the world. We see all of this about us at the present moment. Even religion as we have sometimes apprehended it may delude us. Religion may be thought of as a concrete set of morals, bound to be antiquated. Or again, it may be an emotional substitute for morals. The good, however, blesses the world when it is done and condemns it when it is not done. The fate of our neighbors and ourselves, the destiny of institutions and empires since the world began, has depended upon this more than upon all things besides. There is in the nature of things a right, a good. Man is here to find out about it, to fulfill himself in doing it, or to destroy himself by not doing it. When one thus thinks, one feels that the inquiry as to this particular realm of nature takes precedence over all our other inquiries. To this austerity, this self-evidencing quality, this self-exerting power of the good, in light of which we seek to represent it as the grandest aspect of reality, the history of morals presents a melancholy contrast.

One reads of a dreamland republic as in Plato, or again, a profound philosophy of real government as in Aristotle. One reads the "Meditations" of Marcus Aurelius. What one finds in those "Meditations" is a good deal of despair of the world. He had so profound a knowledge of it and, at moments, felt also his utter impotence for the guidance of it. He retires into the ideal and moral world of the individual. He would do his duty. I doubt if in any man moral sense was ever stronger. But he practically gave up the problem of the world. The satirists of his own time record enormities in his own palace. They never spoke disrespectfully of him. Their testimony and Gibbon's narrative sometimes make us ask ourselves how such a man happened to come to such a post in the world, and what in that world he could have done. Rising Christianity with its apocalyptic expectation of the end of the world, and then, presently, its repudiation of a world which appeared to be too bad even to go to its appropriate end—Christian asceticism, also, gave up the world. Yet Christian organization kept at least one foot in the world to discipline it for the world's own good. Incidentally, it sometimes made of itself a very worldly thing. This, and the wearing of the Roman purple a thousand years after the Empire was dead, sometimes makes us think that the Church had not learned much even of the spirit of the great Emperor, and still less of the spirit of Christ. Calvinism and our own ancestral Puritanism had something of the same trait. Divine authority for lawgivers and law-enforcers, rigid morality enforced by pains and penalties far outside the area of the moral life, transferred no small part of true religion to the inner life, and then, the rest of it, to the future state. We have gained liberty by their strife. But it is long since clear that, if liberty is all that we have gained, it will lead us nowhither. We have built up an empire largely by trade in which, strange as it sometimes seems, the Puritans were adepts. We have built it up more largely still by aid of science. It is sometimes now a fair question as to whether we have morals and manners, or even physique enough to live with the civilization which we have gained. We have achieved unexampled liberty for masses of men. The question now is, What are they going to do with that liberty? We have been told that the voice of the people is the voice of God. Rarely. We have a saying that "One with God is a majority"—a saying which is apt to be quoted by a man who thinks himself that one. We have lapses sometimes into the making of more laws to insure more morality. Sometimes we discover that such laws are more likely to insure their own desperate infraction. Most of law is, of course, conventional. Freedom is essential to morality. Apparently also morality is essential to freedom. To the apprehension of that fact Hebraism worked itself through in a thousand years of history—most of them sad years. Jesus and Paul started from that vantage. But how long did Christianity remain true to that truth? How soon did it fall back into the claim of a divine warrant for its authorities even when these were not very good, and occasionally when they were very, very bad?

It is to be admitted that, on any plane, the pursuit of the sort of truth with which the sciences mainly deal is the task of a limited number of men. The practical interest in science is universal, as is also some participation in benefits which science confers. A commitment of the whole life to it is reserved for some, and these of a more or less defined type. The same sort of thing may be said of the pursuit of beauty. With morals it is different. Every man in every relation in life is touched by morals. In some way or another, morals—either our own or those of the men with whom we have to deal—or both—enter into almost every conceivable relation. The thing is vastly complicated. The process is age-long. "The decay of stocks," as President Eliot called it, stocks which have earned for a few generations power of resistance to evil, an outgoing creative quality for the venture of the good, is a phenomenon nowhere more evident than in the portion of the world in which we live—as also the contrary is nobly evident. On a larger scale the rise and decline of great races is only the same phenomenon covering longer intervals of time. Much ground is gained in ethical perception and control, only to be lost again. On the whole, perhaps altruism, the care of the other man, the care for all men, is the thing which has chronically failed. Yet, on the other hand, self-abnegation, self-immolation, is certainly not all good, for it is the good self which is the driving force. All the rest is only apparatus for the good self to work with. In the last analysis, it is not good conditions, except in a very subordinate way, it is good selves that we hope and strive to create or to re-create in others which determines the issue. And indeed, it is the good self, perpetually re-created, which alone is secure against "going bad." All the rest, government, laws, institutions, reforms, are only instruments. They are all only falsified when they are operated by bad selves if, indeed, they can do more than merely seem to be operated by bad selves. When we have said this we have said again the thing which is parallel to that which we said touching the beautiful, or that which we acknowledged as to the true, only we seem to have said it with greater emphasis and in more universal relations. In the light of a history so long and an obligation so wide as is that of moral evolution, there must be that in the universe which puts all men under obligation to find out what it is, and then to do it. There must be something which has sustained men in an age-long effort which embodies the ultimate hope that we can rationally cherish for mankind. This is the only explanation of the ceaseless struggle of mankind to know and to do the good, namely, that there is in our universe a reality, the most imperious of all of those of which we speak. It corresponds to the best in man, and something in man corresponds to it. The oldest, hardest struggle in the world has been the struggle for the good. The deplorable and pathetic and, after so much experience, the ridiculous errors which we make in the pursuit would long since have overwhelmed even so dull, so obstinate but so indomitable a thing as is mankind, if there were nothing there to justify pursuit. The struggle for the moral is so august, it has been conducted under such terrific odds, it has, after all, achieved such a measure of success! Life would have to be given over as irrational if we did not believe that there is something in common, and exactly at this point, between man and the universe. It is this which makes the struggle for its achievement the expression of the nature of both the universe and of man.

4. THE HOLY

When one thinks of the majesty which we have thus ascribed to the moral, one might ask, What is there beyond? Can there be anything "beyond good and evil?" Nietzsche raised that question, but answered it hardly satisfactorily. The answer is one which postulates religion, and this was the answer which Nietzsche could not give. On the other hand, have not religions, to support their cause, sometimes called evil good? Have they not summoned to their aid fears of an evil more dreadful than the worst things in life? Have they not also promised rewards which are imaged as extensions of what some people take for sources of happiness in this life? But also these have often been happinesses which would hardly seem such to deeper natures. And if, as we declared, the moral order is equipped with such relentless power for its own execution, what is the need of anything beyond? And yet, it is just that need of reparation, restoration, which the religious man feels and which, all of itself, the moral order once broken, does not seem to promise. It is this for which man hopes. And it is this which religion offers. Perhaps in face of his own ideal, damaged or defeated by himself, this is the deepest feeling that man has at all. Otto wrote some years ago a book entitled, "The Holy." The book was promptly translated into English. It has exerted influence both in his land and ours. A Roman poet long ago said that fear is the source of religion. Nor can it be denied that fear has been a source of some of its manifestations ever since. But fear is not the only source. It is not the noblest source. Fear is not the thing which differentiates religion. And if modern man, with the better understanding of nature which science gives, and with wider knowledge of the experience of the race, may, nevertheless, be overtaken by fear, what have we to think of primitive man? All his simple provisions for safety were liable, momentarily, to destruction by powers to which he could offer no resistance. He himself grew ill and old and saw those dear to him a prey to death. How could he fail to live in fear? Yet with his fear seems to have lain also a deeper, a neutral emotion, that of awe. And awe was the parent also of a feeling quite different from fear, that of reverence, trust. In trust he might take refuge from his fear. Man wondered in face of a world so almost totally unknown to him. His wonder might in one train of circumstances be turned to fear. It might in another sequence take the form of reverence. Trust might, indeed, still alternate with mistrust. Even as toward his fellows, trust was as natural toward some as distrust was natural toward others. Expectation of good had place in his mind along with awareness of the possibilities of evil. For that matter, both good and evil had share in his outward state, in his relation to his tribe, to his family, to all the conditions of nature in which his life was involved. If persons, some of his fellows, were sources of his trust, what wonder if he endowed some powers of nature, also, with dispositions like those which he knew among his fellows. Persons among his enemies were also the most real sources of his distrust. Goethe once said, "Man never knows how anthropomorphic he is." What other semblance than that of magnified man would things naturally wear to the great children that primitive men seem to us to have been? Things benevolent and malevolent bear the same semblance of the personal to children and childlike minds even now. Traditions, mythologies and theologies have perpetuated this same semblance, and this for both the religious and the non-religious among us. At this level the devil is as natural as God. And all this is because myths and traditions are more than just semblances for certain aspects of truth. The deeper reason lies in the fact that we ourselves are persons. Those truths, which are also values, are values only to persons.

Granted, however, the naturalness, perhaps inevitableness, of this impersonation of mysterious powers, one fact is only the more surprising, if it is true. Some anthropologists have judged that the thing sought to be compassed, whether by magic or by prayer, was not just favor of persons, malignant or benevolent. It was advantage of which a man could possess himself, and this whether by force or by deceit, as in magic, or by cajoling, as in prayer, and therewith he would have all that he desired. There seems to me something more than ordinarily imaginative in Frazer's effort to set forth magic as the rudiment of science, the beginning of that which has flowered so magnificently in our day. The effort of the magician was not to understand nature. It is not the effort of people of that mind nowadays to understand nature, and so to benefit by putting themselves under its laws. Quite the contrary. The effort seems to be by incantation, gestures, spells, which can have no scientific meaning whatever, to force nature to do the will of the magician. Only this fantasy as to the meaning of magic makes it possible for Frazer to proceed with his argument. He esteems that it was only after the futility of this effort, by magic, to force nature to do man's will became evident, that men betook themselves to prayer. Prayer is accordingly viewed as the effort to persuade deities whom one had not been able to force. These deities were either malignant or benevolent but having power, both of them, over the lives of men. In this sense, it is not probable that magic gave way to prayer. In fact, magic does not seem altogether to have given way to prayer, even yet, either in Papua or elsewhere. It is still with us, if one may believe the signs on our streets. The point is that there is no such sequence of magic and religion. Rather, both are expressions, the one dominantly of the attitude of fear, the other preponderantly of the attitude of trust. These attitudes, as we have said, have a common root in what we call awe. But prayer has had by far the nobler history. It expresses the worthier attitude. It calls out the better qualities of men. It conforms more nearly to the truth as to both man and his universe. Therewith is not said but that prayer also has, at times and for some men, borne the aspect almost, one might say, of conjuring. Men have made a sort of piety of believing in its power, as if, for example, our interpretation of promises of God bound God to do our will. Incidentally, can we be sure of our interpretations? Tennyson's noble line, "More things are wrought by prayer than this world dreams of," may easily be misunderstood. We can but think of such views of our communion with God as survivals of phases of thought almost unimaginably old and surely now discredited. But certainly an ennobling of the souls of men, through aspiration after and submission to that aspect of reality which is most really determinant of ourselves, is the very point of departure for the phase of our discussion upon which we now enter. Whether we call it prayer, or not, is perhaps only a question of definition. It is sensitiveness to, outgoing toward, receptivity of, empowerment by, that aspect of the Great Reality which is related to the vitality and direction, the responsibility and creativity, of our own spirits. It is not the desire of something beyond the moral. It is the solicitude that we may be enabled to know and to do, to be and to bear, all that corresponds to the moral and the spiritual in ourselves, and thus to enter upon a relation loftier even than that which is merely the moral.

Most certainly it is to upright souls a solace, a ground of confidence in the integrity of the universe, that the right gets itself done in the manner which the last paragraph implied. Most certainly there is a comfort if men have given their lives for a good cause and have seen it only in part accomplished, or not accomplished at all. This comfort is to think that, even so, the effort has been by no means vain. If not in their time then in some other time, if not in their way, then in some other way, the good will come to pass. Other men will dedicate themselves to the endeavor. Circumstances will be more propitious. Time will be more ripe. The thing brave spirits dreamed will yet be done. Prophets of old, heroic persons of all time, believed that iniquity will not forever triumph, injustice reign, peace be violated, hope of good be trampled on. The literature they left becomes the language of repentance and renewal to tens of generations, words by which not only they but people of all lands and times have lifted themselves up again from their disasters. Did not Jesus, last of the prophets, some would say, first of the heralds of the new embodiment of an old power, others say—did not Jesus cry, as almost for the last time, he looked down upon the "city of his solemnities,"—"O Jerusalem, thou that killest the prophets and stonest them that are sent unto thee, how often would I have gathered thy children as a hen gathereth her brood beneath her wings, but ye would not." When the mob in their enthusiasm would have taken him by force to make him a king, he fled. When Pilate asked him, "Art thou a king?" he said, "Yes,"—but made haste to explain that it was in a sense which the Procurator could hardly have been expected to understand. It was a meaning which priests, with scribes and Pharisees, rejected in a bitter scorn. Somewhat so, Savonarola must have thought as they bound him to the stake. One reads that amazing book of his, "The Victory of the Cross," one feels the varied currents of his enthusiasm, his pathetic misconceptions, errors of judgment, trust of broken reeds which pierced his hand, his bewilderment in critical moments. He had no friend but God, and God said nothing, only fortified his soul for that he was to suffer. The feet of Savonarola's image were of clay. But are not the feet of our grandest enthusiasms for the good always of clay, even though they may be also, let us hope, mingled with iron? Savonarola had no children. Jesus had no children, that is, in the flesh. Both had children of their spirit, Jesus twenty centuries of them. If one grieves for one's nation when the inexorable right overtakes it, how poignantly must one grieve in pathetically smaller ways over the circle of his intimates, whom he has failed to persuade. This cup has one more drop of bitterness. It is compounded of too many elements. If things come too close to us, we cannot easily take the long look which in the other case may compensate. And what if, in addition to all the rest, we are haunted by the sense that, with all our zeal, we, too, have made mistakes? And who can rise to passion and not make mistakes? Time is on God's side. Nations and races have relatively long time, our children little, and we less. There is hardly anything more certain in life than that it is love that causes us to make some of our blunders, and then it is love which adds bitterness to our contrition. "I have been zealous for the Lord my God," cried Elijah, "and I alone am left." In that mood one is on the road to cease to be good. Our compromises —what we have done in the days when we thought that the road was going to be short and the end sure—those haunt us. Jesus cried from the cross, "My God, why hast thou forsaken me?" But it was to God that he cried.

In times like these, it is not enough to say, "I have loved righteousness and hated iniquity." Still less is it enough to say, "Oh, my opponents will have their reward." Some prophets are rather too full of that kind of confidence. Denunciatory saints impair the beauty of their haloes. If ethics has nothing to say beyond that, then there is need of something beyond ethics. Religion is that thing. If the universe had nothing to say but, "They have their own reward who fail," then few of us would escape that condemnation. For all of us fail partially, and some of us think we fail completely. It is of the very essence of religion to put before us aims so great that in part we must fail. If a man is too sure that he has understood all the good and given himself absolutely to pursuit of it, then we almost feel sure that we understand why he failed. It is from this point of view that we have to think of religion, not as a supplement to the ethical for those who would value such a supplement—or, for that matter, even believe in it. And most certainly it is not a substitute for the ethical. It is an element in it, a necessity of it, if the moral life is to be lived upon ever higher planes. It is rather common that our successes reveal to us our failures—that is, to those who are open to such revelation. What religion postulates in the universe is the counterpart of something which we find within ourselves. Better put, we are, both in our best endeavors and our direst necessities, the counterparts of it. We are souls, and when we feel that, we seek the soul in the universe.

That religion has been used as a source of comfort in this life, or a ground of hope in the next, in matters in which we do not so much need to be comforted as to be "stabbed awake," is true. This is but to say that all good may be misinterpreted and most truths misapplied. This is just one of several ways in which in the long life of mankind, religion has been misapplied. But if it serves not to relax the austerity of the moral—of that which Kant called the "categorical imperative" of it—if, rather, it tends to make us, being only men, more nearly equal to that austerity and more obedient to that imperative—the imperative of that which is beyond the strength of men—then religion has its own place. It does its work, a work which exactly the best men most need to have done. If we are bidden to do that which is beyond our strength, then we have to find a strength beyond our own in which to do it. "Behold, we know not anything but are as children crying in the night." The pride of religion, or at least of some of the religious, has indeed been a stumbling block. There are some tasks so great that pride is the last mood in which they should be approached. Yet self-depreciation also is a snare. True humility is something different from either. It is the mind turned outward, onward, which is at its best and in which we have most confidence. The essence of religion is this outward look.

It is in this virile trust in that which is above ourselves that religion presents its own parallel to the scientific man's belief in the truth, to the artist's surrender to beauty, to the moralist's sense of the inexorableness of the good. That trust—all these trusts—have value for us. They make us capable of becoming what we are not, of doing what we cannot, and of being happy in doing it. And yet, we say again, this trust can have this value for us only on condition that it corresponds to fact. It must itself be a counterpart of reality. It is that reality finding response in our best selves. Furthermore, all these things can have this value for us only if we are of those for whom they have this value. It is no great wonder that religion is not very real to a great many people. How should it be? But again, to how many people is science real? I do not mean the mere benefits which science confers. Anybody can believe in those. I mean the mind which has been re-created after the pattern which obtains in the pursuit of the truth of science. To how many people is music real? To how many people is the supreme magnitude of morals real? I mean real in the sense of something far beyond rewards and punishments. In any deeper sense all these things are real to those only in whom there is something real responding to their reality. You cannot get on at the highest levels of life without them. We all have moments when we may feel that we cannot get on with them. And when once we begin to live for them, they seem to have taken possession of us and not we of them.

We may perhaps doubt the surmises of which we spoke a few pages back, which argued that the object of desire was not necessarily thought of in earliest magic as quality of persons, but just as some thing to be gained possession of. But no one ever thought of a realm of right remotely like that of which we spoke, a world of principles which inexorably execute themselves—no one ever thought of such a kingdom of the good without thinking of it in terms of persons. No such realm would naturally be thought of without a ruler. The more vast the empire, the more necessary the sway. This was the pattern of early sovereignties among men. If there was sovereignty still beyond that, what other pattern would naturally be taken? Such was the model of a tribal leadership like that of Jahve for Israel, of the gods of each nation over their own nation. If arbitrariness was allowed to early sovereigns, how much more to the Universal Sovereign? Even Paul would seem once to have slipped into a reminiscence when he said, "Shall not God do as He will with his own?" It was a lapse, for behind him were generations of a nobler view of God than that. Far and wide kings among men had been made a model for God. Worst and best qualities of earthly rulers were sometimes ascribed to the Eternal King. And so much of the Heavenly King's omnipotence as the earthly sovereign could imitate or arrogate was allowed him. Human lawgivers gave laws, initiated reforms, executed penalties, in God's name. That was the formula as old as anything we know about mankind. Government had to be upheld. How long it took the human race to learn that nothing can have a divine right to be wrong! The passing of such notions is almost of yesterday. And some who think that they have passed beyond this ancient view may merely have substituted for it the will of an ignorant or selfishly interested majority. But in this case the divergence of authority from the right is quite as easy as in the other. How little all of this comports with the thought of an immanent universe such as the knowledge we now have, whether of nature or of man, impresses upon us! The essential thing is not that we deplore the fact that these images so long ruled imaginations of men. The essential thing is that we recognize that they were just images. But, again, there is nothing to surprise us here. Interpretations of science have also been just images, plays of imagination over facts but partly understood. Mechanism, vitalism, all theories of nature of that sort, were just solutions of an unfinished problem. They have fallen into desuetude because they do not solve. When, however, we discard the image, we do not necessarily discard the thing imaged. The divine sovereignty, as Calvin thought it and our New England ancestors mainly adhered to it, was in general the majestic imagery of an ancient world. It was harder for Calvin and men like him to throw off this imagery in part at least because of their view of the nature of inspiration. All that was found in the Bible they took literally as from God. But it is rather vain for us to discant against Calvin, the Scotch and the Puritans. The thing which they imaged remains as true for those of us who do not image it in the same way.

What in all this tragic history of the association of religion with law and government impresses us is that men who have made much of it seem to have failed to note that in all the nobler literature of Israel, and still more essentially in the Gospels, there is, almost perpetually, another image running side by side with the first—a fact which, all of itself, ought to prove to us that both are images. This other is not the image of a king. It is, however, an image which, equally, was taken from men's actual outward relations. It was the image of a father and of man as God's son. This image puts another cast upon a man's environment and his relation to it. It is the atmosphere of affection, solicitude and mutual responsibility. The image does not seem to lie more remote from the experience of early men than was the image of a chief or king. In fact, one might say that it lies nearer, because the family was even more rudimentary than the most rudimentary state. One remembers how tribes of men, other than Israel, either actually were or claimed to be descendants of a common father in the flesh. The very names of the constituent groups in early Attica survived into the great history of Athens. One knows how the early Romans felt about the Etruscans and men of other tribes. The Old Testament has made everyone familiar with what might be called the family feeling of the Jews. And this feeling, in part, alas, because of Christian persecutions, persists to a certain extent among Jews to this day. Whether all Israelites were really descended from Abraham, it was what might be called the ideal of their past, that they should think they were. The ferocious conduct of the tribes against the inhabitants of the land when they came into Canaan, gets what justification it can ever have from what was felt to be the necessity of keeping the clan pure. Certainly we do not need the testimony of the Jews alone to show how great was the authority, the actual power, of the father. Everyone knows what the *patria potestas* meant with the Romans, and again, how its waning among the Greeks was felt by Pindar, for example. Much of the great poetry of the Bible is oriented from this point of view. This is true even when, as with the last and greatest of the prophets, the thing uppermost in their minds was that the family of God was no longer to be thought of as if it were only the tribes of Jacob. Now it is the whole human race under this ideal fatherhood of God and sonship of man. Jesus is in this fully within the prophetic inheritance.

It is not at all confusion of epithets that Jesus talks continually of the kingdom of God, and rarely speaks of God as a king. Both the outward sovereignty of God and the inward rule of a man over himself are thought of at the level not merely of power and obedience, but of affection. It is the level of identification and fulfillment. It is the level at which mere manifestations of authority are done away, because the meaning of that authority has sunk so deeply into the hearts of God's children. In this curious contrast of the kingdom with the fatherhood of God, one may say that Jesus sets forth the rule of God over man as, indeed, outward. But its ideal is a rule in which its quality as mere rule disappears, man having made God's will his own. The contrast with other faiths is highly interesting at this point. Islam conquered, at one time or another, a great part of the world which we identify with the ancient civilizations. In fact, it failed to encircle the Mediterranean at one time or another, only by the distance from Tours to Vienna. It was indeed in the name of the Prophet, of one who claimed to be the vicegerent of God, that this was done. There was terrific power in those Arabian clansmen and the races which surrendered to the new faith, as these gave themselves through centuries to conquest. It must be owned that by Mohammed's time the Christian empire had progressed so far that Mohammed might be excused for thinking that the way to deal with it was by force. But the sentiment of the brotherhood of man as Jesus taught it is certainly not in the Koran. India was ploughed over by successive conquests, among them a Moslem conquest of parts of it. But more than by the entail of many racial bitternesses, its people are still held apart by caste. One cannot speak of God but of hundreds of gods. The great contribution to inner religion which India has made, Buddhism, it conferred, sooner or later, upon other peoples and hardly so much as kept for itself. There was no joy and hope in work for the life and light of all men. And, as for brotherhood, caste under the Brahmans began in denying brotherhood. It would be grossly unjust to say that there was no sense of brotherhood in India. Moreover, contact with the rest of the world, progress of knowledge within the last century and a half, has roused India to a sense of its own unity, which it is hardly too much to say that it never had before. But caste is still too largely unbroken, and caste is the very denial of brotherhood, as Gandhi himself declares. The Buddhist and Brahman view of life and the world have so long dominated their history that it is at present, and primarily, the influence and example of the outside world which would express itself among Indians in the terms of brotherhood today.

The point of all this is to reassert for religion that which, in God, corresponds to personality in man. To us who inherit the Jewish-Christian tradition of religion, it would seem that incomparably the most adequate symbol —and we must remember that we have no language but that of symbols—for the relation of God and man is that of father and son. And the notable thing about the period of the growth of this idea, of the universal sonship, is that it commenced with the time of the destruction of the Jewish kingdom as an earthly sovereignty. Paul could say to his Galatians, "Because ye are sons, God hath sent forth the spirit of his son into your hearts." All down the course of Christian history one can trace alternative influences of given situations, and again, of powerful personalities. Temperaments have their claim. Experiences in life have their play. In morals one may advance—if one has been advancing. In religion, at its best, there is always a chance to recover, even if one has been going back. The ruler may, perhaps must, look mainly at the offense. The father may look—perhaps he may look too much—at the offender. But he is free to pardon sins and in love to renew sinners. He may indulge that high quality once described as man's highest, "to look before and after and consider." By that same token the heights to which the religious man may be led may, in the end, be higher than those which the merely moral man attains. Shakespeare's word in the "Merchant of Venice", rings true, "The quality of mercy is not strain'd. . . . 'Tis mightiest in the mightiest. It becomes the throned monarch better than his crown. . . . It is an attribute to God himself . . . when mercy seasons justice." There is a humanness about religion which helps us to a morale which is, indeed, required of us, but to which perhaps we should not attain, were it not for belief in a personal God, our Father, one who, "like as a father pitieth his children." There are qualities which are lent to human life and personality by the belief that, among things which are real in our universe, is also personality. Not quite all even of the religions have believed that. Many of the religions have believed it in forms in which the weaknesses and even vices of human personalities have been attributed to gods. But it remains that religion has been able to point the way to men perplexed and beaten down, and, as well, to those who have risen to great deeds and sacrifice for their fellows, through the belief that the highest in the universe has also the quality which we find the highest in ourselves, this mystery of personality. Mystery it is. We leave it at that. The worst of our sorrows come to us through our being personalities. Buddha was right in that. But also the purest of our joys and the supreme power of giving light and joy to others come almost solely through our being personalities. We cannot think that the universe is without being and qualities of which these highest things in ourselves may lay hold. It is difficult to think of God as personality. It is more difficult still to think of man at his highest without a God who is personality. It may be that this also is imagery. But if so, that must be because God is more, rather than less, than personality as we know it. The reason is that man, at his highest, always thinks of that which is higher than himself, "the highest and most human, too."